T0333767

COMMODITY PRICE DYNAMICS

Commodities have become an important component of many investors' portfolios and the focus of much political controversy over the past decade. This book utilizes structural models to provide a better understanding of how commodities' prices behave and what drives them. It exploits differences across commodities and examines a variety of predictions of the models to identify where they work and where they fail. The findings of the analysis are useful to scholars, traders, and policy makers who want to better understand often puzzling – and extreme – movements in the prices of commodities from aluminum to oil to soybeans to zinc.

Craig Pirrong is Professor of Finance and Energy Markets Director for the Global Energy Management Institute at the Bauer College of Business at the University of Houston. He was previously Watson Family Professor of Commodity and Financial Risk Management at Oklahoma State University and a faculty member at the University of Michigan, the University of Chicago, and Washington University. Professor Pirrong's research focuses on commodities and commodity derivative pricing, the relation between market fundamentals and commodity price dynamics and the implications of this relation for the pricing of commodity derivatives, derivatives market regulation, commodity market manipulation, and the organization of commodity markets. He has published more than thirty-five articles in professional publications and is the author of four books. He has consulted widely with financial exchanges around the world, testified before Congress on energy pricing, and served as an expert witness in a variety of cases involving commodity markets. He holds a Ph.D. in business economics from the University of Chicago.

Commodity Price Dynamics

A Structural Approach

CRAIG PIRRONG

University of Houston

CAMBRIDGE UNIVERSITY PRESS

CAMBRIDGE UNIVERSITY PRESS
Cambridge, New York, Melbourne, Madrid, Cape Town,
Singapore, São Paulo, Delhi, Mexico City

Cambridge University Press
32 Avenue of the Americas, New York, NY 10013-2473, USA

www.cambridge.org
Information on this title: www.cambridge.org/9780521195898

First published 2012
Reprinted 2012

A catalog record for this publication is available from the British Library.

Library of Congress Cataloging in Publication Data

Pirrong, Stephen Craig, 1959–
Commodity price dynamics : a structural approach / Craig Pirrong.
p.   cm.
Includes bibliographical references and indexes.
ISBN 978-0-521-19589-8
1. Prices. 2. Prices – Forecasting. 3. Commodity exchanges. I. Title.
HB221.P47   2012
332.63'28–dc22   2011016595

ISBN 978-0-521-19589-8 Hardback

Contents

Preface

This book weaves strands of research that date back more than 20 years, to approximately 1990–1991. Although I worked at a futures commission merchant (that is, a brokerage firm) while in graduate school, that work involved financial futures exclusively. Deciding to leave that business in mid-October 1987 (thereby causing the 1987 crash), first for a stint in litigation support consulting and then on to academia at the Michigan Business School, I worked on research completely unrelated to futures markets. But in spring and summer 1989, the Italian conglomerate Ferruzzi cornered the soybean market in Chicago. The corner, and the Chicago Board of Trade's response to it, resulted in sharp criticism of the exchange. To address this criticism, the CBOT decided to commission an academic study of the grain market delivery mechanism.

My senior colleague at Michigan who was primarily responsible for bringing me there, the late Roger Kormendi, succeeded in wrangling a grant from the CBOT to carry out the study. He walked into my office and said: "I know nothing about commodity markets. You worked in them. Would you be part of the team on this study?" I responded: "Well, I know nothing about commodity futures, but I'm game to learn."

This nudge completely changed the trajectory of my research, and virtually everything I have worked on since relates to commodities and derivatives in one way or another. My formal training is as an industrial organization economist, and so my research initially focused on trying to understand the causes and effects of market power in commodity markets and commodity derivatives. Classical manipulations – corners and squeezes, such as the Ferruzzi episode – are exercises of market power, so I examined in detail how various economic "frictions" such as transportation costs could affect a particular market's vulnerability to market power.

I was particularly interested in how to detect manipulations, for the purpose of improving the ability of the courts and regulators to deter manipulation. It has long been known that market-power manipulation distorts price *relationships*, notably the relation between forward (or futures) prices on the same commodity with different maturities. For instance, Ferruzzi's exercise of market power raised the price of July 1989 soybean futures relative to the price of September 1989 soybean futures. But, to identify distortions, it is necessary to understand how "normal," undistorted prices behave in a competitive market. Thus began the inquiries that have culminated in this book.

When I began my research, there were basically two theories on offer, both somewhat confusingly called the "theory of storage." One invokes the concept of a "convenience yield" to explain why forward prices in commodity markets often fail to cover the costs of holding inventories even when inventories are positive. The other uses dynamic programming methods that explicitly incorporate the real-world constraint that inventories cannot be negative to derive implications about the behavior of commodity prices in a competitive market with rational expectations.

The convenience-yield concept struck me as an ad hoc way to rationalize an empirical regularity. The dynamic programming–based approach struck me as more rigorous, with more well-developed microfoundations. The dynamic programming methods were also familiar to me, having been exposed to them in Robert Lucas's macro courses at Chicago. Consequently, I concentrated my research efforts on these models.

There was a flurry of publications in this area around this time (the early to mid-1990s), including work by Deaton and Laroque and that by Williams and Wright. This work clearly laid the foundation for my research, and I gratefully acknowledge having learned a good deal from it. But its focus on low-frequency (e.g., annual) prices, its relative lack of attention to higher moments of prices, and correlations between forward prices with different maturities left unexploited many important sources of data. They also did not exploit fully the potentially quite informative cross-sectional variation in commodity markets: corn and copper are very different things, with different production and consumption patterns and drivers, and such differences are potentially quite revealing sources of information that can be used to test commodity pricing models.

My background in finance, and in options pricing in particular, made me quite attuned to the importance and informativeness of higher moments. Consequently, I focused my attention on this issue, first in empirical work with my former Michigan colleague Victor Ng, then in more theoretical work based on the dynamic programming approach. It is that work that is the basis for most of the material in this book.

My finance background also exposed me to some computational techniques, notably finite difference methods, used in option pricing that are routine in finance but which have seldom been employed in commodity pricing models. The book embodies a fusion between the methods commonly employed in the dynamic programming literature and the quantitative methods routinely employed in options pricing.

I hope that the book conveys several important lessons.

First, the structural approach provides valuable insights into the drivers of commodity prices. One novel insight explored in Chapter 5 is that it is necessary to incorporate stochastic volatility of *fundamentals* to explain salient features of commodity price dynamics. This is a finding that points out the value of looking at higher moments of prices and at the prices of derivatives other than forwards and futures – notably, options of various types.

Second, the structural approach informs as much through its failures as its successes. The chapter on seasonal commodities (Chapter 6) demonstrates that the conventional approach cannot explain salient aspects of price dynamics – most important, price correlations. This should motivate a search for improvements and extensions of the approach; Chapter 6 offers a few suggestions along these lines, but much more needs to be done. The current binding constraint on progress is computational but, fortunately, that is a constraint that is easing steadily over time.

Third, the structural models make quite plain the value of looking beyond prices alone and incorporating data on quantities – especially inventories – into any empirical analysis of commodity markets. After all, the role of prices is to guide the allocation of resources, so it is natural – but all too uncommon – to incorporate data on actual resource allocations in any empirical examination of the theory. Because forward prices guide the allocation of resources over time, and because inventories are a way of shifting resources through time, it is particularly revealing to incorporate inventory data into any analysis. This is also true to the origins of the academic study of commodity markets. The first major scholar in this area, Holbrook Working, was particularly interested in the relation between differences in the forward prices for commodities with different maturity dates (i.e., futures spreads) and the amount of commodity in storage.

I envision three audiences for this book. The first, of course, is scholars engaged in research on commodity markets and commodity prices, and graduate students looking for a self-contained and fairly comprehensive treatment of the subject.

The second is practitioners, most notably those in commodity trading and risk management. I believe that the material in the book provides an intellectual framework that can help traders understand the fundamental factors that influence prices and how they do so. Even the model failures can be helpful: they help identify potentially important factors omitted from the models, and it is useful to understand the known unknowns. I also expect that even though it is presently impractical to utilize the fundamentals-based structural models for pricing contingent claims as a replacement for Black-type models (except for, perhaps, electricity), this will not always be the case. Improvements in computational power, and improvements in data available to estimate and calibrate the models, hold out the prospect that structural models may someday replace reduced-form models as the preferred way to price commodity options of all types.

The third is policy makers. Commodity prices have always been a bone of political contention, although the intensity of commodity-related controversies has waxed and waned over time. The years since 2005 or so have been a time of waxing. Commodity price spikes and crashes have sparked widespread condemnation of the malign effects of speculation in commodities, and this condemnation has resulted in regulatory and legislative action. As of the present time (November 2010), the U.S. Congress has directed regulators to impose limits on commodity speculation and the European Union has made constraining commodity speculation a policy priority.

Too often, debates over the effects of commodity speculation have not been grounded in a scientific understanding of how the commodity prices are determined and how these prices behave. The models in the book can help provide such a grounding. For instance, Chapter 5 on stochastic fundamental volatility shows that some apparent anomalies are in fact quite consistent with rational pricing. Moreover, the emphasis on the importance of looking at quantities as well as prices is invaluable in identifying distortions. Because prices guide the allocation of resources, if prices are distorted, quantities should be distorted too. The models in the book help characterize how prices *and quantities* in undistorted markets should behave, thereby making it easier to identify distortions that may justify a policy intervention.

Because this book represents the work of decades, there are many people to whom I owe a debt of gratitude for making it possible. Professionally, I have profited immensely from collaborating with my co-authors Victor Ng and Martin Jermakyan. They taught me a great deal, and I hope that some of what they taught me shines through every page. Our work demonstrates how complementary skills and knowledge can produce something that is bigger than the sum of its parts. I am also grateful to many practitioners who have shared their wisdom, experience, and insight with me. Two who had a very great impact on my thinking as I was just beginning my explorations of these matters were Frank Sims, then of Cargill, and Paul Krug, first of Continental Grain and subsequently of ADM Investor Services.

I am also very appreciative of the support of the various schools where I have had the privilege to serve as a faculty member. My current academic home, the Bauer College of Business of the University of Houston, deserves special notice. I deeply appreciate that Dean Arthur Warga and Finance Department Chair Praveen Kumar understand the value and relevance of research on commodity markets in a finance department and have supported my research accordingly.

One individual deserves particular thanks. My thesis advisor and mentor, Lester Telser, is an amazing scholar who has made contributions to myriad areas of economics, including industrial organization, the theory of the core, and even macroeconomics. But his first major contribution was in the area of commodity futures pricing. He has taught me so much about so many things, including commodities. It is gratifying to be able to make my own contribution to a subject that he helped pioneer.

Finally, I owe so much to my family for their inspiration, support, counsel, and guidance over the years. My parents, Kay and Glenn, and my wife and children, Terry, Renee, and Genevieve, are my metaphorical bookends. My parents instilled in me a love of learning and scholarship and provided invaluable educational opportunities that made an academic career possible. Terry and the girls gave me the support and encouragement and understanding – and the time – that are so vital to scholarly endeavors.

ONE

Introduction

1.1 Introduction

Not to put too fine a point on it, but the study of commodity prices has long been something of an academic stepchild. Most work on the subject is in the domain of specific fields, notably agricultural economics. Only a smattering of articles on the subject has appeared in broader publications, such as the *Journal of Political Economy* or the *Journal of Finance*.

Especially in finance, this relative obscurity arguably reflects the niche role of commodities in the broader financial markets, as compared to equity and fixed-income markets. But commodities are in the process of becoming mainstream. In the 1990s, and especially the 2000s, many major banks and investment banks have entered into commodities trading. Indeed, commodity trading – especially in energy – has become an important source of profits for major financial institutions such as Goldman Sachs, Morgan Stanley, and Citibank. Simultaneously, and relatedly, many investors have entered into the commodities market. In particular, pension funds and other portfolio managers have increasingly viewed commodities as a separate asset class that, when combined with traditional stock and bond portfolios, can improve risk-return performance. Furthermore, financial innovation has eased the access of previously atypical participants into the commodity markets. Notably, commodity index products (such as the GSCI, now the S&P Commodity Index) and exchange traded funds (ETFs) have reduced the transaction costs that portfolio managers and individual investors incur to participate in the commodities markets. Thus, a confluence of forces has dramatically increased the importance of, and interest in, commodities and commodity prices.

What is more, this increase in the presence of investors and large financial intermediaries in commodity markets combined with extraordinary price movements in commodities in the mid-2000s to make commodity prices an important political issue. Most notably, the unprecedented spike in the price of oil in 2008 created a political firestorm in the United States (and elsewhere) that has led to numerous calls to regulate the markets more restrictively. Indeed, the coincidence of the entry of new financial players into the markets and rocketing prices led many market participants, politicians, and pundits to attribute the latter phenomenon to the former, and hence to call for limitations on the ability of financial institutions, portfolio investors, and individual investors to buy and sell commodities.

Thus, the 2000s have seen commodities achieve an economic and political prominence that they had lacked since a much earlier era (the nineteenth and early twentieth centuries) in which a far larger portion of the population earned a living producing or processing commodities. Unfortunately, the modeling of commodity prices has not kept pace. Most practitioners have adopted reduced-form models, such as the model that is the basis for the Black-Scholes option pricing formula, to analyze commodity prices and to price commodity derivatives. Structural models of commodity prices that explicitly account for the implications of intertemporal optimization through storage have been around since Gustafson (1958) and have been developed by Scheinkman and Schectman (1983), Williams and Wright (1991), and others. These models, however, have been in a state of relative stasis. Moreover, the empirical analysis of these models has been extremely limited, and little use has been made of them to answer questions related to the effects of speculation.

I intend this book to push the structural modeling of commodity pricing forward, to provide a better understanding of the economics of commodity pricing for the benefit of both academics and practitioners. This book builds on the rational expectations, dynamic programming–based theory of storage epitomized by Williams and Wright (1991), but goes beyond the existing literature in many ways.

First, whereas the received models typically incorporate only a single source of economic uncertainty (e.g., a single net demand shock), I (a) demonstrate that such models are incapable of explaining salient features of commodity price dynamics, and (b) introduce models with multiple shocks that can capture many of these features.

Second, unlike received work, in this book I exploit important cross-sectional differences among commodities to derive empirical implications.[1]

---

[1]   See especially Deaton and Laroque (1995, 1996), which lump together commodities as disparate as copper and corn in a single empirical framework.

As I discuss in more detail later in this introduction, commodities can differ on a wide variety of dimensions. Some, such as copper or oil, are produced continuously and have relatively non-seasonal demands. Others, such as corn or soybeans, are produced seasonally. These fundamental differences lead to distinctive price behaviors; the ability of suitably adapted models to explain these differences sheds a bright light on the strengths and limitations of the received structural approach.

Third, quite curiously, the empirical literature structural models of commodity prices tend to focus on low-frequency (e.g., annual) data.[2] They also tend to focus on the spot prices of commodities, as well as on price levels and the first moments (means) of prices; they typically ignore the behavior of higher moments, such as variances and measures of covariation between different prices. These models particularly tend to ignore time variation in these variances and covariances and the association between these time variations and fundamentals.

These tendencies have several pernicious effects. For one thing, they obscure the potentially illuminating differences between continuously and periodically produced commodities. For another, and perhaps more important, they result in a slighting of a tremendously rich source of data: high-frequency (e.g., daily) data on a wide variety of derivatives on a similarly wide spectrum of commodities. In particular, there are abundant data on commodity futures prices for a wide variety of commodities. Moreover, data on other commodity derivatives are becoming increasingly available. Most notably, commodity options are more widely traded than ever, and hence option price data are becoming commonplace.

To exploit these data, the book focuses on the implications of structural commodity price models for the behavior of commodity spot *and* forward prices at *high frequency*; the variances of these spot and forward prices and the correlations between them; the comovements of quantity variables (e.g., inventories) and prices; and the prices of other commodity derivatives, most notably options. Moreover, I continually confront these implications with the data, to see where the models work – and where they do not.

The basic approach is to see what data are available to test the models, derive the implications of the models for the behavior of these observables, and evaluate the performance of the models when faced with the data.

This presents the models with extreme challenges and, as discussed later, they quite often fail. But that is part of the plan. After breaking the models, we can learn by examining the pieces.

---

[2] See again Deaton and Laroque (1995, 1996).

The transparency of fundamentals in commodity markets (in contrast to equity or currency markets, for instance) holds out the promise of allowing structural models of commodity price behavior to be devised that can illuminate the underlying factors that drive these prices and which perhaps can be used to value contingent claims on commodities. There has been much progress on these models in recent years, but the empirical data show that real-world commodity price behavior is far richer than that predicted by the current generation of models and that except for non-storable commodities, structural models currently cannot be used to price derivatives. The models and empirical evidence do, however, point out the deficiencies in reduced-form commodity derivative pricing models and suggest how reduced-form models must be modified to represent commodity price dynamics more realistically. They also suggest additional factors that may be added to the models (at substantial computational cost) to improve their realism.

As just noted, the cross-sectional diversity of commodities represents a potentially valuable source of variation that can be exploited to gain better understanding of the determinants of commodity prices and their behavior and to inform structural models of commodity markets. To understand this fundamental point more clearly, it is worthwhile to examine this diversity in more detail and, at the same time, introduce some modeling issues that this diversity raises and discuss the received modeling literature.

1.2 A Commodity Taxonomy

Although the catchall term "commodity" is widely applied to any relatively homogeneous good that is not a true asset, it conceals tremendous diversity, diversity that has material impacts on price behavior and modeling.[3]

---

[3] The distinction between a commodity and an asset proper is that an asset (such as a stock or a bond) generates a stream of consumption (à la the "trees" in a Lucas [1978] model) or a stream of cash flows that can be used to buy consumption goods (e.g., a bond), whereas a commodity is itself consumed. An asset represents a "stock" that generates a flow of benefits. There are some potential ambiguities in this distinction, especially inasmuch as this book discusses repeatedly the role of "stocks" of commodities. However, as discussed later, even though there are commodity stocks, commodity forward prices behave differently from asset forward prices. Whereas asset forward prices always reflect full carrying costs (the opportunity cost of capital net of the asset's cash flow), commodity forward prices do not. This distinction between a consumption good and a true asset has important implications for the possibility of bubbles in commodity prices, that is, self-sustaining price increases not justified by fundamentals. Williams et al. (2000) and Gjerstad (2007) show that experimental consumption good markets almost never exhibit

The most basic divide among commodities is between those that are storable and those that are not.

The most important non-storable commodity is electricity (although hydro generation does add an element of storability in some electricity markets). Weather is obviously not storable – and it is increasingly becoming an important underlying in commodity derivatives trading. Shipping services are another non-storable commodity. Although ships are obviously durable, the services of a ship are not: space on a ship that is not used today cannot be stored for use at a later date. Shipping derivatives are also increasingly common; derivatives on bulk commodities began trading in the early 2000s, and the first container derivative trade took place in early 2010.

Most other commodities are storable (at some cost), but there is considerable heterogeneity among goods in this category. This heterogeneity occurs on the dimensions of temporal production patterns, temporal demand patterns, and the nature of the capital used to produce them.

Some commodities are continuously produced and consumed and are not subject to significant seasonality in demand; industrial metals such as copper or aluminum fall into this category. Some are continuously produced and consumed but exhibit substantial seasonality in demand. Heating oil, natural gas, and gasoline are prime examples of this type of commodity.

Other commodities are produced periodically (e.g., seasonally) rather than continuously, but there is also variation within the category of seasonally produced commodities. Grains and oilseeds are produced seasonally, but their production is relatively flexible because a major input – land – is quite flexible; there is a possibility of growing corn on a piece of land one year, and soybeans the next, and an adverse natural event (such as a freeze) may damage one crop, but does not impair the future productivity of land.[4]

In contrast, tree crops such as cocoa or coffee or oranges are seasonally produced but utilize specialized, durable, and inflexible inputs (the trees), and damage to these inputs can have consequences for productivity that last beyond a single crop year.

In sum, there is considerable diversity among commodities. This presents challenges and opportunities for the economic modeler. As to challenges,

---

bubbles; in contrast, Smith, Suchanek, and Williams (1998) show that experimental *asset* markets are chronically prone to bubbles.

[4] Adverse weather events sometimes can have effects that span crop years. For instance, the intense drought of 2010 in central Russia devastated the 2010 crop, but also left the ground very dry. This delayed planting of the 2011 crop, which raises the risk of a smaller-than-normal 2011 harvest.

fundamentals-based theories must take these variations across commodities into account, so one-size-fits-all models are inappropriate. As to opportunities, this cross-sectional variation has empirical implications that can be exploited to test fundamental-based structural models.

1.3 Commodity Markets and Data

Fortunately, just as there are many different commodities, there are many actively traded commodity markets. These markets produce prices that are of interest and important in their own right, but which also can be used to test structural commodity models.

In particular, although with a few limited exceptions there are few liquid and transparent "spot" markets for commodities,[5] there are active, liquid, and transparent futures markets for many commodities. (But not all; some important commodities such as iron ore have no active futures market.)

A futures contract is a financial instrument obligating the buyer (seller) to purchase (sell) a specified quantity of a particular commodity of a particular quality (or qualities) at a particular location (or locations) at a date specified in the contract. For instance, the July 2010 corn futures contract traded at the Chicago Mercantile Exchange requires the buyer (seller) to take (make) delivery of 5,000 bushels of #2 corn at a location along the Illinois River chosen by the seller during the month of July 2010. The buyer and the seller agree on the price terms, but all of the other contract terms are established by formal organizations – futures exchanges.[6]

These futures exchanges operate centralized auction markets where buyers and sellers can negotiate transactions. The exchanges typically host continuous, double-sided auctions. Historically, these auctions were face-to-face affairs that took place on an exchange floor – "the pit." In recent years, most trading has migrated to electronic, computerized exchange systems (although commodities lagged behind financial futures in this regard). The prices negotiated during these auctions are broadcast around the world and represent the primary barometer for commodities prices. Buyers and

---

[5] A spot market is a market for immediate delivery. Practically speaking, even a spot transaction involves a separation in time between the consummation of a transaction and the delivery of the commodity, so spot trades are properly very short-term forward transactions.

[6] A futures contract is a particular kind of forward contract. A forward contract is any contract that specifies performance at a future date. A futures contract is a forward contract traded on an exchange, where the performance on the contract is guaranteed by an exchange clearinghouse. The terms "future" and "forward" and "futures price" and "forward price" are often used interchangeably.

sellers of physical commodities base the prices of their transactions on these futures exchange prices.

At present, futures markets exist for many physical commodities, including energy products (especially oil, heating oil, gasoil, natural gas, and gasoline); grains and oilseeds (including wheat, corn, and soybeans); industrial metals (such as copper, aluminum, lead, and nickel); precious metals (gold, silver, platinum, and palladium); fibers (notably cotton); meats (live hogs, live cattle, and pork bellies); and non-grain and non-meat food products (such as coffee, cocoa, and sugar). In some cases, there are futures contracts traded on different varieties of the same commodity; for instance, Brent crude oil futures and West Texas Intermediate (WTI) crude oil futures are both traded.

For most of these commodities, futures contracts with different delivery dates are traded. In the WTI crude market, for instance, contracts calling for delivery in every month for the next several years are traded simultaneously. In the corn market in Chicago, contracts are actively traded for delivery in March, May, July, September, and December.

Thus, for most active commodity futures, at any time there are multiple prices, each corresponding to a different delivery date. The locus of forward prices on the same commodity for different delivery dates is called the "forward curve."

Forward curves exhibit a variety of shapes. Some slope up (i.e., prices rise with time to expiration). Such markets are said to be in "contango" or to exhibit "carry." Others slope down; these are said to be "inverted" or "in backwardation." Others are humped, rising over some range of delivery dates, falling over others. Some exhibit seasonality, with highs and lows corresponding to different seasons.

Any good theory should be able to generate forward curves that exhibit the observed diversity in these curves in actual markets. Moreover, any good theory should demonstrate how these curves evolve with changes in fundamental conditions.

In sum, there are vast amounts of futures price data for commodities that exhibit the diverse characteristics discussed in the taxonomy. Because the markets operate continuously, these data are of very high frequency. There are at least daily data on futures contracts for a variety of delivery dates for many commodities; for some commodities, intra-day data are also available. This represents a vast repository of information that can be used to test, challenge, and potentially break structural commodity models.

But although futures markets provide the most extensive source of price data, there are other commodity markets and hence other data sources.

Many commodity forwards are traded on a bilateral basis in over-the-counter (OTC) markets; that is, they are traded off exchange. Moreover, options on commodities are traded both on exchange and in OTC markets. Some of these options are vanilla puts and calls. Others are more exotic instruments, such as spread options that have a payoff dependent on the difference between futures prices on a particular commodity, with different delivery dates, or swaptions that are effectively options on the forward curve for a particular commodity.

It is well known that the prices of options depend on the characteristics of the dynamics of the underlying price, most notably on the volatility (and perhaps higher moments) of the underlying price. Thus, a copper option's price depends on the volatility (and perhaps higher moments) of the forward price of copper. This means that options prices incorporate information about commodity price dynamics, and hence these options prices can be used to test predictions of commodity price models.

As discussed later, structural models for storable commodities also make predictions about the behavior of commodity inventories, that is, commodity stocks. Indeed, the behavior of stocks is of particular interest because it speaks to long-standing and ongoing battles over whether speculation on futures markets distorts prices. An important economic role of prices is to guide the allocation of resources, so distortions in prices will manifest themselves in distortions in the allocation of real things – such as commodity stocks.

Unfortunately, with a few exceptions, data on commodity stocks are far less abundant than data on prices. Nonetheless, there are some markets – notably the London Metal Exchange's markets for industrial metals – that produce high-quality, high-frequency data on stocks. I will use these data where available.

There is, in brief, a plethora of data that can be used to test commodity price models. This book develops models tailored to the specific features of particular commodities, generates predictions from these models, and uses some of this bounty of data to test these predictions.

1.4 An Overview of the Remainder of the Book

The objective of this book is to develop models customized to capture the salient features of particular commodities (e.g., storability, production frequency), derive the implications of these models for the behavior of commodity prices and stocks, and then examine how well these predictions stack up against the data.

The term "behavior" is meant to be very encompassing. In this book I derive and test the implications of structural models not just for the level of forward curves, but also for the variances of forward prices of different maturities, the correlations between forward prices of different maturities, and the pricing of options. Moreover, I focus on *high-frequency* commodity price behavior. That is, I derive and test implications about the day-to-day behavior of commodity prices. This focus allows me to mine the rich seams of futures data and should also make the work of particular interest to commodity market participants who trade every day.

The rest of the book is organized as follows.

1.4.1 Modeling Storable Commodity Prices

The received theory of storage, based on the stochastic dynamic programming rational expectations modeling framework, is an economically grounded approach for understanding how commodity prices behave and how fundamentals affect commodity prices. This framework can be adapted to each particular commodity. In this chapter, I review the basics of the model and the computational approach to solving it. This chapter also introduces the partial differential equation (PDE) approach to solving for forward prices that is an important part of the solution algorithm. The chapter reviews PDE methods and shows how these methods can be used to determine the prices of more complicated contingent claims in the storage economy. These claims include vanilla options, swaptions, and spread options. Because multiple sources of risk are necessary to provide a reasonable characterization of commodity price behavior, the chapter focuses on modern PDE approaches (such as splitting techniques) for high-dimension problems.

1.4.2 A Two-Factor Model of a Continuously Produced Commodity

The conventional commodity price modeling approach assumes a single source of uncertainty. This approach cannot explain the imperfect and time-varying correlation between forward prices with different maturities. This chapter explores the implications of multiple risk sources with different time series properties; that is, two demand shocks of differing persistence. The chapter focuses on the implications of this framework for the behavior of forward curves, the variances of prices, the correlations between different forward prices, and the dependence of these moments on supply and demand conditions. It also explores the pricing of options in the storage economy with multiple demand shocks, including an analysis of commodity volatility surfaces and how these volatility surfaces depend on underlying supply and demand conditions.

1.4.3 The Empirical Performance of the Two-Factor Model

Formal econometric testing of rational expectations models is challenging, so techniques that mix calibration and estimation are common in macroeconomics where rational expectations models are the most widely used theoretical tool. This chapter adapts those techniques to the study of an important commodity market – the copper market. I use the Extended Kalman Filter (EKF) and a search over the relevant parameter space to determine the persistences and volatilities of the demand shocks of the model of Chapter 3 that best capture the dynamics of copper prices. I show that the extended, multi-shock model captures salient features of copper price behavior, but that the model cannot capture well the behavior of long-term (e.g., 27-month) forward prices; moreover, even though the model accurately characterizes the dynamics of the variance of the spot price (as documented by Ng-Pirrong), it does a poor job of capturing the behavior of longer-dated variances (e.g., 3-month futures price variances) and the volatility implied from copper options prices. This motivates an analysis of what changes to the model are necessary to capture these dynamics.

1.4.4 Commodity Pricing with Stochastic Fundamental Volatility

Traditional storage models (and the model of Chapter 3) assume homoskedastic net demand disturbances; that is, the variance of the fundamental shocks remains constant over time. This chapter explores the implications of stochastic demand variability. Such stochastic variability is plausible. The chapter shows that a model that incorporates stochastic demand volatility can explain otherwise anomalous behavior in commodity markets, namely, episodes where both inventories and prices rise and fall together (whereas the traditional storage model implies that they should typically move in the opposite direction). This is an important finding, because some critics of commodity speculation have asserted that such comovements are symptomatic of speculative price distortions. Moreover, adding stochastic fundamental volatility results in a more accurate characterization of the behavior of forward price variances and option implied volatilities.

1.4.5 The Pricing of Seasonally Produced Commodities

The traditional storage model with independent, identically distributed (i.i.d.) demand shocks cannot explain the high autocorrelation in commodity prices. Deaton and Laroque (1996) suggest that high demand persistence can explain this phenomenon. This chapter explores this issue in the context of a seasonal storage model. The intuition is that it is often optimal to consume all of a seasonally produced commodity before the next harvest. The absence of carryover between years breaks the connection between prices across the harvest; for example, July and December corn prices. Thus, the storage model implies that even in the presence of high demand autocorrelation, "new crop" and "old crop" futures prices should exhibit little correlation. Moreover, the solved model implies that news about the impending harvest should have a large effect on "new crop" futures prices and little effect on "old crop" prices. I examine empirical evidence on new crop–old crop correlations and the sensitivity of old crop prices to information about harvests for a variety of seasonal commodities and find that these correlations and price sensitivities are far higher than predicted by the storage model. This means that neither storage nor demand autocorrelation can explain the high persistence in prices. I then explore alternative explanations for these phenomena, including intertemporal substitution and general equilibrium considerations. I conclude that seasonal commodity prices demonstrate the limitations of partial equilibrium structural models because they do not fully capture all of the intertemporal choices available to agents. Instead, it is likely that general equilibrium models with multiple storable commodities are required to provide a more accurate characterization of commodity prices.

1.4.6 The Pricing of Pollution Credits

Pollution credits – most notably, CO_2 credits – are the newest commodity. Indeed, CO_2 credits are forecast to become the largest commodity market in the world. This chapter adopts the two-shock seasonal storage model to analyze the pricing of pollution credits. (Under existing and proposed trading schemes, pollution credits are effectively seasonal commodities because new credits are issued annually – just as a new corn crop is produced.) The model shows that the variability of the price of these credits should evolve systematically over time (as the credits approach their expiration), and that their price behavior depends crucially on the persistence of demand shocks.

The model also implies that options pricing should vary systematically with supply and demand fundamentals and time to expiration of the credits. It also notes that whereas physical commodities such as corn or copper have certain immutable physical features (e.g., the seasonality of production), salient features of carbon as a commodity can be designed. For instance, the frequency of production of CO_2 credits can be chosen by a legislature enacting a cap-and-trade system. The chapter compares the behavior of pollution credits under various alternative designs.

1.4.7 Non-Storable Commodities Pricing: The Case of Electricity

Electricity is another large commodity market. Unlike commodities such as corn and copper, electricity is effectively non-storable. This chapter incorporates and extends the Pirrong-Jermakyan model of electricity forward and option pricing. This is a fundamentals-based model in which spot prices, and hence forward and options prices, depend on electricity demand and fuel prices. I show how options prices vary systematically with fundamentals. The chapter also shows that the market price of risk is an important determinant of electricity forward prices.

1.5 Where This Book Fits in the Literature

Serious academic attention to the issue of commodity pricing, and the role of storage, dates to the work of Holbrook Working. Working was the first to identify spreads between spot and futures prices as a measure of the return to storage and to derive a "supply of storage" curve relating these spreads to the amount of commodity in store. Working's research posed a serious puzzle. Simple no-arbitrage analysis implies that futures prices should exceed spot prices by the cost of carrying inventory (i.e., the cost of funds, plus warehousing fees, plus insurance) to the future's expiration date. But Working found that (a) futures prices typically fell short of this "full carry" level, and (b) the deviation between the observed spread and the full carry spread varies systematically with inventories.

This puzzle motivated a search for an explanation. Kaldor (1939) advanced the idea of a "convenience yield": those holding stocks receive an implicit stream of benefits from holding inventories (analogous to a dividend), and the marginal value of this stream is declining in stocks. This theory was intuitively appealing and has informed much research in commodity markets (Pindyck 1994, for example), but it is ad hoc. Moreover, as Williams and Wright (1991) have pointed out, even individual firms receive an implicit benefit from stocks; this does not necessarily imply a supply-of-storage relationship in market prices.

The convenience yield approach represents one way of analyzing commodity prices and commodity price relations. Although it is quite popular and, indeed, is the approach taken in most textbooks that discuss commodity pricing, and although it is the motivation for one of the most widely used reduced-form commodity derivatives pricing models (Schwartz 1997), it is a dead end in my view. It is ad hoc, and as Williams and Wright point out, it makes assertions about market-wide phenomena based on constructs that apply to the individual firm, without examining the market equilibrium implications of the behavior of these firms.

The other approach, which I follow in this book, is a structural one that dates from the pathbreaking work of Gustafson (1958).

Gustafson implemented a structural model of the optimal storage of a commodity. He recognized the fundamentally dynamic nature of the problem and utilized dynamic programming techniques and numerical solutions to these programs. He used a piecewise function to approximate price as a function of storage. Subsequently, Newbery and Stiglitz (1982) and Gilbert (1988) employed this approximation to derive storage rules and prices.

The structural modeling of commodity prices and the dynamic programming approach were elegantly formalized by Scheinkman and Schectman (1983) under the assumption of a single i.i.d. demand shock. This work demonstrates the existence of an equilibrium. The most comprehensive application of this approach is in Williams and Wright (1991), who focus on numerical solutions to a wide variety of storage-related problems, including the effects of price controls and public storage. Deaton and Laroque (1995, 1996) introduce autocorrelation into the single-shock model and prove the existence of an equilibrium in a storage economy with such a demand shock. Routledge, Seppi, and Spatt (RSS; 2000) take a similar approach.

The foregoing analyses all (implicitly) assume that the commodity is produced continuously; there is production and consumption in every decision period in these models. Chambers and Bailey (1996), Pirrong (1999), and Osborne (2004) introduce periodic production appropriate for the study of agriculture commodities.

The theoretical structure and numerical analysis of structural models for storable commodities is highly refined. In contrast, empirical analysis of commodity prices based on structural storage models has lagged behind. Empirical work on the competitive storage model has focused on low-frequency (e.g., annual) data (Deaton-Laroque) or relatively simple calibrations using higher-frequency data (Routledge et al., 2000).

Deaton-Laroque fit a one-factor storage model to a variety of commodity price time series. Their maximum likelihood approach exploits an implication of the simple one-factor model: namely, that there is a "cutoff price" such that inventories fall to zero when the spot price exceeds the cutoff, but inventories are positive when the price is lower than the cutoff. Deaton and Laroque (1992) posit that demand shocks are i.i.d. They find that although theoretically storage can cause prices to exhibit positive autocorrelation even when demand shocks are independent, the level of autocorrelation implied by their fitted model is far below that observed in practice. Deaton and Laroque (1995, 1996) allow for autocorrelated demand shocks (again in a one-factor model). Based on an analysis of annual data, they find that virtually all the autocorrelation in commodity prices is attributable to autocorrelation in the underlying demand disturbances, and very little is attributable to the smoothing effects of speculative storage.

The Deaton-Laroque empirical analyses are problematic for several reasons. First, they utilize low-frequency (annual) data for a wide variety of very heterogeneous commodities. Because in reality economic agents make decisions regarding storage daily, if not intra-day, the frequency of their data is poorly aligned with the frequency of the economic decisions they are trying to assess empirically. Moreover, Deaton-Laroque impose a single model on very different commodities. Their commodities include those that are produced continuously and have non-seasonal demand (e.g., industrial metals such as tin and copper), those that are planted and produced seasonally (e.g., corn and wheat), and others that are produced seasonally from perennial plants (e.g., coffee and cocoa). As the analysis of this book will demonstrate in detail, the economics of storage differ substantially among these various products, but the Deaton-Laroque empirical specification does not reflect these differences. Finally, their use of annual data forces them to estimate their model with decades of data encompassing periods of major changes in income, technology, policy regimes, and trade patterns (not to mention wars), but they do not allow for structural shifts.

Routledge et al. present a one-factor model of commodity storage and calibrate this model to certain moments of oil futures prices. Specifically, they choose the parameters of the storage model (the autocorrelation and variance of the demand shock, and the parameters of the net demand curve) to minimize the mean squared errors in the means and variances of oil futures prices with maturities between 1 and 10 months.

They find that the basic one-factor model does a poor job of explaining the variances of longer-tenor futures prices. To mitigate this problem, they propose a model with an additional, and permanent, demand shock that does not affect optimal storage decisions and which is not priced in equilibrium. They calibrate the variance of this parameter so as to match the variance of the 10-month oil futures price, and then choose the remaining parameters to minimize mean squared errors in the means and variances of the remaining futures prices. These scholars do not examine the behavior of correlations between futures prices of different maturities.

Fama and French (1988) and Ng and Pirrong (1994, 1996) do not test a specific model of commodity prices but examine the implications of the convenience yield and structural models for the volatility of commodity prices, and the correlations between futures prices with different maturities. Each of these articles finds that commodity prices tend to be more volatile when markets are in backwardation; that spot prices are more volatile than futures prices; that the disparity between spot and futures volatilities becomes greater when the market is in backwardation; and that correlations between spot and futures prices are near 1 when markets are at full carry and well below 1 when markets are in backwardation.

This book builds on the structural models in the Gustafson tradition, as refined by Scheinkman-Schechtman and their followers; attempts to determine whether the model can explain the empirical regularities documented by Fama-French and Ng-Pirrong; and derives and investigates additional empirical implications. It advances the literature in several ways.

First, it exploits the cross-sectional diversity of commodities, derives models specific to continuously produced and periodically produced commodities, and tests novel implications of these models. Most notably, I show that the predictions of the standard storage model for seasonal commodity prices differ substantially from the observed behavior of these prices. These findings demonstrate that the Deaton-Laroque conjecture for the cause of high commodity autocorrelation is incorrect. This, in turn, motivates suggested lines of future research to explain this high autocorrelation and other aspects of commodity price behavior.

Second, whereas earlier work either ignored issues related to production and decision frequency or focused on low-frequency data, in this book, I focus almost exclusively on the implications of storage models for high-frequency – daily – prices, and use high-frequency data to test these models.

Third, to a much greater degree than in the received literature, in this book, I pay particular attention to the implications of storage models for higher moments of prices, covariation between prices of different maturities, the pricing of commodity options (including more exotic options), and the empirical behavior of stocks.

Fourth, I introduce a new feature into the fundamental shocks in the storage model. Specifically, I examine the implications of stochastic fundamental volatility.

Fifth, I add some numerical and computational wrinkles. Most notably, I draw from the derivatives pricer's toolbox and employ partial differential equation techniques in ways not done heretofore in the storage literature. Moreover, in the empirical work, I implement EKF methods.

Together, these innovations help shed new light on the behavior of storable commodity prices and on the strengths and weaknesses of the structural modeling approach.

The literature on non-storable commodity prices, notably electricity, is far less extensive and far more recent in origin than that on storable commodity prices, primarily because the most important non-storable commodity – electricity – has been traded in spot and forward markets for a very short period of time. Two approaches have dominated this (relatively limited) literature.

The first is to specify reduced-form characterizations of electricity prices. That is, as in the standard approach in derivatives pricing à la Black-Scholes, in this approach, researchers posit a stochastic process that characterizes the evolution of the electricity spot price over time. Given the empirical behavior of these prices – which exhibit pronounced discontinuities – many of the articles in this stream of the literature have posited jump diffusion-type processes for electricity prices. Johnson and Barz (1999) and Geman and Roncoroni (2006) are examples of this. Another reduced-form approach incorporates regime shifts, as in Barone-Adesi and Gigli (2002).

The second approach is structural. The main examples of this approach include Eydeland and Wolyniec (2002) and Pirrong and Jermakyan (2008). These models specify that the spot price of electricity depends on fundamental demand factors (e.g., weather, or "load") and cost factors (e.g., fuel prices); specify stochastic processes for these fundamental factors; and then use standard derivatives pricing methods to solve for the prices of electricity forward contracts and options.

Not surprisingly, I follow the second approach in this book. I go beyond Pirrong-Jermakyan to analyze the pricing of electricity options – including exotic options – in detail.

In sum, this book pushes an established approach for modeling commodity prices to its limits. In so doing, it demonstrates the strengths and weaknesses of these models and, I hope, paves the way for future improvements of our understanding of the behavior of goods that are playing an increasingly important role in world financial markets. Moreover, I also hope that it provides a basis for more reasoned analyses of the contentious policy issues relating to the role of speculation that have dogged commodity markets since the birth of modern futures markets in the years after the American Civil War.

TWO

The Basics of Storable Commodity Modeling

2.1 Introduction

Many important commodities are storable. These include grains, many energy products such as oil and natural gas, and industrial and precious metals. Because of the ability to store, agents have the ability to influence the allocation of consumption of these products over time. Moreover, they typically do so under conditions of uncertainty. Because finance is at root the study of the allocation of resources over time in risky circumstances, the commodity storage problem is fundamentally a problem in finance. Indeed, it is the Ur problem (or pre-Ur problem) of finance: humans have had to make decisions about how to allocate consumption of commodities over time since the dawn of agriculture.

Even a brief consideration of the economics of storage demonstrates that although the problem is a very old one, it is a very challenging one analytically. The problem is inherently a dynamic one with complicated intertemporal dependencies. Storage involves an opportunity cost. If I own a bushel of wheat, I can consume it today or store it for consumption tomorrow – or later. The opportunity cost of consumption today is the value of the commodity tomorrow. I must also pay a physical storage cost and forego any interest I could earn on the money I spend to buy the economy. But under conditions of uncertainty (about future supply or demand, say), the value of the commodity tomorrow is uncertain. What is more, the price tomorrow depends on how much I consume then, which depends on how much I store tomorrow, which depends on my estimate of the value of the commodity the day after tomorrow, which depends on my estimate of its price the day after the day after tomorrow, and on and on.

That is, the storage problem is a dynamic programming problem. These problems are not trivial to solve, but scholars in a variety of disciplines have developed a standard machinery for doing so. In this chapter, I review that machinery, discuss the particular method that I use to solve a variety of storage problems, and examine some specific numerical techniques that I employ repeatedly in this endeavor.

In that regard, it must be emphasized that the solution of storage problems is inherently a numerical and computational exercise. The closed-form solutions so near and dear to the hearts of most academics are few and far between. In my view, this is a feature, not a bug.

It is a feature because numerical methods provide enormous flexibility that permits the answering of a variety of important questions about commodities. These include:

- How do commodity prices behave?
- What does the forward curve for a commodity look like, and how does its shape change as fundamental economic conditions change?
- How does the amount of a commodity stored change over time in response to fundamental economic conditions?
- How do the higher moments of commodity prices behave?
- How do commodity forward prices with different maturity dates co-vary?
- How should the prices of more complicated commodity derivatives (e.g., options) behave?
- How can we determine whether a particular commodity's price has been distorted; that is, does not reflect fundamental supply and demand conditions in a competitive market, but instead reflects distortions resulting from market power, or excessive speculation?

The models that I review in this chapter, and analyze in detail in subsequent ones, are capable of answering these questions when harnessed to efficient numerical techniques. Indeed, numerical methods are so much more flexible, and restricting attention to closed forms is so constraining, that it would be impossible to answer these questions without numerical methods.

More generally, I am interested in matching the model to data on prices and stocks. Numerical methods produce theoretical prices and stocks that can be compared to actual prices and stocks. Because the ultimate objective is to get numbers to compare to actual data, numerical methods are essential rather than restrictive.

This chapter covers a good deal of ground and provides a basis for the analysis of the rest of the book. It covers the basic storage problem and the economic implications of optimal storage decisions. It provides an overview of how to solve the storage problem and then delves into the numerical

techniques necessary to solve it. This requires an introduction to a variety
of computational techniques, including interpolation methods, numerical
integration, and partial differential equation solvers. This introduction is
only sufficient to provide the reader a basic idea of the approach, but there
are numerous specialized works (cited in the text) that provide the necessary
details.

The remainder of this chapter is organized as follows. Section 2.2 provides an overview of dynamic programming as applied to the commodity
storage problem and outlines a specific, economically intuitive solution
approach. Section 2.3 discusses some of the numerical techniques necessary to implement this solution method. Section 2.4 briefly summarizes the
chapter.

2.2 Dynamic Programming and the Storage Problem: An Overview

2.2.1 Model Overview

This section presents an overview of the basic commodity model that I will
analyze in detail in subsequent chapters. This model focuses on a commodity that is produced and consumed continuously over time. Moreover, as
is the case with most of the received literature, the model is a partial equilibrium one. This greatly simplifies the analysis and permits the derivation
of numerous testable implications, but the choice of a partial equilibrium
framework is not an innocuous one; the results for periodically produced
commodities presented in Chapter 6 demonstrate the limits of the partial equilibrium approach and suggest that a general equilibrium approach
with multiple storable commodities is necessary to explain certain aspects
of commodity price behavior. The model also assumes rationality and rational expectations. These assumptions are often controversial and throughout
history, right up to the very present, there have been widespread allegations
that commodity pricing is irrational. However, the proof is in the empirical
pudding: one of the objectives of this modeling approach is to see whether
commodity models grounded in this rationality assumption can explain the
often extreme behavior of commodities prices.

Now the specifics. Consider a commodity that is produced and consumed
continuously under conditions of uncertainty. The market is perfectly competitive, and transactions costs are zero.

The flow demand for the commodity at time t is denoted by $P = D(q_t^D, \mathbf{Z_t})$, where q_t^D is the quantity of the commodity consumed at t,
and $\mathbf{Z_t}$ is a vector of random variables; these are demand shocks. The flow

supply of the commodity is given by the function $P = S(q_t^S, \mathbf{Y_t})$, where q_t^S is the quantity of the commodity produced at t, and $\mathbf{Y_t}$ is a vector of random variables; these are supply shocks, such as the weather, labor strikes, changes in wages or other input costs, or political disturbances.

All agents in the economy have the same information about the demand and supply shocks. At t, they agree that the joint probability distribution of these shocks at some future date $t' > t$ that is relevant for evaluating risky flows is $\tilde{G}(\mathbf{Z_{t'}}, \mathbf{Y_{t'}}|\mathbf{Z_t}, \mathbf{Y_t})$; for simplicity, I will sometimes denote this function as $\tilde{G}_t(\mathbf{Z_{t'}}, \mathbf{Y_{t'}})$. Moreover, all agents form their expectations rationally based on this probability distribution.[1]

The commodity is storable. For simplicity, I will assume that physical costs of storage are zero. However, agents have an opportunity cost of funds, given by the (continuously compounded) interest rate r. Note that storage is constrained to be non-negative.

Given the assumptions relating to competition and rationality, a competitive equilibrium in this economy solves a social programmer's problem. Specifically, the competitive allocation of production and consumption over time maximizes the expected present value of the stream of consumer surplus minus producer surplus. Formally, for all t, a social planner chooses $\{q_t^D, q_t^S\}$ to solve the following problem:

$$V(x_0, \mathbf{Z_0}, \mathbf{Y_0}) = \max_{q_t^D, q_t^S} \int_0^\infty e^{-rt} \tilde{E}_0[CS(q_t^D, \mathbf{Z_t}) - PS(q_t^S, \mathbf{Y_t})]dt \quad (2.1)$$

where:

- $\tilde{E}$ is the expectation operator associated with $\tilde{G}(.)$.
- $CS(.)$ is the consumer surplus function:

$$CS(q, \mathbf{Z}) = \int_0^q D(q, \mathbf{Z})dq$$

- $PS(.)$ is the producer surplus function:

$$PS(q, \mathbf{Y}) = \int_0^q S(q, \mathbf{Y})dq$$

- x_0 is the initial inventory of the commodity, and

[1] I defer a detailed discussion of the meaning of the perhaps obscure phrase "relevant for evaluating risky flows." For now, it is sufficient to note that if agents are *not* risk neutral, the probability measure used to calculate expectations for valuation purposes may differ from the "physical" probability measure that describes the real-world behavior of the demand and supply shocks.

- the problem is solved subject to the constraints:

$$x_t = \lim_{\Delta t \to 0} [x_{t-\Delta t} + q_t^S - q_t^D]$$

$$x_t \geq 0$$

The first constraint says that carry-out at time t (i.e., the amount of inventory at t) is the amount carried in ($x_{t-\Delta t}$) plus production minus consumption at t. The second constraint means that inventory cannot be negative. Carry-out is either positive or zero. If it is equal to zero, it is said that there is a "stockout."

In the maximization problem, the time-zero expectation $E_0(.)$ is conditional on Y_0 and Z_0.

There are a variety of methods for solving problems of this type. These methods all derive from the Optimality Principle originally introduced by Bellman (1957). There are numerous extended treatments of the Bellman approach, so I will not go into detail about it here. The interested reader can consult Judd (1998) or Fackler and Miranda (2002) for recent and accessible treatments.[2]

Instead, I will focus on an economically intuitive way to frame and solve this problem that was employed by Williams and Wright (1991). This approach views the problem from the perspective of the individual, atomistic agents in the economy who use prices to guide their decisions. The analysis follows the typical steps of partial equilibrium analysis. The optimizing decisions of competitive agents *conditional on prices* are characterized; equilibrium constraints (quantity supplied equals quantity demanded) are imposed; and equilibrium prices generate individual behavior that is consistent with these constraints. It is also attractive because it works with the things that are potentially observable: spot and futures prices.

2.2.2 Competitive Equilibrium

As already noted, under the assumptions made herein, the First and Second Welfare Theorems imply that a competitive equilibrium is a social optimum (i.e., solves equation (2.1)), and vice versa. So, consider the choices facing a competitive agent in this economy.

To advance the analysis, I will assume that there is a frictionless forward market where market participants can trade contracts for future delivery on

---

[2] Stachurski (2009) provides a more technical, but still accessible, introduction. Lucas and Stokey (1989) give a very thorough, self-contained treatment of the subject.

the commodity. Because the empirical research will focus on commodities with active forward markets, this is a natural assumption. Moreover, I assume that there are forward markets for every possible delivery date. This assumption is obviously unrealistic, but it greatly facilitates the analysis.

One important decision that agents make is how much of the commodity to store. When making this decision, price-taking agents can compare spot and forward prices. When the spot price is P and the forward price for delivery an instant later is F, there is an arbitrage opportunity available to market participants if:

$$e^{-rdt} F > P$$

They can buy the spot commodity for P and sell a forward contract at F. This locks in a riskless cash flow with present value of $e^{-rdt} F - P$. Thus, if the foregoing inequality holds, agents can make a riskless profit.

This is inconsistent with a competitive equilibrium in the forward and spot markets for the commodity. This strategy is available to everyone, meaning that all agents would try to purchase the commodity on the spot market at P and sell on the forward market at F. This would drive up the spot price and drive down the forward price until the arbitrage opportunity disappears. Thus, in equilibrium:

$$e^{-rdt} F \le P$$

Now consider the opposite situation, with:

$$e^{-rdt} F < P$$

This may or may not represent an arbitrage opportunity. *If* there are inventories of the commodity (meaning that there is an agent who does not want to consume today at current prices, but wants to consume in the future), this *does* represent an arbitrage. The would-be storer can sell the commodity from inventory, at P, and buy the forward contract at F. The next instant, he has $P - e^{-rdt} F$ dollars and a unit of the commodity (which is delivered to him under the forward contract). This strategy dominates just holding the good in storage. By following the latter strategy, the agent has a unit of the commodity but does not have the $P - e^{-rdt} F$ dollars.

Note that this opportunity is available as long as inventories are positive. Recall, however, that there is a non-negativity constraint on storage. Hence, if inventories are zero, but $P - e^{-rdt} F > 0$, there is *no* arbitrage opportunity. Exploiting the arbitrage opportunity would require selling from inventory, but if inventories are zero (i.e., everyone consumes all that is available on the spot market), it is impossible to implement the strategy. Thus, at t, it is possible for $P > e^{-rdt} F$ only if $x_t = 0$.

Putting this all together implies the following restrictions on prices in a competitive market:

$$x_t > 0 \Rightarrow P = e^{-rdt} F \tag{2.2}$$

$$x_t = 0 \Rightarrow P \geq e^{-rdt} F \tag{2.3}$$

This can also be expressed as:

$$0 = \min(x_t, P - e^{-rdt} F)$$

Equations (2.2) and (2.3) provide a characterization of spot-forward price relations in competitive equilibrium. Moreover, spot prices also determine equilibrium consumption and production. If the equilibrium price at t is P, the equilibrium consumption q_t^D solves:

$$P = D(q_t^D, \mathbf{Z_t})$$

and the equilibrium consumption q_t^S solves:

$$P = S(q_t^S, \mathbf{Y_t})$$

Moreover (with a slight abuse of notation), recall that carry-out x_t, carry-in x_{t-dt}, and production and consumption are related:

$$x_t = \lim_{\Delta t \to 0} [x_{t-\Delta t} + q_t^S - q_t^D]$$

Equilibrium spot and forward prices must solve all of these equations simultaneously. These prices thus determine the allocation of the resource over time, and because the competitive equilibrium is optimal, this allocation also solves (2.1).

2.2.3 The Next Step: Determining the Forward Price

Before proceeding further, it is worthwhile to step back and remember what we are really interested in knowing. One of the things we want to know is how prices vary with the state variables of the problem: the demand shocks, the supply shocks, and inventory. Looking over the previous subsection, it might appear that to solve for the equilibrium, we actually have to solve for *two* price functions: a spot price function and a forward price function.

In fact, our problem is less difficult, because finance theory implies that there is a link between spot prices and forward prices. Specifically, as of date t, the forward price for delivery on some date $T > t$ is the expectation, under some probability measure, of the spot price at T.[3] Thus, if we have a spot price function, we can apply the expectation operator to it to determine the forward price.

One phrase that jumps out in the previous paragraph is "under some probability measure." It is conventional in the storage literature to use the "natural" or "physical" probability measure in taking expectations.[4] The natural measure is the one that characterizes the actual probability distribution of the supply and demand shocks in the model. I call the probability distribution associated with the physical measure $G(.)$.

This choice is correct if and only if there are risk-neutral agents in the economy. In this case, if forward prices deviate from the expected spot price, the risk-neutral agents can speculate profitably. They buy (sell) the forward contract when the forward price is less than (higher than) the expected spot price. This strategy generates a profit on average, because agents expect to reverse their forward position at the expected spot price in the future. This strategy subjects them to risk, but if they are risk neutral, they do not care; the deviation between the forward price generates a positive expected profit, which is all that matters to them.

Unless all agents in the economy are risk neutral, however, it is inappropriate to use the physical measure to take expectations when determining the forward price. If agents are risk averse, they would not necessarily want to buy (sell) a forward contract when the forward contract is below (above) the expectation of the spot price (under the physical measure). By so doing, they would earn a profit on average, but this average profit may be insufficient to compensate these risk-averse agents for the risk that they incur by following this strategy.

Finance theory implies the existence of a so-called equivalent martingale measure (sometimes shortened to "equivalent measure" or called a "pricing measure") such that forward prices are the expectation of the future spot price, where the expectation is calculated using this measure. This is probability distribution function $\tilde{G}(\mathbf{Z}, \mathbf{Y})$ introduced before. This distribution is equivalent to the physical measure $G(.)$, but is appropriate for taking expectations for the purpose of calculating forward prices (and the prices of other contingent claims). The word "equivalent" means that events that are impossible under the physical measure are impossible under the pricing measure. Using as before the notation $\tilde{E}$

---

[3] There are too many useful references to list here. Some representative ones are Shreve (2004), Duffie (1996), Elliott and Kopp (2004), and Nielsen (1999).

[4] See, for instance, Williams and Wright (1991).

to indicate expectations under the equivalent measure,

$$F_{t,T} = \tilde{E}_t(P_T)$$

where $F_{t,T}$ means the forward price, quoted at time t for delivery at time T, and P_T is the spot price at time T.

In essence, the pricing measure incorporates risk aversion into the analysis. It is important to note that in the storage problem, this measure is not unique because the supply and demand shocks are not traded assets. This means that the pricing measure that prevails in the market depends on the particular risk preferences of market participants.

With the concept of a pricing measure in hand, we have reduced the complexity of our problem. We need to solve only for the spot price as a function of the state variables; we can then determine the forward price as the expectation under the equivalent measure.

This allows us to recast the problem that must be solved. Specifically, we are searching for a function $P(\mathbf{Z}, \mathbf{Y}, x_{t-dt})$ that solves:

$$P(\mathbf{Z_t}, \mathbf{Y_t}, x_{t-dt}) \geq e^{-rdt} \tilde{E}_t P(\mathbf{Z_{t+dt}}, \mathbf{Y_{t+dt}}, x_t)$$

$$P = D(q_t^D, \mathbf{Z})$$

and the equilibrium output q_t^S solves:

$$P = S(q_t^S, \mathbf{Y})$$

Moreover, carry-out x_t, carry-in x_{t-dt}, and production and consumption are related:

$$x_t = x_{t-dt} + q_t^S - q_t^D$$

Our way forward is now somewhat clearer. We need to solve for an unknown *function*. Specifically, we need to solve for the spot price as a function of the state variables. The spot price function must satisfy the foregoing equations and constraints.

Solving for an unknown function is not a trivial task. Doing so typically requires recursive techniques by which an initial guess is progressively refined until the function converges (i.e., until additional refinements lead to very small changes in the function). Previous scholars in this area have mapped out a specific course for solving this problem[5]:

1. Make an initial guess for the spot price function.
2. Given the assumed spot price function and the equivalent measure, solve for the forward price as a function of the state variables.

[5] See, especially, Williams and Wright (1991).

3. For each possible value of the state variables, find the production and consumption, and hence the amount of carry-out, that equates the spot price to the discounted forward price.
4. If the solution to (3) implies a negative inventory, set inventory to zero and solve for the price such that consumption at that price equals production at that price plus carry-in.
5. Given the consumption level determined q^D for all possible values of the state variables, determine the spot price $D(q^D, \mathbf{Z}, \mathbf{Y})$. Use this as the new guess for the spot price function.
6. Check to see whether the newly solved-for spot price function differs from the spot price function originally assumed by more than some pre-specified amount. If it does not, the analysis is complete. If it does differ by more than the pre-specified tolerance, use the new spot price function and return to step 2.

Sounds easy, no?

2.2.4 Specifying Functional Forms and Shock Dynamics

Actually, it is not that easy. To follow the road map, it is necessary to make more specific assumptions about functional forms and, perhaps more important, about the behavior of the demand and supply shocks: that is, about the relevant pricing measure.

In so doing, it is first necessary to acknowledge that we operate under the curse of dimensionality. Thus, although heretofore I have proceeded as if there is an arbitrary number of random shocks in the economy, practical computational considerations – the curse of dimensionality – effectively make it necessary to limit the analysis to one or two.

Most of the extant literature assumes one shock but, as I discuss in more detail in the next chapter, such a model cannot accurately characterize the high-frequency dynamics of commodity prices; most notably, it cannot generate imperfect correlations between forward prices with different maturities. So, because one shock is inadequate, and three is too many because of computational constraints, I will play Goldilocks and decide that two shocks are just right. I call the shocks y_t and z_t.

Given this choice, I specify the following constant elasticity demand function:

$$D(q, z_t, y_t) = \Phi e^{z_t + y_t} q^\beta$$

where Φ is a constant and the demand elasticity β is also a constant. Moreover, I specify the following supply function:

$$S(q) = \theta + \frac{v}{(Q - q)^\psi}$$

where Q is production capacity and ψ and θ are parameters. This specification exhibits convex and increasing marginal costs (the competitive supply curve being the industry marginal cost curve). Marginal cost approaches infinity as output approaches capacity. ψ determines how sharply marginal cost rises as output approaches capacity. As ψ grows arbitrarily large, the marginal cost curve becomes L-shaped.

Note that these specifications place all of the uncertainty in the demand function. This is an immaterial choice, made purely for expositional and programming convenience.

Now for the behavior of the demand shocks. Following the well-established example of drunks looking for their wallets under the lamp-post, most scholars in the storage literature, and the finance literature more broadly, assume Gaussian ("normal") dynamics for random shocks. That is, they assume that demand disturbances (or the analogous disturbances in the problem of interest) obey a normal distribution. I will do the same here.

Specifically, I assume that under the physical measure, the demand shocks are Ito processes with a particular form:

$$dz_t = -\mu_z z_t dt + \sigma_z d B_t \qquad (2.4)$$

$$dy_t = -\mu_y y_t dt + \sigma_y d C_t \qquad (2.5)$$

where B_t and C_t are Brownian motions. The instantaneous correlation between these Brownian motions is ρdt. The use of Brownian motions as the sole source of uncertainty in the demand shocks means that increments to these demand shocks have a normal distribution.

Several comments are in order. First, (2.4) and (2.5) specify that the demand shocks follow an Orenstein-Uhlenbeck (OU) process. This process "mean reverts." That is, for instance, when z_t is above (below) zero, it tends to drift down (up). The persistence of the demand shocks depends on the sizes of μ_z and μ_y. The smaller the values of these coefficients, the less rapidly the shocks tend to revert to their long-run mean of zero; that is, the more persistent they are.

Intuitively, persistence should affect storage decisions. Storage is used to even out the effects of supply and demand fluctuations over time. If these fluctuations are very rapid, storage is likely to be more useful than if supply or demand take long excursions above or below their long-run means. Put differently, storage is used to shift resources over time in response to changes in economic conditions. The objective is to take resources from times when they are relatively abundant to times when they are scarce. If demand is highly persistent, a demand shock affects current and future scarcity almost equally, meaning that a demand shock of this type should have little effect on the amount of the commodity stored because there is little to be gained by shifting the allocation of consumption over time. Conversely, if a demand shock is expected to damp out rapidly, such a shock affects the scarcity of the commodity today relative to its expected future scarcity; adjusting storage in response to such a demand shock, therefore, is an economical response.

Second, μ_y and μ_z are the values of the OU parameters under the physical measure. If the shocks follow an OU process under the physical measure, then the Girsanov Theorem implies that under the pricing measure, the shocks also follow an OU process, but with different drift terms; however, σ_z, σ_y, and ρ are the same under the physical and pricing measures.[6] Specifically, standard arguments imply that under the equivalent (pricing) measure:

$$dz_t = (\lambda_z - \mu_z z_t)dt + \sigma_z d\tilde{B}_t \tag{2.6}$$

$$dy_t = (\lambda_y - \mu_y y_t)dt + \sigma_y d\tilde{C}_t \tag{2.7}$$

In these expressions, the shift to the pricing measure results in the addition of a market price of risk adjustment to the drift terms in the demand shock Ito processes. These adjustments reflect the risk preferences of the marginal participants in the market. The $\tilde{B}_t$ and $\tilde{C}_t$ are Brownian motions under the equivalent measure, but not under the physical measure; relatedly, B_t and C_t are not Brownian motions under the equivalent measure.

Third, it is possible that μ_z, μ_y, σ_z, σ_y, ρ, λ_z, and λ_y are functions of z_t, y_t, and t. That said, in all of the analysis of this book, I assume that these are constants.

Fourth, the normality assumption is made for convenience. It is possible to specify different dynamics for these shock variables. For instance, the Brownian motion assumption made earlier means that the state variables are continuous in time: they do not exhibit discontinuous "jumps." It is possible, however, to specify other dynamics, such as a jump-diffusion process, in which such discontinuities can occur. More generally, it would be possible to specify that the demand shocks follow Levy processes, which can be decomposed into a continuous "diffusion" component and two discontinuous jump components.[7]

---

[6] See Shreve (2004) for a statement of the Girsanov Theorem.

[7] For applications of Levy processes in finance, see Schoutens (2003) and Cont and Takov (2003).

The normality assumption permits me to draw on a vast array of existing numerical tools, most important methods for solving partial differential equations; the reasons for this importance will become clear momentarily. That said, the effects of more complex demand shock dynamics are a worthy subject for future research. Storage is a means of responding to uncertainty, so presumably the nature of that uncertainty matters. For instance, presumably, agents will make different storage decisions when demand can jump discontinuously than when it cannot. Exploration of this possibility will have to wait for the future, however, as even the simpler Gaussian case presents enough practical challenges, and can provide enough valuable insights, for one book.[8]

2.3 A More Detailed Look at the Numerical Implementation

I have now laid out the basic storage problem, the equations that this storage problem implies, and an overview of the method for solving these equations. I have also pared down the problem to a numerically manageable one with two sources of uncertainty. Given this specification, it is now possible to delve into the details of the numerical methods for solving this problem.

The objective of the analysis is to determine the spot price function $P(y, z, \hat{x})$ and a carry-out function $x(y, z, \hat{x})$, where here $\hat{x}$ denotes the carry-in. The $P(.)$ and $x(.)$ functions, respectively, describe how prices and carry-in depend on the three state variables.

Because $\hat{x}$, y, and z are real numbers, it is not practical to solve for these functions exactly for every possible value of these variables as suggested in the road map in the prior section. Instead, these functions are approximated on a grid. That is, the analyst discretizes the problem and evaluates the functions for N_y values of y, N_z values of z, and N_x values of $\hat{x}$.

A conventional approach is to create evenly spaced grids in all three variables. For instance, the y grid is $\{y_0, y_0 + \delta y, \ldots, y_0 + (N_y - 1)\delta y\}$, the z grid is $\{z_0, z_0 + \delta z, \ldots, z_0 + (N_z - 1)\delta z\}$, and the carry-in grid is $\{\hat{x}_0, \hat{x}_0 + \delta x, \ldots, \hat{x}_0 + (N_x - 1)\delta x\}$. The lowest and highest values in each grid should be chosen so that the grids span the values likely to occur in practice. For y and z, therefore, these low and high values will depend on the statistical properties of these variables, namely their mean and standard deviation. For $\hat{x}$, the choice for the lower value is easy: it is the lower bound

---

[8] When jumps can occur, the forward price function solves a partial integro-differential equation ("PIDE"). These present considerable numerical challenges.

on storage, zero.[9] Determining the upper bound typically requires some trial and error: solve the problem given a guess for the carry-in grid, simulate the behavior of this variable, and check to see whether the simulated carry-out frequently exceeds the maximum value in the carry-in grid. If it is, increase the maximum value of $\hat{x}$ and try again.

The fineness of the grids (that is, N_y, N_z, and N_x) involves a trade-off. The greater these values – that is, the finer the grids – the more accurate the approximation of the functions of interest. At the same time, however, the greater these values, the more computationally costly and time-consuming the analysis. In particular, because (a) it is necessary to solve for the equilibrium at every grid point, and (b) this involves numerical solution of a fixed point problem, computation costs rise rapidly with the number of grid points.

Given the grids, the analysis can begin in earnest. One starts with a guess for a spot price function. One then uses this spot price function to derive forward price function, $F(y, z, x)$.[10] Now, a forward price is a price for delivery of the commodity at some future date, which raises the question: What date? As specified previously, the problem is in continuous time, and agents can make decisions continuously, so F would be the price of a contract that expires in an instant. Just as it is impractical to treat the y, z, and x_0 as continuous, however, it is also computationally impractical to treat time as continuous. Instead, it is also necessary to discretize time and solve for a forward contract that expires some (finite) time hence, in δt years. Put differently, although as in many finance problems it is convenient to derive results in continuous time under the assumption that markets trade claims for all possible delivery dates continuously, numerical solution must be in discrete time.

Recall that a primary goal of the analysis is to make predictions about the high-frequency behavior of commodity prices, so as to match the model predictions with observable, high-frequency data. Because daily data are available for many commodities, this motivates a choice of δt of a day (i.e., $\delta t = 1/365$). For commodities for which time homogeneity is not reasonable, notably seasonally produced ones, this choice is typically not computationally practical because it is necessary to estimate a separate function for every point in the time grid corresponding to a single production

---

[9] This is for "natural" commodities, for which there is a non-negativity constraint on storage. As will be seen for an "artificial" commodity, namely an environmental commodity such as carbon permits, depending on market design this minimum value could be negative.

[10] The methods for using the spot price function to determine a forward price function are discussed later.

cycle (e.g., a year for corn); estimating 365 such functions is time consuming and tests computer memory constraints.

It should also be noted that the choice of the fineness of the time discretization affects the choice of the carry-in discretization. If the $\hat{x}$ grid is so coarse that for $\delta t = 1/365$, carry-out is always positive when carry-in is $\hat{x}_0 + \delta x$ (i.e., the lowest positive value in the carry-in grid), it is impossible to estimate with any accuracy the exact value of $\hat{x}$ for which a stockout will occur. Because stockouts are critically important for determining the behavior of prices, this is highly undesirable. Thus, for a choice of δt, it is necessary to check after solving the problem that the $\hat{x}$ grid is fine enough (i.e., δx is small enough) that $x(y, z, \hat{x})$ is zero for combinations of y and z that are likely to occur with non-trivial frequency. If this is not the case, it is necessary to make the $\hat{x}$ grid finer.[11]

Once the state variable and time grids are in place, and a guess for a forward price function has been made, the analysis proceeds in several steps:

1. Loop over all of the values of y, z, and $\hat{x}$ in the grids.
2. For each value of y, z, and $\hat{x}$, solve for the value of carry-out x such that $P(y, z, \hat{x}, x) = e^{-r\delta t} F(y, z, x)$. If this value of $x \geq 0$, this is the equilibrium value of carry-out. If $x < 0$, indicating a violation of the non-negativity constraint on storage, set $x(y, z, \hat{x}) = 0$. Note that because the forward price function is only known at grid points, when solving this equation, it is necessary to interpolate between x grid points. I discuss the interpolation issue in more detail later.
3. Check to see whether the spot price function thus determined is sufficiently close to the initially assumed spot price function. If it is, stop. If not, use the new spot price function as the initial guess, solve for a new forward price function, and return to step 1.

Steps 2 and 3 require some additional explanation.

First consider step 2. In equilibrium, the spot price equals the marginal value of the commodity to consumers, and the marginal cost of producing it. The marginal value depends on the amount consumed, q_c, and the marginal cost depends on the amount produced, q_s. Moreover, carry-out is carry-in plus the difference between the amount produced and the amount

---

[11] It can also be desirable to use an unevenly spaced $\hat{x}$ grid, with points closer together for small values of $\hat{x}$ and more distantly spaced for large values of $\hat{x}$. As it turns out, when carry-in is large, carry-out is a nearly linear function of carry-in, so a coarse grid for large values of $\hat{x}$ is acceptable (because linear interpolation is quite accurate). The finer grid for small values of carry-in permits more accurate approximation of the non-linear carry-out function for such values.

consumed. Thus, if carry-out is x, q_c and q_s must satisfy the following equations:

$$x = \hat{x} + q_s - q_c$$

and

$$D(q_c, z) = S(q_s, y)$$

The solution to these equations defines an implicit function $P(y, z, \hat{x}, x)$. This function is increasing in carry-out x. As x increases, it is necessary to increase quantity supplied q_s and reduce quantity demanded q_d. These, in turn, require a rise in the spot price.

Given this implicit function $P(.)$ and the guess for the forward price function (which will be decreasing in x because a higher carry-out today involves a higher carry-in tomorrow and, hence, a lower price then), it is necessary to solve a fixed point problem to complete step 2. Because for a well-behaved $F(.)$ function, $P(x) - e^{-r\delta t} F(x)$ will be strictly increasing in x, this problem can be solved readily using conventional root-finding techniques such as Newton-Raphson, or the zero-finding routines in software such as MATLAB. Although $P(x)$ can be evaluated to a user-defined level of accuracy for any value of x (although this also entails a root-finding exercise to solve the set of equations just discussed), $F(x)$ must be determined by interpolation because the F function is known exactly only for the points on the $\hat{x}$ grid. This solution gives both the spot price and carry-out for every value of the shocks and carry-in in the grid.

There are a variety of interpolation methods. Williams and Wright (1991) employ a polynomial technique. Specifically, they estimate a regression:

$$F(x) = \sum_{j=0}^{N_o} \alpha_j x^j + \epsilon$$

using least squares. In this expression, N_o is the order of the polynomial; for example, $N_o = 3$ for a cubic fit. The x values used in the regression correspond to the points in the x grid. Thus, the number of data points in the regression is the number of points in the carry-in grid.

Given the estimated α parameters, the value of the forward price for an arbitrary value of x is just:

$$F(x) = \sum_{j=0}^{N_o} \alpha_j x^j$$

Although the polynomial approach is easily implemented, there are other interpolation methods that have more desirable properties. These include spline methods and colocation methods. Rather than re-inventing the wheel, I refer the reader to careful discussions of these methods in Fackler and Miranda (2002). What is more, high-level mathematical software packages, such as MATLAB, include interpolation routines that permit the user to choose a variety of interpolation methods, including splines.

Now consider step 3. Once step 2 is solved, one has a spot price defined for each y, z, and $\hat{x}$ in the valuation grid. Recall that a forward price is the expectation of the spot price under the equivalent measure. This expectation, in turn, is given by an integral.

There are a variety of numerical techniques to estimate this integral.[12] In general, in these methods, the forward price for y^0, z^0, and $\hat{x}^0$ values in their respective grids can be determined by:

$$F(y^0, z^0, \hat{x}^0) = \sum_{i=1}^{N_y} \sum_{j=1}^{N_z} p(y_i, z_j | y^0, z^0) P(y_i, z_j, x(y_i, z_j, \hat{x}^0))$$

where $p(y_i, z_j | y^0, z^0)$ is the probability that tomorrow's value of y will equal y_i (a value in the grid), and tomorrow's value of z will equal z_j (again, in the grid), given that the current values of these shocks are y^0 and z^0 (both grid values), respectively. These probabilities are derived from the dynamics of y and z.

Note that estimating this integral involves an estimation of the spot price for a value of x *not* necessarily on the x grid. This is because $x(y_i, z_j, \hat{x})$ is not necessarily (and will almost never be) one of the N_x values in the x grid.

Although this integral method is widely employed, I prefer another method and use it hereafter. Specifically, this method solves a partial differential equation to determine the forward price.

The Feynman-Kac Theorem implies that the forward price function that solves the integral must solve a particular partial differential equation (PDE) and vice versa.[13] Specifically, the F function must solve:

$$0 = \frac{\partial F_{t,\tau}}{\partial t} + \mu_z^* \frac{\partial F_{t,\tau}}{\partial x} + \mu_y^* \frac{\partial F_{t,\tau}}{\partial y} + \frac{1}{2}\sigma_z^2 \frac{\partial^2 F_{t,\tau}}{\partial z^2}$$

$$+ \frac{1}{2}\sigma_y^2 \frac{\partial^2 F_{t,\tau}}{\partial y^2} + \rho\sigma_z\sigma_y \frac{\partial^2 F_{t,\tau}}{\partial z \partial y} \qquad (2.8)$$

[12] Common methods include Simpson's rule and Gaussian quadratures. See Fackler and Miranda (2002).

[13] See Oskendal (2003) for a discussion of the Feynman-Kac Theorem. This is a generalization of Kolmogorov's backward equation, which can also be used to produce the PDE. Arbitrage arguments can also be employed to derive this equation. See Wilmott, Dewynne, and Howison (1993).

where $\mu_z^* = \lambda_z - \mu_z z_t$ and $\mu_z^* = \lambda_y - \mu_y y_t$. The right-hand side of (2.8) is called the infinitesimal generator of F.

Therefore, one can determine the forward price function by solving the valuation PDE (2.8) subject to the initial boundary condition $F(y, z, x, 0) = P(y, z, x)$, where I have expanded the notation to include a fourth argument in the forward price function to represent time to expiration. This condition means that at expiration, the forward price equals the spot price.[14]

The PDE approach is attractive because there are robust, well-known methods to solve such equations. Specifically, finite difference methods are widely employed in finance, engineering, and the physical sciences to solve PDEs. These methods have been the subject of intense study and, as a result, it is possible to draw on a vast body of work and greatly refined and experience-tested techniques. Moreover, the fact that partial derivatives are estimated along with the values of the contingent claim of interest is quite useful. These partial derivatives are important determinants of price dynamics, and the accurate and simultaneous estimation of these partial derivatives facilitates the analysis of these dynamics.

I will go into the details of these methods momentarily, but before doing so, I will briefly describe what these methods do and show how to apply them in the storage problem. In brief, a finite difference method will produce $F(y, z, x)$ for *every* point in the $\{y, z\}$ grid, for a given value of x. Thus, in the storage problem, one starts with a matrix of values of the spot price, where the values in the matrix correspond to the values for each y and z point, for a given value of carry-in x (where, recall, this is the carry-in at the expiration of the forward contract). The finite difference method then provides the value of the forward price δt years *prior to* expiration, again for each y and z value for this value of carry-in at expiration. It is necessary to solve this PDE – and, hence, produce a value matrix – for every possible value of carry-in in the x grid.

Note, however, that this forward price at δt years prior to expiration is conditional on carry-in in δt years, not for carry-in at the valuation date, which is δt years prior to expiration. Because (a) carry-in in δt years is carry-out at the valuation date, and (b) carry-out and valuation date carry-out ("current date" carry-out) can differ (and usually do), an additional step is required to determine the current date forward price for every point in the y, z, and x grid. Specifically, it is necessary to implement a so-called jump condition to find the forward price.

---

[14] Two other boundary conditions are required. I discuss these further later.

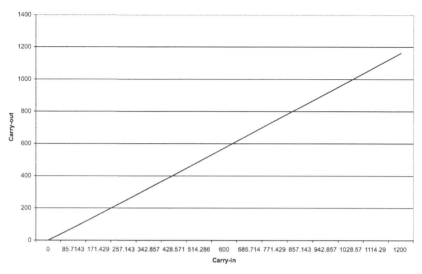

Figure 2.1.

This involves another interpolation. Recall that in step 2, one has solved for carry-out $x(y, z, \hat{x})$ for $\hat{x}$ values in the grid. By solving the PDE, one has determined $F(y, z, \hat{x}')$ for each $\hat{x}'$ in the grid. To implement the jump condition, for each $\hat{x}$ in the grid, (a) find $x(y, z, \hat{x})$, and (b) interpolate to find $F(y, z, x(y, z, \hat{x}))$. This is a one-dimensional interpolation and must be executed for each y and z value. Once this jump condition is implemented, step 3 is complete.

This can be illustrated by a figure. Figure 2.1 represents current carry-out, for those same current values of z and y, as a function of current carry-in. Figure 2.2 represents the forward price in δt years, for given current values of z and y, as a function of carry-in (depicted on the horizontal axis). The grid points at which the carry-in values are located are indicated by hash marks on the x−axis. Assume that current carry-in takes the value of $\hat{x} = 600$. The current carry-out graph indicates that given a carry-in of $\hat{x}$, carry-out will equal $x^* = 573$. Because x^* falls between grid points in the forward price graph, to determine the forward price corresponding to current carry-in of $\hat{x}$, it is necessary to interpolate using the forward price values corresponding to the grid points.

2.3.1 Solving a PDE Using Finite Differences:
The One-Dimensional Case

As already noted, to make the solution to the storage problem interesting and realistic, it is necessary to assume at least two sources of uncertainty.

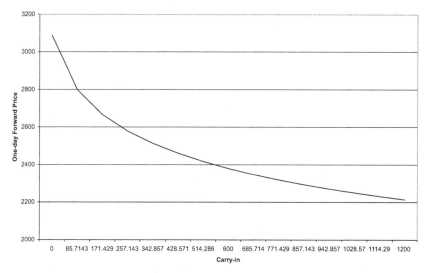

Figure 2.2.

Thus, it is necessary to solve a two-dimensional PDE in y and z. Before discussing the methods for doing this, to get familiar with the method, it is worthwhile to study its implementation in the simpler, one-dimensional case. Here, I briefly outline an unconditionally numerically stable solution technique: the implicit method.[15]

In the 1D case, one solves a PDE in, say, z:

$$0 = \frac{\partial F}{\partial t} + \mu_z^* \frac{\partial F}{\partial z} + \frac{1}{2}\sigma_z^2 \frac{\partial^2 F}{\partial z^2}$$

To solve this equation, one needs to determine the partial derivatives. These are done by finite difference approximations in the time and z grids. Specifically, for the time partial derivative:

$$\frac{\partial F}{\partial t} \approx \frac{F^0 - F^1}{\delta t}$$

[15] Explicit methods (such as the binomial method) are well known and very easy to implement. However, they are not unconditionally numerically stable. This means that for particular choices of the time step δt and the z step δz, the method may give nonsensical, explosive solutions. Thus, achieving stability requires the imposition of constraints on δz and δt. Implicit methods do not impose such a constraint. The necessary constraint is even more costly in 2D problems, so avoiding it is computationally attractive. The Crank-Nicolson method combines explicit and implicit methods. Although this method is unconditionally stable and is more accurate than the implicit method, it exhibits some undesirable properties. See Duffy (2006). As a result, I avoid it and use the implicit method.

where F^0 is the forward price at expiration (one time step hence, because when implementing step 3 shown earlier, the PDE is always solved for δt years prior to expiration) and F^1 is the forward price one time step prior to expiration.

For the z partials, it is conventional to employ central finite differences. Specifically, for point z_i, $i = \{2, \ldots, N_z - 1\}$ in the z grid:

$$\frac{\partial F}{\partial z} \approx \frac{F^1_{i+1} - F^1_{i-1}}{2\delta z}$$

and

$$\frac{\partial^2 F}{\partial z^2} \approx \frac{F^1_{i+1} - 2F^1_i + F^1_{i-1}}{\delta z^2}$$

where F^1_i is the value of the forward price at the ith z grid point, δt years prior to expiration.

Plugging these approximations back into the PDE equation and simplifying produces equations such as:

$$F^0_i = AF^1_{i-1} + BF^1_i + CF^1_{i+1}$$

for $i = 2, \ldots, N_z - 1$. That is, with the approximations for the partial derivatives, the PDE produces a system of linear equations. The values on the left-hand side of each equation are known: they are the spot prices at expiration. The coefficients A, B, and C depend on δt, δz, μ_z, and σ_z.[16]

Note, however, that there are $N_z - 2$ equations, but N_z unknowns, the F^1_i. Thus, additional information is required to solve the system. This comes in the form of boundary conditions that specify the behavior of the forward price for the highest and lowest values of z in the grid. Boundary conditions for the storage problem require a detailed discussion, which I defer for a bit. For now, to advance the exposition, I just specify the following lower and upper conditions:

$$0 = A_1 F^1_1 + B_1 F^1_2 + C_1 F^1_3 + D_1 F^1_4$$

and

$$0 = A_N F^1_{N_z} + B_N F^1_{N_z-1} + C_N F^1_{N_z-2} + D_N F^1_{N_z-3}$$

These are, in the argot of finite difference methods, boundary conditions of the von Neumann type.

---

[16] If μ_z and σ_z depend on z, these coefficients also depend on the grid location; that is, on the i.

We now have N_z equations in N_z unknowns. $N_z - 2$ of the equations come from the PDE and the finite difference approximations. The remaining two come from the boundary conditions. It is straightforward to solve these N_z equations. Once this is done, one has solved for the forward price as of δt years prior to expiration for each $\hat{x}$ in the carry-in grid and each z in its grid. With these values, it is possible to perform the interpolations in step 2 and solve for optimal carry-out.

2.3.2 Solving the 2D PDE

The interesting and relevant 2D storage problem can be solved using finite difference methods as well, but the move from one dimension to two is anything but trivial. The same basic approach of using finite differences to approximate partial derivatives is applicable, but the number of equations that must be solved increases by a factor of $N_y \times N_z$, the product of the number of z points and the number of y points. This increases computational costs substantially and requires the development of additional techniques.

The most widely employed method for solving 2D PDEs is called the alternating direction implicit method, or ADI. Although widely employed, it has some deficiencies that arise from (a) its reliance on explicit finite differences as well as implicit ones, and (b) its inability to handle problems where the y and z variables have a non-zero correlation.

There is another and, in my view, highly superior way to solve 2D PDEs. This method, called the splitting technique, was developed by Soviet mathematicians in the 1960s.[17] In a nutshell, as the name suggests, the method involves splitting the 2D PDE into pieces. For each y, one solves a 1D PDE in z: this is the "z-split." Then, given this solution, for each z, one solves a 1D PDE in y: this is the "y-split." Finally, if y and z are correlated, one solves a PDE in z and y: this is the "correlation" split.

In more detail, the method proceeds as follows. As its name suggests, the splitting method works by splitting the PDE (2.7) into three parts at each time step. The first PDE "split," which captures the effect of the purely z-related terms, is:

$$0 = \frac{\partial F_{t,\tau}}{\partial t} + \mu_z^* \frac{\partial F_{t,\tau}}{\partial x} + \frac{1}{2}\sigma_z^2 \frac{\partial^2 F_{t,\tau}}{\partial z^2} \tag{2.9}$$

---

[17] This method is described in Yanenko (1971), Ikonen and Toivanen (2009), and Duffy (2006).

The second split handles the cross derivative term:

$$0 = \frac{\partial F_{t,\tau}}{\partial t} + \rho \sigma_z \sigma_y \frac{\partial^2 F_{t,\tau}}{\partial z \partial y} \tag{2.10}$$

The third PDE split, which handles the purely y-related terms, is:

$$0 = \frac{\partial F_{t,\tau}}{\partial t} + \mu_y^* \frac{\partial F_{t,\tau}}{\partial y} + \frac{1}{2} \sigma_y^2 \frac{\partial^2 F_{t,\tau}}{\partial y^2} \tag{2.11}$$

One time step prior to expiry, (2.9) is solved using an implicit method for each different y value from the lowest to the highest. At each time step, the solution to (2.9) is used as the initial boundary condition in the solution for (2.10), which is again solved implicitly. Then, the solution for (2.10) is used as the initial condition for (2.11), which is solved implicitly for each z from highest to lowest. At all time steps but the one immediately preceding expiration, the solution to (2.11) from the prior time step is used as the initial condition for (2.9).

The effect of the curse of dimensionality is evident here. Whereas solving a 1D PDE requires solving one set of linear equations, in the splitting method, the z split requires the solution of N_y sets of linear equations; the y split requires the solution of N_z sets of linear equations; and the correlation split requires the solution of a set of $N_z \times N_y$ linear equations. Despite this additional computation effort, this method is well worth it. It is stable, efficient, and facilitates the calculation of sensitivities that are essential to understanding the dynamics of commodity prices.

2.3.3 Boundary Conditions

In many financial applications of finite difference methods, economic considerations dictate the boundary conditions. For instance, when solving for the value of a call option on a stock, one knows that as the stock price goes to zero, the call becomes worthless. This information can be used to fix the lower boundary condition; a related condition can be used to fix the boundary condition for high stock prices.

Unfortunately, in the commodity storage problem, there are often no such obvious, economically motivated boundary conditions.[18] Thus, one must proceed with caution. Most important, one must experiment to ensure that the solution is not particularly sensitive to the assumed boundary

---

[18] In the stochastic fundamental volatility model of Chapter 5, economic considerations can inform the choice of the volatility boundary conditions.

conditions. If it is, one must be concerned that the (inherently) arbitrary assumptions about boundary conditions are driving the results.

There are two basic types of boundary conditions: von Neumann and Dirichlet. Von Neumann conditions fix the shape of the F^1 function at the boundaries. Dirichlet conditions fix their exact values at the boundaries.

One common type of von Neumann condition is that the function is linear at the boundary. That is, its second derivative is zero:

$$0 = \frac{F_{i+1}^1 - 2F_i^1 + F_{i-1}^1}{\delta z^2}$$

This implies, in terms of the notation used earlier, that $A_1 = -2$, $B_1 = 1$, $C_1 = 1$, and $D_1 = 0$; similar results obtain for the upper boundary condition.

Given the lack of economic guidance about the likely shape of the F^1 function at the boundary, this condition may be unduly restrictive: that is, the function may not be linear at the boundary. Therefore, I typically use a boundary condition that effectively assumes that the third derivative is zero at the boundary:

$$\frac{F_3^1 - 2F_2^1 + F_1^1}{\delta z^2} = \frac{F_4^1 - 2F_3^1 + F_2^1}{\delta z^2}$$

with a similar condition for the upper boundary. This expression implies, in terms of the earlier notation, $A_1 = 1$, $B_1 = -3$, $C_1 = 3$, and $D_1 = -1$.[19]

This approximation is admittedly arbitrary because there is no economic motivation for it. However, I have found that it performs well. For the solution of carry-out and spot price functions, it does not have a big impact on the solution because there is little time (only δt years) for the information from the boundaries to diffuse into the interior of the valuation grid. As a result, the solutions for the spot price and carry-out functions are almost identical regardless of whether one uses this boundary condition or the more restrictive linearity-at-the-boundary condition. Because for some applications it is necessary to solve for forward prices with longer times to expiration, where there is more time for information from the boundaries to affect – and distort, if they are unrealistic – values in the interior of the valuation grid, I also check the behavior of these longer-tenor forward prices at the boundary. Practically, bad boundary conditions give rise to visible problems in forward price functions for longer tenors. For instance, a bad boundary condition can result in a 1-year forward price decreasing

---

[19] Of course, the signs on all of these coefficients can be reversed.

as the demand shock increases. This is not economically sensible. But even for fairly long tenors of 3 or more years, the constant-convexity-at-the-boundary condition does not generate such perverse behavior. Thus, I rely on it for the bulk of the analysis in the book.

The alternative is to specify Dirichlet conditions. Unlike the stock option case, however, there is no economic logic that tells us what those conditions are. One way to address this is to combine the expectation (integral) and PDE methods. Specifically, one can set the value of the forward price at the upper (or lower) boundary as the expectation of the spot price, conditional on being at that boundary, and use numerical integration to determine this expectation. Calling this expectation $\hat{F}_1^1$ for the lower boundary, one gets a boundary condition:

$$\hat{F}_1^1 = F_1^1$$

with a similar expression for the upper boundary.

The main issue that must be confronted in this method is that if one starts at the lower z boundary, for instance (i.e., one is determining the expected spot price conditional on the current value of z being z_1), there is a positive probability that in δt years, the realized z will fall outside the z grid. Thus, to calculate the expectation, one has to extrapolate the spot price function for such out-of-bounds z values. Extrapolation is always more problematic than interpolation. This effectively requires making assumptions about the shape of the spot price function outside the grid, and hence is not so different from the von Neumann conditions that also impose shape restrictions. Thus, a priori there are no strong reasons to favor one method over the other. Based on the good behavior of the constant-convexity-at-the-boundary approach, I let computational considerations prevail: because the Dirichlet approach requires additional computational steps – the calculations of the expectations at four boundaries – I typically rely on the von Neumann approach.[20]

2.4 Summary

The foundations for the detailed analysis of storage problems are now in place: the (partial equilibrium) model economy, the no-arbitrage-based equations relating spot and forward prices that must hold in this model economy, the basic recursive technique for solving these equations, and the

---

[20] I have compared the results from the Dirichlet and von Neumann approaches and find that they give very similar results.

numerical method for solving for forward price functions given a terminal spot price function. It should be noted that there is more than one way to skin the storage model cat. At virtually every step of the analysis, I could have chosen different solution methods. The methods presented here, however, are economically intuitive, well matched with observable quantities that we want to study, and computationally flexible *and* sturdy. With the methods out of the way, I can now turn attention to the presentation of specific models for specific types of commodities, beginning with continuously produced ones subject to homoscedastic demand shocks, the subject of the next two chapters.

THREE

High-Frequency Price Dynamics for Continuously Produced Commodities in a Two-Factor Storage Economy: Implications for Derivatives Pricing

3.1 Introduction

Many important commodities are produced and consumed continuously and exhibit little seasonality in demand. These include the industrial metals (such as copper and lead) and some important energy products (such as crude oil). These products are important (representing a large fraction of total traded commodity production, value, and trading volume). Moreover, it is easiest to analyze the high-frequency price behavior of these commodities in the structural storage model framework because the continuous nature of product and non-seasonality of demand makes it reasonable to impose time homogeneity, which makes numerical solution simpler; it is not reasonable to impose such homogeneity for seasonally produced commodities, such as corn. Therefore, considerations of importance and tractability make it desirable to focus initially on continuously produced commodities. These will be the subject of the next three chapters.

Most received storage models posit a single source of uncertainty. Sometimes this single source is portrayed as a "net demand shock." Whatever its interpretation, it is readily evident that a one-shock model is inadequate to describe the rich behavior of actual commodity prices.

This is most evident when one looks at correlations between commodity futures prices with different times to expiration, or correlations between spot and futures prices. In a single factor model, *all* prices on the same commodity, regardless of expiration date, are instantaneously perfectly correlated. If there is only one source of uncertainty, futures prices with different times to expiration may exhibit different variances because they have different sensitivities to shocks to these uncertainties. But correlation scales for these different sensitivities, and if only one factor drives all prices, they will all respond only to that factor. Thus, completely sharing exposure to a single factor, all prices must be instantaneously perfectly correlated.

But the data tell a very different story. Empirical work by Fama and French (1988), Ng and Pirrong (1994, 1996), and Pirrong (1996) demonstrates that (a) correlations between spot prices and futures prices, and between futures with different tenors, are frequently far below 1; and (b) these correlations are time varying, and vary systematically with measures of the tightness of supply and demand conditions, as summarized by the spread between spot and futures prices. These empirical studies are based on daily data, and although perfect instantaneous correlation can result in empirical correlations slightly below 1 in finitely sampled data, the deviations of correlations from 1 observed in the empirical data are too large to be caused by finite sampling if the true instantaneous correlations are 1. Furthermore, if instantaneous correlations are truly equal to 1, finite sampling cannot explain the substantial time variation in the empirical correlations or their co-variation with spot-futures spreads.

This means that to have any chance at describing the data, a model must involve at least two factors. This chapter analyzes a two-factor model. In the specific two-factor model examined here (a subsequent chapter explores a different two factor model), there are two net demand shocks. Each shock has different persistence.

In what follows, I set out the model and then examine the implications of the model for the behavior of high-frequency commodity prices. Specifically, I investigate the behavior of the volatilities of spot and futures prices of different maturities; how these volatilities relate to fundamental supply and demand conditions and to observable variables such as the spread between spot and futures prices that reflect these fundamental conditions; the correlation between spot and futures prices; and the relations between these correlations and fundamental supply and demand conditions and observables such as the spread.

The analysis demonstrates that the two-factor model can produce several stylized behaviors demonstrated empirically by Ng and Pirrong (1994) and Fama and French (1988). Specifically, the model predicts:

- Spot and futures volatilities are time varying.
- Spot volatilities exceed forward volatilities.
- Volatilities are highest when supply and demand conditions are tight, and because in the model the spread between spot and futures prices also depend on the tightness of fundamental conditions, volatilities

are high when the market is in backwardation and are low when the market is in full carry.

- The difference between spot and future volatilities is very small when the market is at full carry and largest when the market is in backwardation (i.e., when supply and demand conditions are tight).
- Correlations between spot and forward prices are time varying.
- Correlations between spot and forward price are effectively 1 when the market is in full carry and decline monotonically as spot-forward spreads fall progressively below full carry.

All of these features have been documented in empirical data from important commodity markets, such as the industrial metals and oil markets.

These implications of a structural model also imply that many reduced-form models commonly used to price commodity contingent claims (such as commodity options and commodity swaps) are mis-specified, and hence likely to mis-price these claims. The most common models assume that volatilities are constant over time. Others permit some time variation in volatility, and a relation between volatility and the spread, but do not capture the behavior of correlations. Thus, the structural model casts serious doubt on the reliability of even the most sophisticated reduced-form model to price contingent claims on continuously produced commodities, especially those (such as swaptions) that are correlation-sensitive.

I explore these issues by examining the implications of the two-factor model for commonly used metrics used to summarize the behavior of option prices. In particular, I examine the implications of the two-factor structural model for the behavior of the implied volatility smile in commodity options. I also examine the implications of the model for implied correlations in correlation-sensitive claims, such as swaptions and spread options.

These comparisons are useful as a means of diagnosing the deficiencies of reduced-form models. They also generate hypotheses that can be tested on options data.

The remainder of this chapter is organized as follows. Section 3.2 reviews the basic model described in more detail in Chapter 2. Section 3.3 describes the implications of the model for volatilities and correlations. Section 3.4 studies the ramifications of the model for the behavior of commodity options prices. Section 3.5 extends the model to permit capacity constraints on storage; this became a practically important issue in oil markets after the financial crisis. Section 3.6 uses the model to analyze the effects of increased speculation on commodity prices; this has long been, and remains, a hot-button issue. Section 3.7 provides a brief summary.

3.2 A Model of the Storage Economy with a Continuously Produced Commodity

3.2.1 Introduction

This section lays out the basic two-factor model. Its details are actually quite straightforward. There is a constant elasticity flow demand for the commodity. This demand is subject to two stochastic shocks of differing persistence. One can think of the more persistent shock as reflecting macroeconomic factors affecting demand (i.e., GDP, which is highly persistent). The more transitory shock reflects disruptions unique to that market (e.g., an increase in the demand for oil resulting from a sudden cold snap that drives up the demand for heating oil). Moreover, the commodity is produced continuously. Producers are competitive, and the industry supply curve is increasing and convex and is subject to a capacity constraint.

The commodity can be stored, at some cost. There are competitive agents who can store the commodity; these agents may be risk averse.

In a competitive market, production, consumption, and storage will implement a first-best allocation of resources. Moreover, this first-best allocation will result in an equation of the spot price and the discounted forward price of the commodity *if* this allocation requires positive storage: the spot price will exceed the discounted forward price if a stockout occurs under the optimum plan.

Solving for the first-best numerically produces optimal storage rules and a spot price function that relates the spot price to the state variables in the problem: inventories and the demand shocks. Moreover, given these spot price and inventory functions, it is possible to solve for forward price functions for arbitrary time to expiration. Given all of these functions, it is possible to determine how prices behave as state variables change, how these behaviors depend on the levels of the state variables, and how prices covary.

3.2.2 Framework and Numerical Solution

In this chapter, I implement the same model discussed in detail in Chapter 2. The numerical solution technique is also that described in Chapter 2. I make an initial guess for a function that gives the spot price as a function of the state variables, the demand shocks z and y, and carry-in $\hat{x}$. I then use the splitting technique to solve a partial differential equation that (after implementing a jump condition) gives the forward price as a function of these state variables. I then solve for the equilibrium production and consumption of the commodity (and hence carry-out); this equilibrium equates the spot price and the discounted forward price if the carry-out that results in this equation is positive and is equal to zero if equating the spot and discounted forward prices would entail a negative carry-out. The equilibrium production and consumption imply a new spot price function, which is compared to the assumed spot price function. This process continues until the spot price function converges.

In what follows, I assume that the market prices of risk λ_y and λ_z are zero. The specific numerical values used for the mean reversion parameters μ_z and μ_y and for the demand shock volatilities σ_y and σ_z are those determined in the estimation-calibration exercise described in the next chapter.

Given this solution for the spot price, it is possible to use this spot price function as a boundary condition and then solve the basic valuation equation (2.8) for the forward price function for an arbitrary maturity forward contract.

This approach in the two-factor model is computationally burdensome because it involves solving for the spot price for every value of the demand shocks in the numerical grids. To mitigate the computational burden, RSS (2000) propose an alternative model in which there is a permanent demand shock, z, uncorrelated with a transitory shock y, and is not priced. In essence, the Routledge et al. (2000) z shock causes a parallel shift in the entire forward price structure. Moreover, in the Routledge et al. (2000) specification, this permanent demand shock does not affect the optimal storage decision. This eases the computational burden substantially because it effectively reduces the dimensionality of the storer's decision problem: it only requires solution of the spot price function for the values of the y shock and the carry-in $\hat{x}$ in the grids. In terms of the notation of Chapter 2, this means that whereas the model solved in this chapter requires solving for optimal storage at $N_z \times N_y \times N_x$ values, the Routledge et al. (2000) model requires solution at only $N_y \times N_x$ values.

Despite its relative numerical simplicity, the RSS setup is problematic. The RSS permanent shock shifts the supply and demand curves up in parallel. This could be interpreted as a pure price level shock, which would imply that deflated commodity prices exhibit relatively little persistence. This is not consistent with extant evidence. An alternative interpretation is that a permanent (or highly persistent) shock is related to the business cycle; note that it is difficult to reject the hypothesis that GDP and aggregate consumption are integrated processes. However, under the RSS specification, the permanent shock does not affect output. This is inconsistent with the fact that the output of many continuously produced commodities is strongly pro-cyclical. Moreover, a permanent shock risk (presumably related to the business cycle and hence systematic) should be priced in equilibrium, which is inconsistent with the RSS assumption that the expected value of the future shock is its current value. Finally, spot and forward prices simulated from the solved RSS model calibrated to match the volatilities and correlations of copper futures prices (see the next subsection for a more detailed discussion of calibration) frequently move upward to very high levels (to a level well above that necessary to attract additional investment) or downward to very low levels (below any reasonable minimum production cost) and stay there for years. This is unsurprising given the salience of a permanent shock in determining the levels of prices in the RSS model, but it is an unsatisfactory characterization of real-world commodity price data.

Given these concerns, I focus on a two-shock model that does not adhere to the RSS assumptions.

3.3 Moments and the State Variables

Once the model is solved for an equilibrium spot price function $P^*(z, y, \hat{x})$ and for forward price functions, it is possible to utilize them to characterize their high frequency dynamics. Of particular interest are the behaviors of price variances (for both spot and forward prices) and the correlations between these prices. These are of such interest because there is some empirical evidence on the behaviors of these quantities.[1]

The values of the spot and forward price functions in the valuation grid can be used, with finite difference methods, to calculate variances and correlations for different values of the state variables. These solutions demonstrate whether these moments depend on the state variables, and if so, how.

Specifically, consider the variance of the spot price. Using the notation of Chapter 2 and $P^*(z, y, \hat{x})$ to indicate the equilibrium spot price function, Ito's Lemma implies:

$$dP^* = \mu_z^* \frac{\partial P^*}{\partial z} dz + \mu_y^* \frac{\partial P^*}{\partial y} dy + \mathcal{A} dt$$

where

$$\mathcal{A} = \frac{\partial P^*}{\partial t} + \frac{1}{2} \frac{\partial^2 P^*}{\partial z^2} \sigma_z^2 + \frac{1}{2} \frac{\partial^2 P^*}{\partial y^2} \sigma_y^2 + \frac{\partial^2 P^*}{\partial z \partial y} \sigma_z \sigma_y \rho$$

---

[1] Notably Fama and French (1988), Ng and Pirrong (1994, 1996), and Pirrong (1996).

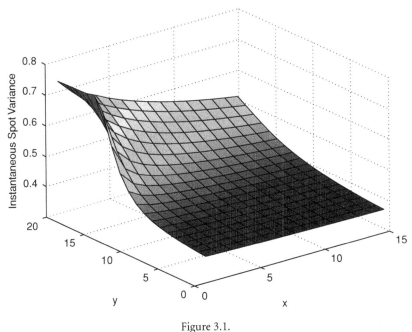

Figure 3.1.

Squaring dP^* implies:

$$\frac{var(dP_t^*)}{dt} = (\frac{\partial P_t^*}{\partial z})^2\sigma_z^2 + (\frac{\partial P_t^*}{\partial y})^2\sigma_y^2 + 2\frac{\partial P_t^*}{\partial z}\frac{\partial P_t^*}{\partial y}\rho\sigma_z\sigma_y \qquad (3.1)$$

The relevant partial derivatives can be calculated from the spot prices determined by the solution of the dynamic program. They are calculated using central finite differences.

An examination of this instantaneous variance implies that it is state dependent. Specifically, Figure 3.1 depicts the relation between the instantaneous variance of the spot price and y_t and x_t, given a $z_t = 0$ (i.e., the mean value of the more persistent demand shock).

Note that (a) given the short-memory demand shock y_t, increasing carry-in x_t (moving into the figure) reduces the variance of the spot price; and (b) given carry-in x_t, increasing demand y_t increases spot variance. Moreover, the sensitivity of spot variance to demand changes is greater the lower are stocks. Similarly, the sensitivity of spot variance to stock changes is greater the greater the demand. The convexity of the surface is evident in the figure.

This result is intuitive. In response to a surprise increase in demand, (a) price adjusts, (b) output adjusts, or (c) stocks adjust. When output is

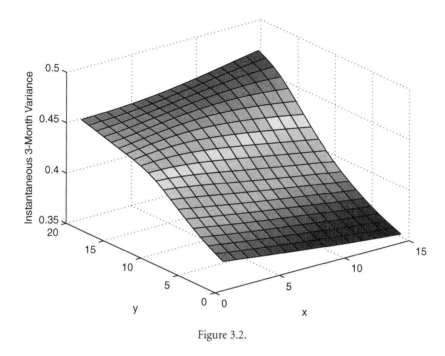

Figure 3.2.

near capacity (because demand is high) and stocks are low, there is limited scope for output and stock adjustments, and prices must bear the main burden of adjustment – hence, the high volatility. Conversely, when output is low and stocks are high, agents can adjust these real variables to cushion the price impact of the demand shock. The convexity of the variance surface reflects in large part the convexity of the marginal cost function.

Not surprisingly, variance levels increase in the level of the more persistent demand shock z_t, and the effect of a change in z_t is greatest for low stock and high transitory demand y_t. Intuitively, when demand is high, output is closer to capacity, where marginal production costs rise more steeply with output. A given change in demand will lead to a larger price move under these circumstances. Moreover, when stocks are low, inventories provide less of a buffer against demand shocks, and prices bear a greater portion of the burden of accommodating the demand shocks.

Figure 3.2 depicts the relation between the 3-month forward price instantaneous variance and y_t and x_t for $z_t = 0$ (drawn to the same scale as Figure 3.1); the same approach used to calculate the spot variance is used to calculate the futures price variance, with the sole exception that the (numerically estimated) 3-month forward price function is used to calculate the relevant sensitivities. Although the forward price variance surface has the

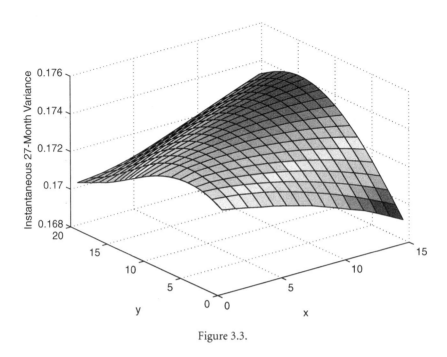

Figure 3.3.

same basic shape as its spot price variance counterpart, there are some key differences. Most notably, ceteris paribus the level of the 3-month variance is lower than that of the spot price. Moreover, this difference in variances is greatest for low x_t and high y_t, and very small for high x_t and low y_t. That is, the forward variance surface is flatter, and less convex, than the spot variance surface.[2]

These results are also intuitive. Although the scope for adjustments to output and stocks is very limited in the very short run (i.e., over the course of a day), it is greater over a period of weeks and months. Hence, variations in current conditions have less impact on forward prices than on spot prices. This is especially true when current conditions are extremely tight (sharply circumscribing the ability to adjust real quantities in the very short run), but less so when current conditions are very bearish (meaning that there is plenty of scope to adjust real quantities even in the very short run). Indeed, the variance surface for the 27-month forward prices (depicted in Figure 3.3) is almost flat, indicating that (a) the stationarity in demand shocks, and (b) the greater ability to adjust real quantities over the longer run make

---

[2] Moreover, although the 3-month variance increases with y_t, it also *increases* with x_t.

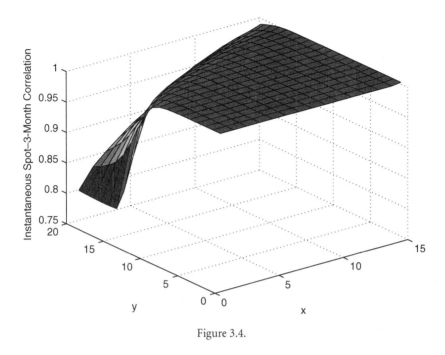

Figure 3.4.

the dynamics of long-tenor forward prices virtually insensitive to current market conditions.[3]

The solutions to the dynamic programming problem can also be used to determine covariances and correlations between different prices. For instance, the covariance between the spot and 3-month forward prices is:

$$cov(dP^*, dF_3) = \frac{\partial P^*}{\partial z}\frac{\partial F_3}{\partial z}\sigma_z^2 dt + \frac{\partial P^*}{\partial y}\frac{\partial F_3}{\partial y}\sigma_y^2 dt$$
$$+ (\frac{\partial P^*}{\partial z}\frac{\partial F_3}{\partial y} + \frac{\partial P^*}{\partial y}\frac{\partial F_3}{\partial z})\sigma_z\sigma_y\rho dt$$

Dividing this covariance by the square root of the product of the variances already calculated produces the instantaneous correlation between the spot and 3-month forward prices.

Figure 3.4 depicts the relation between the instantaneous correlation between the spot price and the 3-month price and y_t and x_t with z_t at its mean value of 0. Note that the correlation is almost exactly 1.00 when x_t

---

[3] The insensitivity of longer-tenor forward prices to shocks indicates that spot prices are stationary. This stationarity arises from two sources: the stationarity in the demand shocks and the equilibrium effects of storage on prices.

is sufficiently large. However, the correlation drops sharply when (a) stocks fall, and (b) transitory demand becomes very large.

Again, this is a sensible result. Storage connects spot and forward prices. When stocks are positive, tomorrow's forward price equals the spot price plus the cost of carrying inventory, and these two prices move in lockstep. When stocks are extremely abundant, it is unlikely that stocks will be exhausted over a 3-month period; therefore, the 3-month price will move almost in lockstep with the spot price. However, when stocks are low or when demand is high, a stockout is more likely over a 3-month horizon. A stockout eliminates cash-and-carry arbitrage as a link between spot and forward prices. Under these circumstances, spot prices respond primarily to current demand shocks, whereas forward prices change primarily in response to expected future demand. Correlations are lower under these circumstances.

3.4 Derivatives Pricing

The analysis in Sections 3.2 and 3.3 demonstrates that the variances of prices in the storage commodity change in response to changes in fundamental market conditions. This suggests that the values of options will also change systematically with fundamentals. The dependence of correlations on market conditions documented earlier also suggests that the values of correlation-sensitive products, such as commodity swaptions and calendar spread options, are similarly sensitive.

The price of any option in the storage economy must satisfy the basic valuation PDE (subject to the appropriate boundary conditions):

$$rV = \frac{\partial V}{\partial t} + \mu_z^* \frac{\partial V}{\partial z} + \mu_y^* \frac{\partial V}{\partial y} + \frac{1}{2}\sigma_z^2 \frac{\partial^2 V}{\partial z^2} + \frac{1}{2}\sigma_y^2 \frac{\partial^2 V}{\partial y^2} + \rho\sigma_z\sigma_y \frac{\partial^2 V}{\partial z \partial y}$$

(3.2)

where V is the price of the option. An equilibrium spot price function P^* implies a payoff function for any vanilla option on the commodity. Given this payoff function, the same finite difference technique used to solve for the forward prices in Chapter 2 can be used solve the option pricing equation.

The most useful way to illustrate the dependence of options prices on fundamentals is to examine the relation between implied volatilities (from the canonical Black model, the most widely used commodity futures option pricing model) and fundamentals. Figure 3.5 illustrates the relation between the at-the-money (ATM) implied volatility for a 1-month option and y_t and

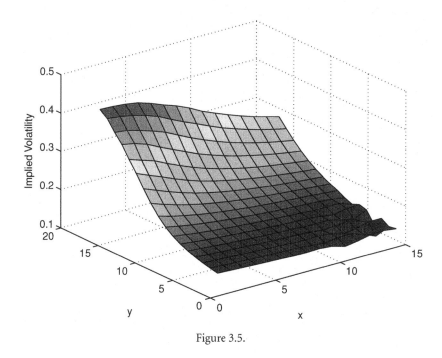

Figure 3.5.

x_t, with $z_t = 0$. The payoff to this option is $\max[S_T - K, 0]$, where S_T is the spot price at expiration.

To perform this analysis, I first solve the relevant valuation PDE to determine the 1-month forward price for each point in the state variable grid. This forward price gives the strike price of the ATM option as a function of the state variables. I then solve the valuation PDE (3.2) to determine the option price for each point in the state variable grid, plug this option value into the Black option pricing equation, and solve for the implied volatility.

Unsurprisingly, the ATM implied volatilities vary with the state variables in much the same way as the instantaneous variances. Implied volatilities are increasing in y_t and decreasing in x_t. Moreover, there is a substantial difference in the level of the implied volatility between slack times and tight ones. When demand is high and stocks low, the volatility is substantially larger than when demand is low and stocks high. Though not pictured, ATM implied volatilities are less sensitive to state variables, the longer the option's maturity. This reflects the same fundamental factors discussed earlier.

It is well known that variations in instantaneous variances can generate a "smile" or "skew" in implied volatilities. The smile depicts, in a graphical form, the relation between the strike price of an option and the option's

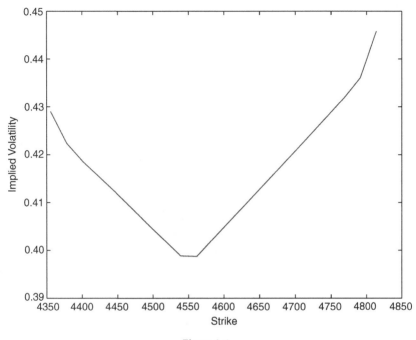

Figure 3.6.

implied volatility. In the Black model with a constant volatility, this relationship would be flat; volatilities would be the same for every strike price.
If, however, the assumptions of the Black model do not hold because, for
instance, volatility varies with the state variables as in the storage economy,
market participants will negotiate options prices that differ from those generated by the Black model with a given value for volatility. Hence, if you
utilize the Black model to back out a volatility estimate from options with
different strike prices, you will estimate different implied volatilities for
options on the same underlying commodity that have the same expiration
date but different strike prices. The variation in implied volatilities across
options of different strikes is an indication that the market is using a model
other than the Black model to price options. The plot of volatilities against
strike prices is often called a smile or a skew because the resulting curve is
often smile-shaped or exhibits a skew (higher values for low strike prices
than high ones, for instance).

Given the fundamentals-driven variations in volatilities, one expects to
observe a smile in implied volatilities in the storage economy because these
variations violate the Black model assumptions. Indeed, Figures 3.6 and 3.7

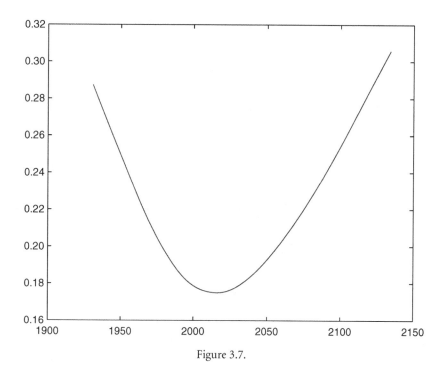

Figure 3.7.

illustrate that storage economy volatilities do smile. Each figure depicts the relation between volatilities and strike price, with the strike price range between 95 percent and 105 percent of the current 1-month forward price.

Figure 3.6 depicts the smile for 1-month options for tight fundamental conditions with low stocks and high demand. The smile reaches a minimum near ATM strike price; the minimum volatility is about 43 percent. The smile reflects the leptokurtosis that arises from the stochastic volatility of prices induced by the dependence of instantaneous variances on the state variables.

There is a slight bias to the "call wing," with the highest strike price options (deep out-of-the-money calls) having a higher implied volatility than call options that are out of the money by an identical percentage.[4] This reflects the effect of supply and demand fundamentals on price variability; a further tightening of supply-and-demand conditions would increase both

---

[4] The "call wing" refers to the part of the smile corresponding to high strike prices, as with out-of-the-money calls. The "put wing" refers to the part of the smile corresponding to low strike prices, such as out-of-the-money puts.

prices and volatility, whereas a relaxation of said conditions would tend to reduce both prices and variability.

Figure 3.7 depicts the volatility smile when y_t, z_t, and x_t are at their long-run means (with the mean of x_t estimated from the simulated sample). Here, the smile is fairly symmetric and reaches a minimum near the ATM strike; not surprisingly, the overall level of volatility is much lower with these moderate-demand conditions as compared to their level under tight-demand conditions. The minimum volatility level is only about 18 percent, in contrast to the 43 percent in Figure 3.6. The smile is again largely symmetric, with a slight bias to the call wing.

This behavior of implied volatilities is difficult for standard reduced-form options pricing models based on Gaussian state variables to capture. The widely used Schwartz (1997) two-factor model provides a standard of comparison.[5] This model permits twists in the term structure of commodity prices by incorporating two state variables: the spot price and the convenience yield. The spot price essentially determines the level of the price curve, and the convenience yield its slope. The spot price process is:

$$\frac{dS_t}{S_t} = (\mu - \delta_t)dt + \sigma_1 dW_1 \tag{3.3}$$

The convenience yield process is:

$$d\delta_t = \kappa(\alpha - \delta_t)dt + \sigma_2 dW_2 \tag{3.4}$$

and W_1 and W_2 are Brownian motions. The appropriate volatility to use in the Black formula to value an option on the spot expiring in τ years in this model is:

$$\sqrt{\sigma_1^2 + \frac{\sigma_2^2}{\tau\kappa^2}[\tau - \frac{2}{\kappa}(1-e^{-\kappa\tau}) + \frac{1}{2\kappa}(1-e^{-2\kappa\tau})] - \frac{2\rho\sigma_1\sigma_2}{\kappa\tau}(\tau - \frac{1-e^{-\kappa\tau}}{\kappa})} \tag{3.5}$$

I fit the Schwartz model (using the Kalman filtering methodology described in Schwartz [1997]) to spot, 3-month, 15-month, and 27-month forward prices simulated from using the same parameters used to create the earlier figures. The parameters produced from this estimation imply a volatility for a 30-day forward price of 0.33. A comparison of the implied volatilities in Figures 3.6 and 3.7 with this figure for the Schwartz 30-day

---

[5] There are a variety of similar models, including Gibson and Schwartz (1990), Miltersen and Schwartz (1998), and Hilliard and Reis (1998). For simplicity, I focus on Schwartz (1997) model 2; models from these other papers exhibit similar properties.

forward price volatility implies that this model misprices options systematically. During average supply-and-demand conditions (illustrated in Figure 3.7), the Schwartz model substantially overprices options because the 33 percent Schwartz model volatility is much higher than the implied volatilities from any but the deepest in- or out-of-the-money options. (Given that the volatility smile is lower for looser supply-and-demand conditions, this means that the Schwartz model overprices options under these conditions too.) During the tight supply-and-demand conditions, the Schwartz model substantially underprices options; note that the entire smile in Figure 3.6 is well above the 0.33 percent Schwartz model volatility. The underpricing is most extreme for deep in- or out-of-the-money options.

It should be noted that these mispricings are most pronounced for short-dated options. Extending the maturity of the options flattens the smile. Indeed, for long-dated options (e.g., a year), the smile is flat at a level approximately equal to the volatility implied by the Schwartz model fit to the calibrated, simulated data. Thus, although a reduced-form, multi-factor Gaussian model may be deficient for pricing and hedging short-dated options, it is a plausible model for pricing longer-dated ones.

There is another way to illustrate the limitations of models that do not take into account the non-linearities in prices that arise from non-linearities in marginal cost and the effects of storage. This is to examine the implications of the "true" storage economy model and the reduced-form Gaussian model for the behavior of very short-dated futures prices. In the industrial metals markets, there is a well-developed overnight borrowing market, so 1-day forward contracts are actively traded.

Figure 3.8 presents a simulation of the "true" daily backwardation from the storage model and the daily backwardation that the Schwartz model generates. The daily backwardation is the difference between the 1-day forward price (net of interest costs) and the spot price, implied by the equilibrium price and storage functions and the simulated series of z and y shocks. Note that this series is almost always zero, but periodically spikes down to very low levels; these spikes occur when inventories are zero, or nearly so.

The other series in Figure 3.8 is the fitted daily backwardation implied by the Schwartz model. To produce this series, I first implement the Schwartz (1997) Kalman filter methodology to fit his Model II to the simulated spot, 3-month, 15-month, and 27-month prices. This fitting procedure produces estimates of the parameters of the Schwartz model and filtered spot price and convenience yield series (the state variables in the model). Given the parameters and the filtered state variables, for each day in the sample I use

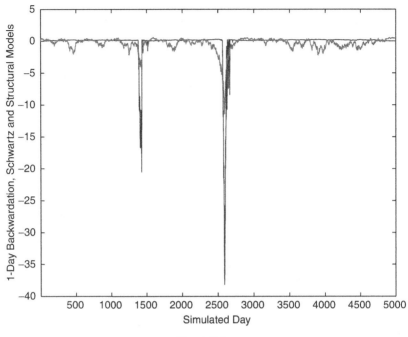

Figure 3.8.

equations 18 and 20 in Schwartz (1997) with $\tau = 1/365$ to determine a series of 1-day forward prices.

Note that in the reduced-form Schwartz model, daily backwardation is almost never zero, is sometimes positive, is much smoother, and never reaches the very low levels achieved by the "true" daily backwardation. It tends to reach its lowest levels at the same time the true daily backwardation does, but the Schwartz daily backwardations never reach the depths of the true daily backwardation. This reflects the linear, diffusive nature of the underlying stochastic processes in this model. These are not capable of handling the sharp twists at the short end of the forward curve that are inherent in the storage economy due to (a) the possibility of stockouts, and (b) capacity constraints. In essence, although a change in tenor has a smaller effect on backwardation for longer tenors than shorter ones in the diffusion model, the relation between backwardation and tenor is flatter for short tenors in this model than in the actual storage economy. In contrast, the stationarity attributable to the stationarity of the state variables and the effects of storage results in nearly diffusive behavior for longer-tenor

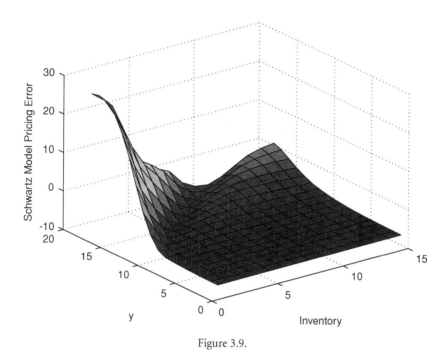

Figure 3.9.

contracts. Hence, the better performance of the Schwartz model in capturing the behavior of these prices.

Schwartz and Nielsen propose a model with state-dependent volatility. This is essentially a Schwartz two-factor model with volatilities of the state variables that depend on the convenience yield. Although this model can address the problems valuing short-dated vanilla options as described earlier, conditional correlations between different tenors are constant and not state dependent. Thus, this model will face difficulties in pricing correlation-sensitive claims that are dependent on the shape of the term structure, such as swaptions or spread options.

One common correlation-sensitive claim is an option on a spread between futures prices with different tenors, such as the spread between 1-month and 2-month futures prices. Figure 3.9 depicts the difference between (a) the price of an ATM option with 1-month to expiration on the difference between the 1-month and 2-month futures prices implied by the solution to the relevant valuation PDE and the calibrated parameters; and (b) the price of such an option implied by the Schwartz model fit to simulated data from the calibrated model. Because there is no analytical expression for spread option value in the Schwartz model setup, this value is determined by numerical integration. The figure holds $z_t = 0$ and depicts the difference between the "true" option value and the Schwartz value for different values of y_t and x_t. Note that the Schwartz model grossly underprices the spread option when y_t is large and x_t is low, but substantially overprices the spread option when y_t is small and x_t is large. That is, the reduced-form model's pricing error is negative (positive) when market conditions are tight (slack).

This reflects the lack of state dependence in the reduced-form diffusion model. In particular, the insensitivity of the correlation to fundamentals in the reduced-form model contributes to the pricing bias. When market conditions are slack, the market is at full carry, and the nearby and deferred futures prices are almost perfectly correlated. Under these circumstances, there is very little variability in the spread; consequently, spread options are virtually valueless. The reduced-form model exhibits a correlation between the nearby and deferred prices of approximately 0.95 regardless of the shape of the term structure; hence, spread options still have some value even when conditions are slack. Relatedly, when market conditions are tight, the reduced-form model's correlation substantially exceeds the true correlation between nearby and deferred prices. Combined with the fact that the reduced-form model understates volatilities under these circumstances (as seen before), this implies that this model underestimates the value of the spread option. Spreads (i.e., the slope of the term structure) are much more volatile when the market is in backwardation than under normal circumstances; hence, spread options are more valuable then.[6]

In sum, options prices and implied volatilities exhibit state dependence in the storage economy. Option values are higher ceteris paribus when supply-demand conditions are tight. Moreover, under these circumstances, options-implied volatilities exhibit a pronounced smirk toward the call wing. In more typical market conditions, options volatilities exhibit a symmetric smile. Correlation-dependent products also exhibit state dependence. These effects are most pronounced for short-dated options. Valuation models with Gaussian state variables do a poor job of pricing short-dated claims in the storage economy. These models can neither capture the huge swings in volatility at the short end of the forward curve, nor can they handle the extreme twists in the short end of the curve. Gaussian models characterize the behavior of longer-dated forward and option prices much

---

[6] Similarly, the reduced-form model does not capture state dependence in swaption-implied volatilities. Swaption values are also correlation sensitive.

more effectively. Given that many exchange-traded and OTC commodity options have relatively short maturities, but many commodity real options have very long ones, this suggests that Gaussian models have a place in pricing real options, but not exchange- and OTC-traded options.

It also should be noted that conventional methods of enriching the dynamics of the spot price, such as adding jumps (Hilliard and Reis 1998), cannot improve the ability of spot price-convenience yield models to capture the dynamics of the short end of the commodity term structure. In the jump-diffusion version of the Hilliard-Reis model, spot price jumps cause the forward price to jump by the same proportion. That is, the term structure of log prices jumps in parallel. Moreover, in this model, neither the probability ("intensity") nor the size of the jump depends on the level of prices or the shape of the term structure. In contrast, in the storage economy, large moves in spot prices typically occur when the market is in backwardation, and such movements are substantially larger (both absolutely and proportionally) than the movements in forward prices (with the difference increasing with tenor). Although a model in which spot price jump probability and intensity depend on the shape of the term structure would perhaps generate more realistic spot-price dynamics, even such a model would not accurately characterize the dynamics of the shape of the term structure, especially at the short end.[7]

The dependence of the volatilities and correlations on fundamental factors suggests that a generalized Ito process may provide a better representation of price dynamics. One candidate is:

$$\frac{dS_t}{S_t} = \mu(S_t) + \sigma(S_t)dZ_t$$

The idea here is that prices tend to be high when supply-and-demand conditions are tight, which is when spot volatility is high as well.

There are some problems with this characterization. Figure 3.10 depicts a scatter plot from simulated data of the instantaneous variance against the spot price. Note that although variance is generally increasing in price, there is considerable dispersion of points. This reflects the existence of three state variables (the demand shocks and inventories), all of which affect both

---

[7] Prices in the storage economy as modeled herein are continuous but can exhibit large movements in discretely sampled data that look like "jumps" to the naked eye. The storage model implies that the likelihood in discretely sampled data of these large price movements is state dependent. Standard jump models do not capture this dependence, and it would be a substantial challenge to estimate a model in which the characteristics of jumps depend on measures of the tightness of supplies.

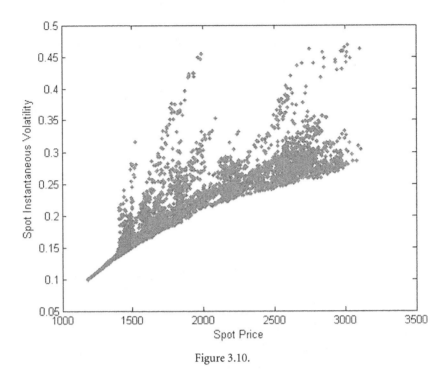

Figure 3.10.

the prices and instantaneous variances. Hence, there is no simple mapping between price and variance. Figure 3.11 illustrates that there is a much tighter relation between a measure of the slope of the term structure and instantaneous variance.[8] Both are based on simulations of the storage economy. The horizontal axis depicts the percentage interest-adjusted spread between the spot and 3-month forward prices $(\ln(P_t^*/F_{t,.25}) + .25r)$. The vertical axis depicts the instantaneous variance. Capturing this relation requires a model in which variance is a function of the slope of the term structure. The two-factor (spot price and convenience yield) model of Schwartz-Nielsen (2004) incorporates such an effect. Their specification implies a constant

---

[8] Note that in the storage model, the variance must be spanned by the forward prices. There are two shocks in the model, the variations in which induce variations in volatility *and* prices. Thus, it is possible to hedge the volatility changes with dynamically adjusted positions in forward contracts. Note that in the two-factor model, at least two futures are required to achieve this hedge. For this reason, variance cannot be spanned by the spot price (or any individual forward price alone). This explains the lack of any close relation between volatility and the spot price alone, as illustrated in Figure 3.10, and the much closer relation between a spot-futures spread and volatility in Figure 3.11. I provide evidence in the next chapter, however, that empirical volatility is *not* spanned by the forward curve.

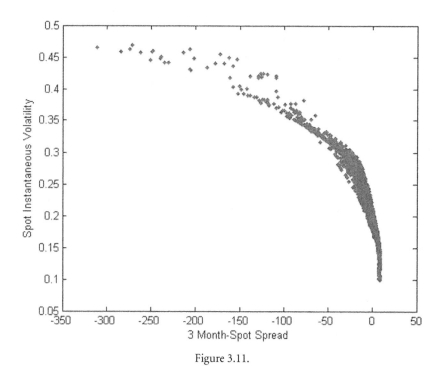

Figure 3.11.

correlation between the spot price and forward prices. As noted earlier, however, in the storage economy the correlation between the spot price and forward prices is state dependent, with low correlations when the market is in a strong backwardation. Thus, although models à la Schwartz-Nielsen may do a better job at pricing vanilla options, they are less suited to pricing correlation-sensitive claims including spread options and swaptions.[9]

3.5 Extension: Storage Capacity Constraints

The model presented herein examines price dynamics and derivatives pricing in a storage economy in which the non-negativity constraint on inventory plays an important role. When this constraint binds, or is close to binding, both prices and the shape of the term structure tend to be much more volatile than when inventories are abundant.

There is evidence that for other commodities, most notably petroleum and related products, volatilities can be elevated and correlations depressed

[9] Schwartz-Nielsen point out that their model exhibits the same difficulties as the Schwartz model in capturing the dynamics of very short-term prices.

when inventories are very large. That is, empirically there is sometimes a *V*-shaped relation between the volatility and the spread, with high volatilities when contango is large as well as when backwardation is large.[10] This effect is readily introduced into the storage model by introducing a physical cost of storage that is a convex, increasing function of inventory.

For instance, if the cost of storage is:

$$c_s(x_t) = \frac{\theta_s}{\bar{x} - x_t}$$

where $\bar{x}$ is an upper bound on storage capacity, then (a) the market is in a large contango when x_t is close to $\bar{x}$, and (b) spot and forward volatilities are high and correlations between spot and forwards are low when x_t nears $\bar{x}$. In this model, prices and spreads become more volatile as inventories approach either the non-negativity or storage capacity constraints. Thus, the model can produce the *V*-shaped relation between the term structure slope and volatility found in some energy markets.

The existence of an upper bound on storage has implications for conditional price distributions and volatility smiles. Specifically, prices in the storage economy exhibit a negative skew when inventories approach storage capacity. In this circumstance, although the market can respond to a demand increase by drawing down on stocks (thereby mitigating the price impact of the demand change), it cannot respond to a demand decrease by adding to stocks; hence, price bears all of the burden of accommodating the negative demand shock. This produces an asymmetric response to symmetric demand changes, with large price declines more likely than large price increases. This left skew also affects the shape of the volatility smile, with low strike options exhibiting higher implied volatilities than ATM options when the market is in a substantial contango.

An upper bound on storage capacity is plausible, especially in energy markets. Indeed, in the aftermath of the financial crisis, in 2009 especially, oil storage facilities in Cushing, Oklahoma – the WTI delivery point – were

---

[10] Ng and Pirrong (1996) estimate a model for refined petroleum prices similar to the Backwardation Adjusted GARCH model of Ng and Pirrong (1994) but that includes the positive and negative components of $\ln(P_t/F_{t,\tau})$ as separate variables in the variance and covariance equations. I have estimated this model for Brent and WTI crude oil prices for the 1990–2009 period and find that volatilities are high and correlations low during both large contangos and large backwardations. Indeed, oil volatility during 2008–2009 was at historically high levels at the same time that contango was at all-time highs. Kogan, Livdan, and Yaron (2009) also document a *V*-shaped relation between the spread in the market and price volatilities for oil and refined products. There is no similarly strong relation among contango and volatilities and correlations for industrial metals.

effectively full. Despite construction of new storage tanks, increased oil production in Canada and North Dakota and transportation bottlenecks have caused storage in Cushing to remain near capacity. Thus, this is a practically important issue. The predictions of the storage model regarding the V-shaped relation among spreads, volatilities, and correlations are consistent with empirical evidence from these markets.

3.6 Extension: The Effects of Speculation on Price Dynamics in the Storage Economy

The analysis so far has focused on the implications of the storage model for the behavior of prices, particularly higher moments of prices. But it can also shed light on policy issues that have long been contentious and are even more so at present.

Specifically, the storage model can be used to explore the effects of speculation on the behavior of prices. In the past decade, and especially in 2008 when commodity prices skyrocketed, speculators were widely condemned for distorting prices. The storage model can be utilized to predict the effects of speculation. It implies that speculation can indeed affect prices, but that the effects of speculation are typically favorable. Moreover, the model demonstrates that the effects of speculation are typically indirect, namely, through its effect on storage decisions.

This subject is most easily studied in the context of a simpler, one-factor model: the implications carry through to a more complicated multi-factor setting. The Martingale framework readily permits studying the effects of speculation. Speculators willingly take on risk. Innovations that make it easier for speculators to enter commodity markets, such as commodity index swaps and exchange-traded funds, affect the market price of risk. This, in turn, affects the cost of holding and hedging inventories. Changes in the cost of hedging and holding inventories can affect storage decisions, which in turn have implications for price dynamics.

The analysis so far, for simplicity, has assumed that the market price of risk is zero. But, as noted in Chapter 2, a non-zero market price of risk is readily incorporated into the analysis. Recall that in the equivalent measure that is relevant for pricing purposes, the dynamics of the underlying fundamental shock are:

$$dz_t = (\lambda_z - \mu_z z_t)dt + \sigma_z d\bar{B}_t \tag{3.6}$$

where λ_z is the market price of z risk.

Speculation, and in particular the degree of integration between the commodity market and the broader financial markets, affects λ_z.[11] Assume that prior to the entry of new speculators into the market (where the influx occurs because of, for instance, a financial innovation or the elimination of a restriction on market participation), the market price of risk $\lambda_z < 0$. This means that in the equivalent measure, the fundamental demand shock drifts down, as compared to the drift in the process in the physical measure. This, in turn, means that the forward price is "downward biased." The forward price is less than the expected spot price. This occurs because the expected spot price is the expectation of the future spot price taken with respect to the physical measure, but the forward price is the expectation taken with respect to the equivalent measure. The downward drift in the process under the equivalent measure means that the distribution used to determine the forward price is displaced to the left, as compared to the distribution in the physical measure. This displacement of the mean implies a lower value for the expectation.[12]

Assume that the entry of new speculators drives λ_z to zero. This could occur, for instance, if the fundamental factor, z, is perfectly diversifiable and hence should not be priced in equilibrium in an integrated financial market. In the new equilibrium, the forward price is unbiased. That is, it equals the expected spot price.

Prior to the entry of the new speculators, those holding inventories pay the market price of risk. Equivalently, an inventory holder who desires to hedge risk by selling forward incurs a cost of doing so: he incurs a loss on average equal to the bias. In contrast, with the influx of speculators, the market price of risk is zero: equivalently, hedgers pay no cost (incur no loss) on average. Thus, the influx of speculators affects the costs of holding (or

---

[11]　See Hirshleifer (1988) for a formal analysis of how the costs of entry incurred by speculators affect risk premia; that is, the market price of risk.

[12]　In the confusing terminology of Keynes (1930), the forward price exhibits "backwardation," which he considered a normal condition in commodity markets. The terminology is confusing because it is at odds with normal market usage of the term. In market usage, a backwardation refers to a situation where a futures price – a traded price – is below the current spot price – another traded price. In Keynes's usage, a backwardation refers to a situation where the futures price is below the *expected future spot price* – which is *not* a traded price. There is no logical connection between a Keynesian backwardation and a market backwardation. As an example, the futures market for a true asset, such as a stock, will always be at full carry because of cash-and-carry arbitrage. However, the futures price may be backwardated in a Keynesian sense. This would occur, for instance, in a Capital Asset Pricing Model (CAPM) world if the stock has a positive beta.

hedging) inventory. This, in turn, should influence inventory decisions and, through this channel, prices.

This possibility can be investigated using the storage model. Specifically, first solve the model under the assumption that $\lambda_z < 0$. Then, solve it with $\lambda_z = 0$. Then, simulate the two economies under the same sequence of z shocks, and compare the evolution of inventories and prices. To make the difference pronounced, I first assume $\lambda_z = -.05$.

The results of this comparison are readily summarized and are consistent with the foregoing intuition.

First, inventories are smaller in the downward-biased economy. Indeed, in long simulations, the average inventory in the $\lambda_z = -.05$ economy is about 60 percent as large as the average inventory in the $\lambda_z = 0$ economy. This reflects the rather substantial downward bias in the forward price in the former (or, equivalently, the high risk cost incurred to hold inventory). Stockouts are more frequent in the downward-biased economy.

Second, this change in inventories affects prices. The effects on price levels are relatively small. The average spot price in the $\lambda_z = -.05$ is about 3 percent *lower* in long simulations. Thus, speculation can raise prices on average. But, crucially, price volatility is higher in the downward-biased economy: in long simulations, the standard deviation of percentage spot price changes is on the order of 10 percent higher in that economy. Moreover, price spikes are more frequent in the downward-biased, low-storage economy: the skewness of prices in that economy is more than 10 percent greater in long simulations in that economy.

Thus, the model implies that greater speculation that reduces the market price of risk (and eliminates *Keynesian* backwardation) increases inventories, raises prices, but reduces price volatility and the frequency of price spikes. Because these changes reflect a more efficient allocation of risk, they are salutary.[13]

---

[13] Energy economist Philip Verleger claims that this phenomenon has occurred in the heating-oil market. He points out the interesting case of cold snaps in 1989 and 2009. In the earlier episode, the cold snap led to a dramatic increase in the price of heating oil; in the latter, the price effect was mild. Verleger notes that inventory levels and speculation levels were higher in the years leading up to 2009 as compared to 1989 (Verleger 2010). This is broadly consistent with the implications of the model, but it should be noted that heating-oil inventories were also bloated as a result of the precipitous drop in oil demand in the sharp recession that began in late 2008. Regardless of the reason for the higher inventory holdings, this episode does illustrate the effects of inventories on price spikes. To the extent that greater speculation and closer integration of commodity and financial markets leads to higher inventory holdings (as the model predicts), price spikes should be smaller and less frequent.

Third, prices are highly correlated across the two economies. Demand shocks are the main drivers of price movements in both economies, and for an identical set of demand shocks, price movements are highly correlated.

Fourth, spot-forward spreads are affected somewhat (I simulate a spot–3-month spread). Backwardations are more pronounced, and more frequent, in the downward-biased economy. This is because stockouts are more likely in this economy as a result of the smaller stockholdings. But, overall, the differences in calendar spreads between the two economies are not large (although they are larger than the price differences); the time-series plot of the simulated spread for the downward-biased economy is a slight displacement of the simulated spread for the risk-neutral economy. Backwardations peak at about the same times in each simulation, and contangos/full-carry periods exhibit large overlaps (though not complete overlaps because there are times when the downward-biased economy exhibits departures from full carry and the risk-neutral economy does not).

One key result is that almost never in the simulations does a substantial backwardation exist in the downward-biased economy while the risk-neutral economy is at full carry.

Market commentors sometimes attribute the more frequent and persistent contangos in commodity markets (such as oil) since the mid-2000s to increased speculation. These arguments are frequently dubious because they confuse Keynesian backwardation with a market backwardation. The simulation results show that speculation that leads to a reduction in the cost of hedging can indeed mitigate backwardations (properly defined), but this reflects the effect of speculation on the cost of hedging, and the effect of the cost of hedging on inventory levels.

This has implications for the speculation debate. Changes in market structure that lead to increased integration between a commodity market and the broader financial markets can, in theory, have an impact on the behavior of the commodity market. In general, if you believe that a commodity market that is, as in the Keynesian treatment, isolated from the broader financial market exhibits "normal backwardation," then the entry of diversified speculators that results in a dissipation of downward bias will have some effect on prices and spreads and potentially a big effect on inventories.

Identifying such an effect in practice is likely to be hugely challenging. The results presented here assume a downward bias that is far larger than ever documented for any storable commodity; indeed, since Telser (1958), economists have provided little empirical evidence that Keynesian backwardation is at all normal. This reflects, in part, the fact that measuring differences in mean are difficult to estimate precisely even in relatively large samples.

The simulation results permit the examination of these effects in a controlled environment. It is possible to create samples of any size while holding all the structural features of the economy unchanged. It is further possible to compare exactly the behavior of prices and quantities under the same set of demand shocks. Even given this, it is hard to distinguish the two economies; plots of the time series of prices are nearly indistinguishable (although plots of the spreads are more obviously different). Moreover, it is possible to set exactly the effect of speculation on the cost of risk.

Real-world empirical work would have none of these advantages. It is difficult – nigh on impossible – to measure speculation or its effect on risk premia. Difficult-to-control-for structural shifts (e.g., production technology shocks, taste shocks that affect demand elasticities, regulatory changes) occur regularly. The most pronounced effect of speculation is on inventories, but stocks data are far less reliable and more difficult to obtain than price data. These difficulties make any empirical estimation of the effects of speculation on prices highly problematic.

The model is still valuable, however, because it forcefully makes the point that the main effect of speculation is on the price of risk. Its effects on the prices of the commodities themselves flow from this, and these effects are indirect, via an inventory channel.

3.7 Summary and Conclusions

The modern competitive rational expectations theory of storage implies that the prices of continuously produced, storable commodities should exhibit complex dynamics with considerable state dependence. In particular, prices are more volatile when demand is high and/or inventory is sufficiently small. The volatility of the spot price is particularly sensitive to supply-and-demand conditions. Moreover, in a two-factor model such as that studied in this chapter, the correlation between spot prices and forward prices is lower when supply-demand conditions are tight.

These rich dynamics have important implications for pricing of commodity options. In particular, the prices of vanilla options should be strongly state dependent, with higher implied volatilities when market conditions are tight (because of high demand and/or low inventory). Moreover, options-implied volatilities "smile" in the storage economy, and the shape of the smile depends on supply-and-demand conditions. Furthermore, the prices of correlation-sensitive claims depend on the level and shape of the term structure of prices.

Extant reduced-form models of commodity prices cannot capture the rich dynamics of commodity prices in the storage economy. Although such models characterize the behavior of longer-tenor prices fairly well, they are poor representations of the behavior of shorter-term prices. Even models that permit some state dependence in volatilities find it difficult to generate the dynamics of the shape of the short end of the term structure of prices in the storage economy. Indeed, it is doubtful that any variation on the standard reduced-form commodity price modeling framework will adequately characterize the dynamics of actual commodity prices.

The two-factor model makes many predictions about the behavior of commodity spot and forward prices, their volatilities, and their correlations. These predictions match, at least qualitatively, findings in some empirical studies of commodity prices, such as in my work with Victor Ng. But it is desirable to know how well the model predictions match up with the behavior of actual commodity prices. That is, how good a job does the model do in fitting actual data on the prices of continuously produced commodities? The next chapter makes such an evaluation, using data from an important continuously produced commodity: copper.

FOUR

The Empirical Performance of the Two-Factor
Storage Model

4.1 Introduction

The previous chapter showed how continuously produced commodities' prices, volatilities, and correlations behave in a competitive market with two homoscedastic net demand shocks of differing persistences. The model studied there implies that these prices can exhibit rich dynamics, with time-varying correlations and volatilities that depend on the shape of the forward curve and, hence, with underlying fundamental supply-and-demand conditions.

Empirically observed commodity prices also exhibit rich dynamics, including time-varying – and often extreme – volatilities.[1] Commodity forward curves exhibit a variety of shapes, including backwardation, contango, and "humps," and correlations between forward prices of different maturities are time varying (Ng and Pirrong 1994). Hence the question: How well do the dynamics generated by the model match with the dynamics observed for actual commodity prices?

Empirical work on the theory has lagged its theoretical development. In some respects, this is not surprising, given the complexity of the problem and the associated computational costs.

Heretofore, confrontations between the theory and the data have involved modest calibration exercises based on relatively simple one-factor versions of the model of Routledge et al. (2000) (RSS), or more ambitious estimations involving low-frequency (annual) data (Deaton and Laroque 1992, 1995, or 1996). These empirical investigations have not been particularly kind to the theory. RSS find that the theory has difficulty explaining the dynamics of

---

[1] Mandelbrot's early work on non-linearities in price dynamics, since extended to financial markets, was motivated by the study of cotton futures prices (Mandelbrot 1963).

longer-term forward prices. Deaton-Laroque claim that storage apparently has little role in explaining commodity price dynamics; instead, autocorrelation in the underlying net demand process, rather than speculative storage, seems to be the main source of autocorrelation in commodity prices.

In this chapter, I attempt to extend this modest empirical literature in several ways. First, I explore the ability of the model to fit dynamics of the entire term structure of a commodity's price (the commodity studied being copper) in high-frequency (daily) data. Moreover, unlike in previous studies, I utilize inventory data as well as spot and forward price data. Second, I implement the two-factor model analyzed in the previous chapter in order to allow the potential for richer price dynamics (and hence avoid a potential specification error that may result using a one-factor model). Third, I utilize an empirical technique (Extended Kalman Filtering) that is well suited to the study of a market where (a) there are readily observable time series of various quantities (prices and stocks), but (b) the underlying driving variables are latent.

The basic results of this exercise are as follows:

- For copper, the storage model does a good job at explaining the dynamics of spot prices, short-tenor (e.g., 3-month) forward prices, and inventories. The model can match the unconditional volatilities of these prices and the unconditional correlations between them. Moreover, the spot and 3-month prices and inventories fitted by the Kalman Filter match the observed prices quite closely.
- For this commodity, the model does a poorer job of explaining the dynamics of longer-dated forward prices, especially 27-month prices. Observed 27-month forward prices are far more volatile than implied by the fitted model. Moreover, the 27-month prices fitted in the EKF differ noticeably from actual 27-month forward prices.
- The two-factor storage model can capture salient features of the dynamics of copper inventories. In the model, copper inventories are very insensitive to the long-term shock, but are highly sensitive to the dynamics of the short-term shock. Small changes in the persistence and volatility of the short-term shock can produce large changes in the behavior of the inventory variable and the ability of the model to fit the observed inventory data.
- The estimated parameters that describe the dynamics of the net demand shocks imply the existence of one highly persistent demand shock (with a half-life of around 6 years) and another much less persistent shock (with a half-life of around 40 days). Thus, most of the autocorrelation in copper prices results from the fact that

demand is highly persistent. Contrary to the conclusions of Deaton-Laroque, however, this does not imply that storage is unimportant. Storage greatly affects the higher moments of prices and the correlations between spot and forward prices. That is, even though demand autocorrelation predominates in determining commodity price levels, storage is salient in determining commodity price risks. Moreover, a model that incorporates only a single highly persistent shock cannot explain the dynamics of inventories; it is necessary to incorporate a high-frequency shock in order to do so.[2]

- The model cannot generate option-implied volatilities as large as those observed in the data. Moreover, the filtered demand shocks are not homoscedastic. These findings suggest that it is necessary to incorporate stochastic demand volatility into the model.

The remainder of this chapter is organized as follows. Section 4.2 discusses the empirical literature on commodity storage. Section 4.3 outlines the empirical approach adopted herein, and Section 4.4 discusses the results generated by that approach. Section 4.5 discusses the implications of the analysis for the speculation debate. Section 4.6 summarizes the article.

4.2 Empirical Tests of the Theory of Storage: A Brief Literature Review

Empirical work on the competitive storage model has focused on-low frequency (e.g., annual) data or relatively simple calibrations using higher-frequency data.

Deaton-Laroque fit a one-factor storage model to a variety of commodity price time series. Their maximum likelihood approach exploits an implication of the simple one-factor model – namely, that there is a "cutoff price" such that inventories fall to zero when the spot price exceeds the cutoff, but inventories are positive when the price is lower than the cutoff. Deaton and Laroque (1992) posit that demand shocks are i.i.d. They find that although theoretically storage can cause prices to exhibit positive autocorrelation even when demand shocks are independent, the level of autocorrelation implied by their fitted model is far below that observed in practice. Deaton and Laroque (1995, 1996) allow for autocorrelated demand shocks (again in a one-factor model). They find that virtually all the autocorrelation

---

[2] Chapter 6, which analyzes seasonal commodities, provides compelling evidence that high-demand persistence is not sufficient to explain the high autocorrelations observed in the prices of commodities such as corn or soybeans.

in commodity prices is attributable to autocorrelation in the underlying demand disturbances, and very little is attributable to the smoothing effects of speculative storage.

The Deaton-Laroque empirical analyses are problematic for several reasons. First, they utilize low-frequency (annual) data for a wide variety of very heterogeneous commodities. Because in reality economic agents make decisions regarding storage daily, if not intra-day, the frequency of their data is poorly aligned with the frequency of the economic decisions they are trying to assess empirically. Moreover, Deaton-Laroque impose a single model on very different commodities. Their commodities include those that are produced continuously and have non-seasonal demand (e.g., industrial metals such as tin and copper), those that are planted and produced seasonally (e.g., corn and wheat), and others that are produced seasonally from perennial plants (e.g., coffee and cocoa). The economics of storage differ substantially between these various products, but the Deaton-Laroque empirical specification does not reflect these differences. Finally, their use of annual data forces them to estimate their model with decades of data encompassing periods of major changes in income, technology, policy regimes, and trade patterns (not to mention wars), but they do not allow for structural shifts.

RSS present a one-factor model of commodity storage and calibrate this model to certain moments of oil futures prices. Specifically, they choose the parameters of the storage model (the autocorrelation and variance of the demand shock, and the parameters of the net demand curve) to minimize the mean squared errors in the means and variances of oil futures prices with maturities between 1 and 10 months.

RSS find that the basic one-factor model does a poor job at explaining the variances of longer-tenor futures prices. To mitigate this problem, they propose a model with an additional, and permanent, demand shock that does not affect optimal storage decisions and which is not priced in equilibrium. They calibrate the variance of this parameter so as to match the variance of the 10-month oil futures price and then choose the remaining parameters to minimize mean squared errors in the means and variances of the remaining futures prices.

RSS do not examine correlations between different futures prices. The models they examine do not generate the dynamics of correlations documented by Ng and Pirrong (1994). Specifically, their models cannot explain the fact that correlations between spot and forward prices can decline substantially when stocks are low and the market is in backwardation. Moreover, as noted in Chapter 3, the permanent shock has undesirable characteristics.

Specifically, this shock shifts the supply and demand curves up in parallel. This could be interpreted as a pure price-level shock, which would imply that deflated commodity prices exhibit relatively little persistence. This is not consistent with extant evidence. An alternative interpretation is that a permanent (or highly persistent) shock is related to the business cycle; note that it is difficult to reject the hypothesis that GDP and aggregate consumption are integrated processes. However, under the RSS specification, the permanent shock does not affect output. This is inconsistent with the fact that the outputs of many continuously produced commodities are strongly pro-cyclical. Moreover, a permanent shock risk (presumably related to the business cycle and hence systematic) should be priced in equilibrium, which is inconsistent with the RSS assumption that the expected value of the future shock is its current value (as is necessary to ensure that it does not affect storage decisions).

4.3 An Alternative Empirical Approach

4.3.1 Overview

I propose and implement an alternative empirical approach to studying the continuously produced commodity storage economy analyzed in Chapter 3. This approach utilizes high-frequency – daily – data to reflect the fact that economic agents can and do make intertemporal resource allocation decisions almost continuously; an empirical study in which the assumed frequency of decision making matches the actual frequency is better specified than one in which it does not. Moreover, rather than just trying to match only a selected subset of moments of prices, I attempt to fit a daily time series of spot prices, forward prices and – importantly – inventories. Finally, I fit a full-blown two-factor model (rather than the more restrictive RSS two-factor model) that can generate richer price and inventory dynamics.

The requisite data are available only for a small number of commodities – industrial metals traded on the London Metal Exchange (LME). Industrial metals are continuously produced and not subject to seasonal supply or demand. The LME trades very short-dated contracts – 1-day forwards, effectively a true spot contract – and very long-dated ones – as much as 27 months forward.[3] Data on these instruments are available daily

---

[3] Indeed, the LME recently introduced a 63-month forward contract.

going back to the 1980s. These prices are also unique in that they are for a constant maturity (e.g., 15 months) rather than for a particular delivery date (e.g., July 2011) with maturities that change as time passes. This eliminates another empirical challenge. Moreover, since 1997, the LME has reported daily inventories of its commodities held in exchange warehouses; these warehouses contain virtually all of the speculative stocks of metal.[4] No other commodities have equivalent, comprehensive inventory figures at frequencies that match those of available price data.

The LME data have been studied extensively by Ng and Pirrong (1994); hence, it is possible to compare the implications of the models fitted here with the empirical regularities they document. I therefore implement the empirical analysis using copper (the most heavily traded industrial metal). This sample period for this metal presents a serious challenge to the theory. During the early part of the sample period, copper prices were very low – historic lows, when adjusting for inflation. During the latter part of the sample period, copper reached all-time highs – even adjusting for inflation. Then, as the financial crisis kicked in late in 2008, copper prices plunged before making a sharp recovery in mid-2009. In other words, this is a commodity that exhibited sharp and substantial variations over a considerable period of time. It thus poses a tough challenge to any model.

The copper market is also one that was widely alleged to have been unduly affected by excessive speculation, especially in 2005–2008. That is, much of the price action in these years was attributed to speculative distortion rather than changes in fundamentals. Thus, the ability of a fundamentals-based model to accurately reproduce the observed price behavior, especially during this period, is relevant to the debate over the influence of speculation. And as I show later, it is possible to see how well measures of speculative activity relate to the filtered demand estimates that the empirical analysis produces to determine whether the demand that moved prices was speculative or fundamental.

The basic empirical approach involves a mixture of estimation and calibration techniques; a full-blown estimation of all the parameters necessary for a realistic model is not computationally practical. In essence, I fix various parameters (e.g., demand elasticity, production capacity, the shape of the supply curve, storage costs) and estimate others (notably, those describing

---

[4] RSS refer to speculative stocks as "discretionary" stocks, to be distinguished from stocks committed to production or consumption farther down the value chain, such as natural gas in a pipeline near an industrial consumer.

the dynamics of latent net demand shocks). I then test the robustness of the results by varying the fixed parameters.

The method involves several steps, as follows:

1. Establish a grid of parameters. The parameters characterize the dynamics of net demand shocks, specifically their persistence, volatility, and correlation.
2. Choosing a set of parameters from the grid, solve a stochastic dynamic program for a storage economy. Given that this is the same model as that studied in Chapter 3, please refer to that chapter for a detailed discussion of the model and its numerical solution. This program has three state variables: inventories and two net demand shocks with different degrees of persistence. The solution to the program gives spot prices; 3-month, 15-month, and 27-month forward prices; and inventories as functions of these state variables.
3. Given the solution to the storage problem, run an EKF.[5] In the EKF analysis, the observables are LME cash; 3-month, 15-month, and 27-month prices; and LME inventories from 7 April 1997 to 1 July 2009. The EKF provides filtered estimates of the latent net demand shocks. Determine the log-likelihood from the EKF.
4. Choose another set of parameters from the grid and then repeat steps 2–4 for all points in the parameter grid.
5. Choose the set of parameters that generates the highest log likelihood.

This is a very computationally expensive process. Because of the curse of dimensionality, solution of the two-dimensional dynamic programming problem can take as long as 6 hours on a 1.2-GHz computer for each set of parameters. Moreover, each iteration of the EKF takes several minutes (because of the need to interpolate in three dimensions the four price and one inventory functions for each of the 3,709 observations). These computational burdens make a full-blown estimation of all parameters (including the parameters that describe the instantaneous demand curve and the supply curve) impractical.

Given the final demand process parameters, I simulate multiple sets of time series (each with the same number of observations as the empirical data available) of spot, 3-month, 15-month, and 27-month prices and of inventories, and for each set I estimate the variances of these series and the

---

[5] An Extended Kalman Filter is necessary because the observables are non-linear functions of the state variables, and one state variable is a non-linear function of the other state variables.

correlations between them. I then compare the means of these simulated variances and correlations to the corresponding empirical variances and correlations for copper estimated using data from April 1997 to July 2009; the starting date is dictated by the fact that marks when daily inventory data are available from the LME. Finally, I estimate a backwardation-augmented GARCH model like that employed by Ng and Pirrong (1994) using the simulated cash and 3-month prices to see whether the simulated conditional variances and covariances exhibit the features documented by Ng-Pirrong.

The solution of the dynamic programming model is at the heart of the process. The model is the same as studied in the previous chapter, with two net demand shocks, z and y, with the former more persistent than the latter. The cost and demand functions are the same as in Chapter 3. Individual, risk-neutral agents are presumed to make storage decisions on a daily basis. The model is solved recursively and numerically, using the PDE approach to determine the relevant forward prices and the splitting method to solve the PDEs.

The solution to the model for a given set of parameters is then combined with an EKF to extract estimates of the net demand shocks and prices and inventories.

4.3.2 The Extended Kalman Filter

The solution to the dynamic programming problem relates potentially observable quantities (prices and inventories) to state variables, parameters describing the dynamics of those state variables, and parameters that describe supply-and-demand conditions. Using this solution, I utilize a Kalman Filter to extract estimates of latent economic processes (the demand shocks) from observable data on prices and inventories. This method is well suited for the present application. The underlying demand processes are latent, but observable prices (and inventories) are related to these processes via the solution of the dynamic program. Given a choice of parameters, the Kalman Filter permits calculation of a log likelihood that quantifies how well the model fits the data. By choosing the parameters that maximize the log likelihood, it is possible to find the model that best explains the time-series behavior of the price and inventory data.

The state–space representation of the problem is as follows. The state variables are z_t, y_t, "true" speculative stocks x_t, and lagged true speculative stocks x_{t-1}. Thus, there is a vector of state variables, $\mathbf{X_t} = [z_t \ y_t \ x_t \ x_{t-1}]'$. There is also a vector of observables, $\mathbf{Z_t}$. The observables are daily observations of cash, 3-month, 15-month, and 27-month prices; LME inventories;

and 1-day lagged LME inventories. Denote these as P_t, $F_{3,t}$, $F_{15,t}$, $F_{27,t}$, I_t, and I_{t-1}, respectively, so $\mathbf{Z_t} = [\, P_t \; F_{3,t} \; F_{15,t} \; F_{27,t} \; I_t \; I_{t-1}\,]'$. Because the observables are non-linear functions of the state variables, as is x_t, the standard Kalman filter (which assumes a linear relation between state variables and observables) is not applicable. It is therefore necessary to utilize a filtering technique that can handle non-linearity. I therefore employ the EKF to solve this problem. The EKF modifies the standard Kalman machinery to handle non-linearities in relations between state variables and observables.[6]

The data are observed with daily frequency, so it is necessary to discretize in time the processes for z_t and y_t. This is achieved by setting:

$$z_t = \rho_z z_{t-1} + \epsilon_t^z$$

and

$$y_t = \rho_y y_{t-1} + \epsilon_t^y$$

where $\rho_z = exp(-\mu_z/365)$, $\rho_y = exp(-\mu_y/365)$, ϵ_t^z is Gaussian with variance $\sigma_z^2 \delta t$, and ϵ_t^y is Gaussian with variance $\sigma_y^2 \delta t$. Moreover, μ_z and μ_y are coefficients on the drift terms on the z_t and y_t Ornstein-Uhlenbeck processes.[7] $\mathbf{Q}$ denotes the variance-covariance matrix for ϵ_t.

Given this time discretization, the EKF linearizes the state and measurement functions around the current estimate of the state variables based on the partial derivatives of the state and measurement functions. Specifically, $\mathbf{X_t} = f(\mathbf{X_{t-1}}, \epsilon_t^z, \epsilon_t^y)$, where $f(.)$ is a non-linear function determined by the dynamics of z_t and y_t and the solution of the dynamic programming problem for x_t. Similarly, $\mathbf{Z_t} = h(\mathbf{X_t}) + v_t$, where $h(.)$ is a non-linear function determined by the solution to the dynamic programming problem and v_t is a vector of Gaussian measurement errors. $\mathbf{R}$ is the variance-covariance matrix for v_t. Because I assume that observed prices and inventories differ from the true competitive prices and inventories, this matrix has positive elements along the diagonal. Moreover, I assume that measurement errors are uncorrelated across observables, so all off-diagonal elements of $\mathbf{R}$ are zero.

To implement the EKF at a given observation t, one first sets:

$$\tilde{\mathbf{X}}_t = f(\hat{\mathbf{X}}_{t-1}, 0, 0)$$

---

[6] An alternative approach is to utilize the unscented Kalman filter. It generates similar results to those presented here.

[7] See Chapter 3.

where $\hat{\mathbf{X}}_{t-1}$ is an a posteriori estimate of the state vector derived from time $t-1$ (i.e., it is the filtered estimate of the state vector conditional on all information through $t-1$), and:

$$\tilde{\mathbf{Z}}_t = h(\tilde{\mathbf{X}}_t)$$

In essence, the EKF sets the errors in the state and measurement equations equal to zero and then expands these non-linear equations around the lagged, filtered estimate of the state vector as follows:

$$\mathbf{X}_t \approx \tilde{\mathbf{X}}_t + \mathbf{A}_t(\mathbf{X}_t - \hat{\mathbf{X}}_{t-1}) + \mathbf{W}_t\epsilon_t$$

where $\epsilon_t = [\epsilon_t^z \; \epsilon_t^y]'$, and

$$\mathbf{Z}_t = \tilde{\mathbf{Z}}_t + \mathbf{H}_t(\mathbf{X}_t - \mathbf{X}_{t-1}) + v_t$$

In these expressions, $\mathbf{A}_t$ is the Jacobian matrix of partial derivatives of $f(.)$ with respect to $\mathbf{X}_t$; $\mathbf{W}_t$ is the Jacobian of the partial derivatives of $f(.)$ with respect to ϵ; and $\mathbf{H}_t$ is the Jacobian of $h(.)$ with respect to $\mathbf{X}_t$. The various partial derivatives are determined using $\hat{\mathbf{X}}_{t-1}$ and the solutions to the dynamic program.[8] In this specific application:

$$\mathbf{A}_t = \begin{pmatrix} \rho_z & 0 & 0 & 0 \\ 0 & \rho_y & 0 & 0 \\ \frac{\partial x_t}{\partial z_t}\rho_z & \frac{\partial x_t}{\partial y_t}\rho_y & \frac{\partial x_t}{\partial x_{t-1}} & 0 \\ 0 & 0 & 1 & 0 \end{pmatrix}$$

$$\mathbf{W}_t = \begin{pmatrix} 1 & 0 \\ 0 & 1 \\ \frac{\partial x_t}{\partial z_t} & \frac{\partial x_t}{\partial y_t} \\ 0 & 0 \end{pmatrix}$$

and

$$\mathbf{H}_t = \begin{pmatrix} \frac{\partial P}{\partial z_t} & \frac{\partial P}{\partial y_t} & 0 & \frac{\partial P}{\partial x_{t-1}} \\ \frac{\partial F_3}{\partial z_t} & \frac{\partial F_3}{\partial y_t} & 0 & \frac{\partial F_3}{\partial x_{t-1}} \\ \frac{\partial F_{15}}{\partial z_t} & \frac{\partial F_{15}}{\partial y_t} & 0 & \frac{\partial F_{15}}{\partial x_{t-1}} \\ \frac{\partial F_{27}}{\partial z_t} & \frac{\partial F_{27}}{\partial y_t} & 0 & \frac{\partial F_{27}}{\partial x_{t-1}} \\ 0 & 0 & 1 & 0 \\ 0 & 0 & 0 & 1 \end{pmatrix}$$

[8]   The H, W, and A matrices are time varying because the relevant partial derivatives depend on the state variables. These partials are calculated using central difference approximations on the solution grid used in the storage problem.

All of the relevant partial derivatives are estimated using central finite differences from the functions that solve the dynamic programming problem.

Welch and Bishop (2001) show that the filtering process works as follows:

$$P_t = AP_{t-1}A' + WQW'$$

$$K_t = P_tH'(HP_{t-1}H' + VV')^{-1}$$

$$\hat{X}_t = \tilde{X}_t + K_t(Z_t - h(\tilde{X}_t))$$

$$P_{t+1} = (I - K_tH)P_t$$

In these expressions, P_t is the conditional variance matrix for the measurement equations, and K_t is the Kalman gain. The filter starts by setting the initial state vector equal to its unconditional expectation and sets P_0 to the unconditional variance-covariance matrix for the state vector.

4.3.3 Parameter Choices and Data

The main focus of this exercise is to find parameters for the state variable processes (μ_z, μ_y, and Q) that generate solutions to the dynamic program that mimic the behavior of actual commodity prices. I therefore fix the other parameters (relating primarily to the supply-and-demand functions) and then experiment to determine whether changes in these other parameters have a large impact on the parameters for the state variable processes that maximize the log likelihood.

The production capacity, Q_t, for copper is chosen to match the annual daily production capacity for copper in 2004; this figure (of 40,000 metric tons) was obtained from the International Copper Study Group. To reflect capacity growth during the 1998–2009 period, similar capacity figures were obtained for each year. Then, LME copper stocks data were adjusted to reflect capacity growth. First, for each day of data, stocks were divided by daily production capacity for the relevant year to determine the number of days of capacity that the stocks represent. This figure is then multiplied by the 40,000-ton 2004 daily capacity. This effectively makes the stocks variable equal to the number of days of production capacity held in inventory.

θ is chosen to ensure that (given the state variable process parameters) the minimum and maximum observed cash, 3-month, 15-month, and 27-month prices fall within the minimum and maximum prices implied by the solution to the dynamic programming problem on the grid for z and y.

v and ψ are set equal to 1.00. The demand elasticity is set equal to 1.00 as well.

The 1-day simple interest rate r is set equal to the average 1-month LIBOR rate observed over the 1997–2009 period divided by 365 plus the average of the ratio of the LME copper storage charge ($.25 per day) to the cash price of copper. Thus, r captures both the time value of money and warehousing fees.

The variances of the price measurement errors are chosen to reflect differences in liquidity across different maturities, with the near maturities being more liquid than the more distant ones. That is, microstructure effects can cause observed prices to deviate from "true" prices. Because the prices of more actively traded contracts are more likely to reflect accurately true supply-and-demand conditions, measurement errors are plausibly smaller for more liquid instruments. The bid-ask spread is a measure of market liquidity and reflects (in the same units in which prices are measured) the precision of the price-discovery process. The "true" price for a contract with a wide bid-ask spread can differ substantially from the reported price. Consequently, I set the standard deviation of each measurement error equal to the half-spread for the corresponding maturity obtained from the LME. As a result, the variance for the measurement errors on the very liquid cash contract is set equal to .25, whereas for the slightly less liquid 3-month tenor it is set equal to 1. The variances for the errors on the much less liquid 15- and 27-month tenors is set equal to 25.

Some results are sensitive to the choice of the variance of the stock measurement error. Whereas market bid-ask spreads provide a measure of the closeness of the relation between observed prices and "true" prices, there are few a priori considerations to guide the choice of the stock measurement error variance. I therefore experiment with a variety of choices for this parameter.

Data on LME prices and stocks were obtained from the LME. The prices are the official settlement prices for LME copper from 7 April 1997 to 10 July 2009. Stocks are daily LME stocks.

4.4 Results

Given the fixed parameters, the state variable process parameters that maximize the log likelihood that results from the iteration between the solution of the dynamic program and the EKF procedure are $\rho_z = .9997$, $\rho_y = .986$, $\sigma_z = .55$, $\sigma_y = .165$, and $\rho = -.02$. These imply that the more persistent z shock has a half-life of approximately 5.75 years, and the less persistent y

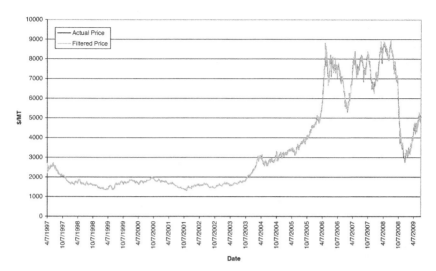

Figure 4.1. Actual and Filtered LME CU Cash Prices–Structural Model.

shock has a half-life of about 52 days. Thus, the copper data are consistent with the results of Deaton-Laroque, who find that a highly autocorrelated demand disturbance is necessary to explain the high persistence of commodity prices.

Figures 4.1–4.4 illustrate the degree of fit between observed and fitted prices; the fitted prices are the light line, the actual prices the dark line. The

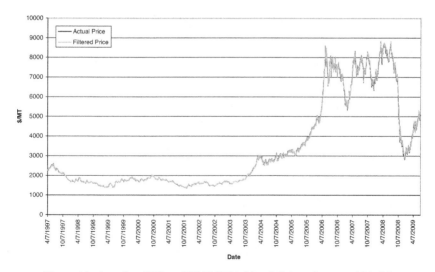

Figure 4.2. Actual and Filtered LME CU 3-Month Prices–Structural Model.

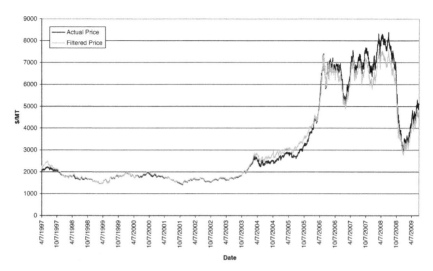

Figure 4.3. Actual and Filtered LME CU 15-Month Prices–Structural Model.

fitted prices are based on the implementation of the EKF for the parameters from the grid search that maximized the likelihood criterion. To determine these prices, I plug the filtered value of the z and y shocks into the price and inventory functions implied by the solution to the dynamic programming problem. The correspondence between the fitted and observed prices is very close for the spot and 3-month time series. The correspondence between

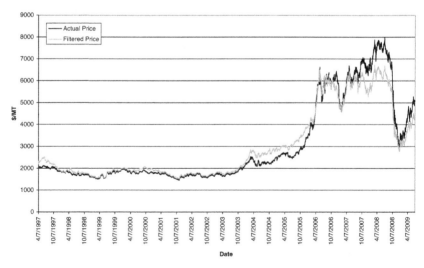

Figure 4.4. Actual and Filtered LME CU 27-Month Prices–Structural Model.

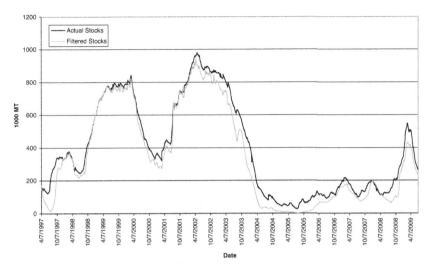

Figure 4.5. Actual and Filtered LME CU Inventories–Structural Model.

the 15-month observed and filtered prices is moderately close. However, there are more marked differences between the filtered and observed prices for the 27-month tenor. The fitted 27-month price and, to a lesser extent, the 15-month price are above the observed price when that price is low and below the observed price when it is high. Thus, the two-shock model has difficulty in capturing the variability of the 27-month price.

Figure 4.5 depicts the fit between observed and fitted stocks. As with the prices, the fitted stocks are derived from (a) the solution to the dynamic programming problem, and (b) the filtered values of the shocks derived from the model and copper data by the EKF. The fitted stocks are close to observed stocks when observed stocks are large.

The behavior of the stocks variable and the ability of the model to fit the evolution of stocks provide some interesting insights on what drives the behavior of the observables. The stocks function is highly sensitive to the persistence and volatility of the less persistent y shock; slight changes in these parameters lead to substantial divergences between observed and filtered stock values. Conversely, stocks are largely insensitive to the persistence and volatility of the longer-lived z shock. Moreover, the fits of the price variables are much more sensitive to the z shock parameters than to the y shock ones.

Changes in the parameters characterizing the demand curve, the supply curve, and inventory costs have little impact on the log likelihood. Moreover,

Table 4.1. *Empirical and Simulated Copper Volatilities (Annualized)*

Tenor	Empirical Including Crisis	Excluding Crisis	Simulated
Cash	.2725	.2378	.2579
3-Month	.2500	.2157	.2350
15-Month	.2418	.2097	.2054
27-Month	.2418	.2097	.1850

changes in the measurement error variances affect the value of the log likelihood, but do not have an impact on the ranking of the log likelihood across different choices of demand process parameters.

Taken together, these results suggest that the storage model does a good job of capturing the dynamics of the short end of the copper forward curve, an adequate job of characterizing the dynamics of stocks and medium-tenor (15-month) forward prices, and a poorer job of describing the evolution of the long end of the term structure. The simulation results confirm this impression. Table 4.1 reports (a) the unconditional annualized volatilities of the actual copper cash and 3-, 15-, and 27-month daily percentage price changes from 7 April 1997 to 10 July 2009; (b) the annualized volatilities of the actual prices from 7 April 1997 to 31 July 2008; and (c) the averages of the annualized volatilities of percentage changes in simulated time series of cash and 3-, 15-, and 27-month forward prices. The first empirical sample includes the period of the financial crisis, whereas the second excludes it. Each simulation run has the same number of simulated observations for each of these prices (3,709) as the actual copper price time series. The table reports the average of each of the four volatilities from 250 simulation runs.[9] The simulated data assume that observed prices equal the "true" price given by the solution to the dynamic programming problem for the parameters that maximize the likelihood criterion. The variance of the measurement error variances are those used in the EKF.

Note that the simulated volatilities match their empirical counterparts quite closely, although the simulated cash volatility is somewhat higher and the simulated 27-month volatility somewhat lower than their empirical counterparts from the sample that excludes the crisis period; the simulated variances are uniformly lower than the empirical estimates from the sample

---

[9] The actual data incorporate weekends, so the daily volatilities are annualized by multiplying them by the square root of 252. The simulated data assume trading takes place every day, so they are annualized by multiplying by the square root of 365.

Table 4.2. *Empirical and Simulated Copper Correlations*

	Empirical – Including Crisis			
Tenor	Cash	3-Month	15-Month	27-Month
Cash	1.00			
3-Month	.9800	1.00		
15-Month	.9544	.9478		
27-Month	.9130	.9366	.9820	1
	Empirical – Excluding Crisis			
Tenor	Cash	3-Month	15-Month	27-Month
Cash	1.00			
3-Month	.9757	1.00		
15-Month	.9416	.9648		
27-Month	.8857	.9127	.9752	1
	Simulated			
Tenor	Cash	3-Month	15-Month	27-Month
Cash	1.00			
3-Month	.9531	1.00		
15-Month	.8733	.9578		
27-Month	.8779	.9485	.9900	1

period that includes the crisis. Experimentation suggests that the volatility of the persistent z shock is the primary determinant of the 27-month volatility, and that the relations between the shorter-tenor volatilities are driven by the persistence and volatility of the transient y shock.

Table 4.2 reports a comparison of correlations between simulated returns for forward prices of different tenors and correlations between actual returns for the same tenors. Again, the simulated correlations are based on simulated prices that equal the "true" price derived from the solution to the dynamic program. The reported simulated correlations are the averages taken from 250 simulations of 3,079 observations each. As with the volatilities, I calculate the empirical correlations on samples including and excluding the period of the 2008–2009 financial crisis.

The simulated correlations match up closely with the empirical correlations. Thus, the storage model can capture some of the dynamics in the shape of the forward curve. The simulated cash correlations are slightly lower than the corresponding actual correlations, and the 27-month simulated correlation is slightly higher than its empirical counterpart. The primary deficiency is that the simulated correlation between the 15- and 27-month prices is almost exactly 1.00, which is considerably higher than the empirical value. One can reduce this correlation by introducing measurement error into the simulation, but this also depresses substantially the correlations between the 15- and 27-month prices on the one hand and the shorter-tenor prices on the other.

In sum, for copper, the empirical performance of the storage model is quite good at the short end of the forward curve. Despite the fact that the estimation/calibration technique fixes certain parameters arbitrarily to reduce the computational burden, the solution to the dynamic programming storage problem based on net demand shock parameters that maximize the likelihood criteria matches cash and 3-month prices quite closely. Similarly, in simulations, it generates volatilities and correlations for these tenors that are quite close to those observed empirically. The performance for the longer-tenor prices, especially the very long 27-month price, is less satisfactory. In particular, it is difficult to match the correlation of the 15- and 27-month prices. Moreover, the path of shocks that creates a close correspondence between the observed and filtered model generated prices leads to noticeable disparities between the fitted and observed 27-month prices.

The results strongly suggest the importance of a very persistent demand shock in explaining the dynamics of copper prices. Log likelihood falls substantially when one restricts the more highly autocorrelated demand shock to have a persistence of much less than 5 years.

This can be seen visually. Figure 4.6 depicts the filtered value of the persistent demand shock z_t (derived from the EKF). Compare the path followed by this demand shock to the paths of the prices depicted in Figures 4.1 through 4.4 – they are almost identical (except for scaling/units). It is evident that the persistent shock is a major price driver.

For some, interest in the theory of storage derives from the ability of storage to transform temporally uncorrelated demand shocks into more persistent price shocks (Deaton and Laroque 1992). Earlier empirical results, and those presented here, suggest that storage is not the primary driver of the persistence of commodity prices; instead, autocorrelation in demand plays the leading role.

This is not to say that storage is unimportant. Instead, as argued by Ng-Pirrong (1994) and demonstrated in Chapter 3, storage can also affect the higher moments in prices (particularly variances and correlations among forward prices of differing maturities). Ng-Pirrong show that empirically, volatilities tend to be high when the market is in backwardation, and that the correlation between the spot and futures prices tends to be near 1 when

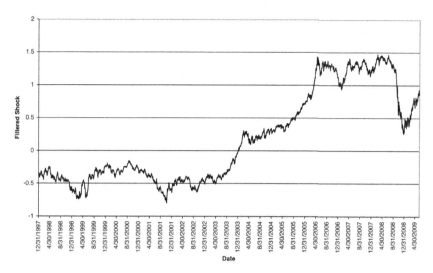

Figure 4.6. Filtered z Shock.

the market is at full carry and inventories are high, but falls well below 1 as the market goes into backwardation.

As documented in Chapter 3, the two-factor storage model generates similar dynamics. Thus, at least qualitatively, the model generates predictions about the behavior of volatilities and correlation that correspond with the empirical findings of Ng-Pirrong. This raises the question of how well the behavior of the second moments from model-generated prices matches with their empirical counterparts.

Ng and Pirrong (1994) investigate the joint dynamics of copper cash and 3-month prices in a bivariate GARCH framework that utilizes the amount of backwardation in the market as a measure of the level of stocks (because their work was done before daily stocks data were available). This "backwardation adjusted GARCH" (BAG) framework allows the variance of the cash and 3-month prices, and the correlation between them, to depend on the degree of backwardation. As illustrated in Figure 4.7, there is a strong relation between backwardation and the level of stocks in the storage model. This figure graphs the backwardation (adjusted for carrying costs) between the cash and 3-month generated by the storage model in a simulated time series of 5,000 observations against the simulated time series of carry-in stocks. Note the classic "supply of storage" relation first documented by Working in the 1930s, with large (small or non-existent) backwardations associated with low (high) stocks.

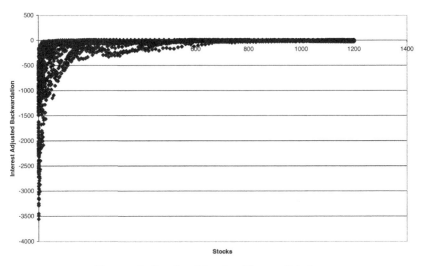

Figure 4.7. Simulated Supply of Storage Relation.

To determine whether the storage model can generate similar dynamics, I estimate the Ng-Pirrong model on both simulated data and data from 1997–2009. Formally, the model is:

$$h_{c,t} = \omega_c + \alpha_c \epsilon_{c,t}^2 + \beta_c h_{c,t-1} + \phi_c \mathcal{B}_{t-1}^2 \tag{4.1}$$

$$h_{3,t} = \omega_3 + \alpha_3 \epsilon_{3,t}^2 + \beta_3 h_{3,t-1} + \phi_3 \mathcal{B}_{t-1}^2 \tag{4.2}$$

$$\sigma_{c,3,t} = \rho \sqrt{h_{c,t} h_{3,t}} + \theta \mathcal{B}_{t-1}^2 \tag{4.3}$$

where $h_{c,t}$ is the variance of the daily unexpected percentage change in the cash price on date t; $h_{3,t}$ is the variance of the daily unexpected percentage change in the 3-month price on date t; $\epsilon_{c,t}$ is the unexpected cash price percentage change on date t; $\epsilon_{3,t}$ is the unexpected 3-month price percentage change on date t; $\sigma_{c,3,t}$ is the covariance between the cash and 3-month unexpected percentage price changes at t; and:

$$\mathcal{B}_t = \ln P_t - \ln(F_{t,.25} - c_t)$$

where P_t is the cash price, $F_{t,.25}$ is the 3-month price, and c_t is the cost of carrying inventory for 3 months. That is, $\mathcal{B}_t$ is the carrying-cost adjusted backwardation between the cash and 3-month prices. This should be non-negative (because spreads should not exceed full carry) and is larger the greater the backwardation in the forward curve.

Table 4.3.

Coefficient	Actual Data	Simulated Data
ω_c	5.71E-6	2.93E-5
α_c	.0437	.1719
β_c	.9479	.8198
ϕ_c	.001534	.0107
ω_3	5.26-E6	2.74E-5
α_3	.0437	.1684
β_3	.9481	.8257
ϕ_3	.001316	.00177
ρ	.9972	.9981
θ	−.00655	−.0315

Table 4.3 presents the BAG model parameters estimated from LME copper cash and 3-month data for the 1997–2009 period and the parameters estimated from simulated price data (using the same structural parameters from the calibration); all coefficients are highly significant, so only the point estimates of the parameters are presented. The results from the estimations on the simulated and actual data exhibit some important similarities. First, each exhibits both ARCH and GARCH effects, and the magnitudes of the ARCH and GARCH parameters are similar, although the persistence of volatility shocks is somewhat lower and the ARCH effects somewhat larger in the simulated data.[10] Second, in both actual and simulated data, the coefficients on the backwardation variable are positive and significant, indicating that prices are more volatile when the market is in backwardation than when it is not. The coefficient on the squared spread in the cash price variance equation is substantially larger in the simulated data. Third, cash price variances are more sensitive to the backwardation measure than 3-month prices for both real and simulated data, but the disparity between these coefficients is much more pronounced in the simulated data.[11] Fourth, when the market is at full carry (i.e., the backwardation variable is zero), spot-3 month correlations are effectively 1.00 for both the real and simulated data; for both series, increasing backwardation reduces the covariance

[10] When estimated on a longer time period of data (1982–2009), the GARCH and ARCH coefficients based on actual data are somewhat smaller than those for the simulated data.

[11] In the longer 1982–2009 sample period, backwardation has a more pronounced effect on the spot volatility than the 3-month volatility, which is not the case in the shorter period, where the coefficients on the backwardation variable in the spot and forward equations are almost equal.

between cash and forward prices. Together, the results for the variances and covariance imply that correlations decline as backwardation increases in both the actual and simulated data.

There are some differences between the estimates gained from the actual and simulated data. One difference is that when the BAG model is estimated under the assumption that the unexpected cash and 3-month percentage price changes are drawn from a t-distribution is that in the actual data, the estimated number of degrees of freedom is 3.36, whereas in the simulated data, the estimated degrees of freedom is near 10. Thus, whereas in the simulated data, leptokurtosis results mainly from heteroscedasticity attributable to changing supply-and-demand conditions, there is an additional source of leptokurtosis in the actual data (the larger degrees of freedom in the simulated data correspond to a less-leptokurtotic conditional price distribution). Another difference is that although in the simulated data both the cash and 3-month volatilities increase when stocks fall and backwardation rises, the effect is much larger for the cash price, whereas in the actual data, the backwardation change has an almost equal effect on the cash and 3-month variances. This finding is robust to changes in the net demand process parameters; regardless of the choice of these parameters, the spot volatility function implied by the solution to the dynamic programming problem is highly sensitive to inventories, but the 3-month volatility is not as responsive as in the empirical data. Thus, the storage model does a very good job at capturing salient features of the conditional variance of the spot price, but a poorer job at capturing the behavior of the conditional variance of forward prices. Furthermore, the impact of backwardation on correlation is negative in both the actual and simulated data sets, but the magnitude of the effect is substantially larger in the simulated data.

Another metric points out some deficiencies in the ability of the storage model to capture fully the dynamics of the higher-order moments of copper returns. Specifically, the storage model cannot generate implied volatilities for copper options similar to those observed during the 1997–2009 time period.

To make this comparison, I first determine Black-model implied volatilities using the solution to the dynamic programming model. Given the parameters for the y and z processes that maximize log likelihood and the spot price function generated by the solution of the dynamic programming problem for these parameter values, I solve the following PDE to determine the value of an ATM call option with 45 days to maturity for each value of z, *y*, and *x* in the valuation grid[12]:

$$rC = \frac{\partial F_{t,\tau}}{\partial t} + \mu_z \frac{\partial F_{t,\tau}}{\partial x} + \mu_y \frac{\partial F_{t,\tau}}{\partial y} + .5\sigma_z^2 \frac{\partial^2 F_{t,\tau}}{\partial z^2}$$

$$+ .5\sigma_y^2 \frac{\partial^2 F_{t,\tau}}{\partial y^2} + \rho\sigma_z\sigma_y \frac{\partial^2 F_{t,\tau}}{\partial z \partial y} \qquad (4.4)$$

where C is the price of the call being valued. Given the C that solves this equation (for each point on the valuation grid), I determine the corresponding implied volatility from the Black model at each point in the grid. I then collect the implied volatilities from ATM copper options traded on COMEX. The available data include volatilities for options with between 0 and 3 months to expiry; I interpolate between the volatilities of options with maturities spanning 45 days to determine an estimate of the implied volatility on an option with a 45-day maturity. Based on the availability of the implied volatility data, I perform this exercise for each day between 2 January 1998 and 17 June 2009.

I then use the COMEX-implied volatility as another observable variable in the EKF setup. That is, I expand the state space to include implied volatility and re-estimate the EKF to determine how well the model can fit not just the observed prices and stocks, but also the observed implied volatilities.

The answer is, not very well. Figure 4.8 depicts the time series of the actual 45-day implied ATM copper volatility (the more jagged and variable series) and the filtered value of the 45-day ATM option implied volatility. Note that the series do not covary even remotely closely. The disparity is particularly pronounced during the period of the financial crisis, beginning in September 2008. At that time, implied volatilities skyrocketed, but the implied volatility generated by the model and the filtered shocks actually declined. This decline was due to the fact that demand declined and stocks ballooned during this period; in the model, both of these developments tend to reduce price variances but, during this period, in the COMEX data, the implied volatility ranges between 50 and 70 percent. It reaches levels of more than 60 percent at times prior to the crisis. In contrast, the largest implied volatility generated by the storage model is approximately 35 percent. The model continues to fit the prices and inventories well when implied volatility

---

[12] Because the 45-day forward price differs at each point in the valuation grid, there is a different strike price for each point in this grid, each corresponding to the 45-day forward price at that grid.

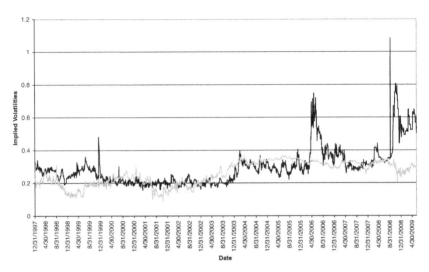

Figure 4.8. Actual and Filtered COMEX CU Implied Volatilities–Structural Model.

is included as an observable, but it cannot fit volatilities. That is, although the model can generate time variation in price volatilities, it cannot generate variations as large as those observed in the data.

Thus, although the storage model can produce time variation in instantaneous and implied volatilities, empirically, the model-predicted variations do not match observed variations. This means that volatility is not spanned by the forward prices – or, indeed, by the forward prices and inventories.[13] Put differently, if the two risk factors (and inventories) were the only determinants of copper prices, a two-factor model that fit the copper prices would also explain the evolution of copper-implied volatilities, and one could hedge the implied volatilities with a portfolio consisting of two different forward contracts (e.g., the 3- and 15-month prices).[14] The model fits prices well, but fails miserably in fitting the implied volatility, indicating that something other than variations in z_t and y_t drive variations in volatility. That is, volatility variations are not subsumed by – explained by or spanned by – these underlying demand variables.

These various results suggest that the model analyzed herein is missing a factor salient for the pricing of options – and for explaining the variances of

---

[13] See Trolle and Schwartz (2009) for a discussion of unspanned volatility and an empirical analysis that demonstrates that oil futures prices do not span oil futures volatilities.

[14] The weights in this portfolio would be determined based on the sensitivities of the 3- and 15-month prices and the implied volatility to the two demand shocks.

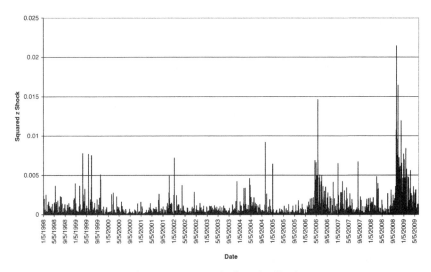

Figure 4.9. Squared Filtered z Shock.

copper prices. One obvious possibility is stochastic volatility in the underlying net demand shocks. The filtered values of the shocks from the solution to the EKF provide some evidence of this. Figure 4.9 depicts the time series of $(\Delta \hat{z}_t)^2$, where $\hat{z}_t$ is the filtered value of z_t. Note that this series exhibits pronounced "waves" of the type characteristic of GARCH processes, or stochastic volatility processes. Indeed, fitting a GARCH(1,1) model to this series produces large and statistically significant coefficients on the lagged variance and the lagged squared shock. Similar results hold for the y process. Thus, the data are not consistent with the assumption (maintained in the model studied herein) that the demand shock processes are homoscedastic. Given the salience of volatility for options prices and the possible dependence of storage decisions on fundamental volatility (because storage is an economic response to risk), this suggests the necessity of extending the model to incorporate stochastic volatility in the demand shock. I explore such a model in the next chapter.

Because it takes a model to beat a model, in addition to comparing the two-factor storage model's performance to the actual data, it is also worthwhile to compare its performance to an alternative model. The main competitors to structural models like those studied here are reduced-form models, such as those used in derivatives-pricing applications. In commodities, a well-known reduced-form model is the two-factor Schwartz model, which is closely related to the Schwartz-Smith and Gibson-Schwartz models.

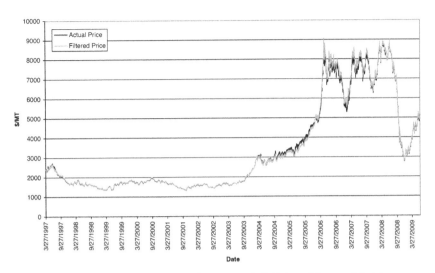

Figure 4.10. Actual and Filtered LME CU Cash Prices–Schwartz Model.

The Schwartz two-factor model posits a spot-price process:

$$\frac{dS_t}{S_t} = (\mu - \delta_t)dt + \sigma_1 dz_{1t}$$

and a convenience-yield process:

$$d\delta_t = \kappa(\alpha - \delta_t)dt + \sigma_2 dz_{2t}$$

Given these SDEs, the solution to partial differential equations with the appropriate boundary conditions gives the forward price for any tenor.

Schwartz (1997) uses Kalman filtering to determine the parameters for the SDEs and to produce filtered estimates of the state variables (the spot price and convenience yield) and forward prices. I use the same methodology on the 1997–2009 copper price data used in my analysis of the structural storage model. The resulting filtered cash, 3-month, 15-month, and 27-month prices are depicted in Figures 4.10 through 4.13 (green lines); these figures also present the actual price data (blue lines). (Stocks are not part of the Schwartz model; hence, there is no filtered-stock series.) A comparison of these figures with Figures 4.1 through 4.4, which present similar data from the structural storage model, reveals that the structural model fits the short-tenor (cash and 3-month) prices slightly better than the Schwartz model, whereas the latter does somewhat better at longer tenors. Furthermore, all returns in the Schwartz model are homoscedastic, meaning that this model cannot generate any time variation in the second moments. Although the

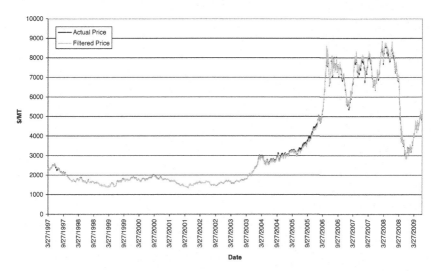

Figure 4.11. Actual and Filtered LME CU 3-Month Prices–Schwartz Model.

storage model cannot generate second moments that match closely the observed behavior of these moments in the actual data, the structural model variances and covariances exhibit some time variation. Thus, the structural model does a better job at capturing the time-series dynamics of copper prices than the Schwartz model, but it is still deficient in some respects.

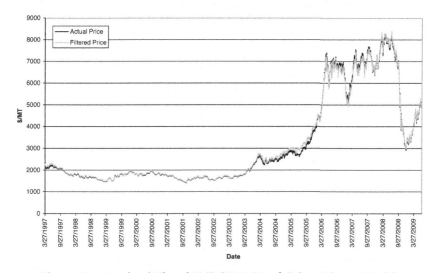

Figure 4.12. Actual and Filtered LME CU 15-Month Prices–Schwartz Model.

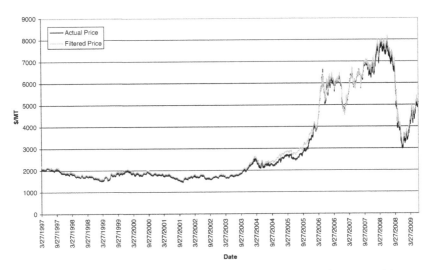

Figure 4.13. Actual and Filtered LME CU 27-Month Prices–Schwartz Model.

The Schwartz model, of course, cannot capture the dynamics of inventories because it does not include this variable.

In sum, the calibrated storage model can capture key features of the empirical behavior of copper prices. The model does a very good job at capturing the behavior of the spot price – the model can match the level, unconditional variance, and the behavior of the conditional variance of the spot price. The model's performance is less satisfactory at the longer end of the forward curve – the model's pricing errors for 27-month copper forward prices are large, and it somewhat underestimates the unconditional variance of this price. The model can match the unconditional variances of shorter-term forward prices and the unconditional correlations between the various forward prices. It does a poorer job at capturing the behavior of the conditional variance of forward prices, even for tenors as short as 3 months; the model predicts smaller fluctuations in the variance of the forward price in response to changes in the slope of the forward curve than are observed in practice. The model also suggests the existence of a highly persistent net demand shock for copper.

4.5 The Implications of the Model for the Speculation Debate

As was the case with many other commodity markets in the mid-2000s, there were numerous allegations that copper prices were driven not by fundamentals but rather by speculative excess. For instance, in mid-2006, the International Wrought Copper Council claimed that the price "had been driven up by a 'feeding frenzy' by hedge funds... 'It may be great for the producers but we feel that a market built on speculation leaves tremendous problems out for our side of the industry'."[15] Barclays Capital opined that a "new class of investors [such as pension funds], who didn't exist three years ago, are a dramatic influence in these markets."[16] Warren Buffett claimed that "like most trends, at the beginning it's driven by fundamentals but at some point speculation takes over."[17] The *Financial Times* stated that

the near-vertical take-off of the copper price this year has created an unstable mix of greed, speculation, and conspiracy theory.... Momentum investors who pile into any rapidly rising market, and have been riding the general boom in commodity prices, have almost certainly played a big role in the massive increase.[18]

The model casts some doubts on these claims. Specifically, it shows that there is a set of demand shocks that can account for virtually the exact course of copper prices during the period when claims of speculative excess were rife. That is, the price movements over the period in question were perfectly consistent with a purely fundamentals-driven model.

But, it might be argued in opposition that the demand estimate – the z_t – that the model filters from the data is not "real" demand, but instead reflects speculative demand: the impact of new monies flowing into the copper market from pension funds, hedge funds, and others.

The model, along with other considerations, casts doubts on this claim as well. To understand why, consider how speculation could affect the *spot* price of copper. If speculators are truly determining price at the margin, they must be those willing to pay the highest price – and, hence, must end up owning the commodity. That is, if they are determining the spot price, they must own the spot commodity.

There is little reason to believe that speculators were indeed accumulating inventories during the period when prices spiked. Note that most of the "new investors" blamed for the price spike do not – and, in some cases, cannot – take delivery of physical metal. They either sell their expiring futures and

[15] Philip Thornton, "Fresh surge in commodity prices raises fears of unsustainable speculative bubble," *The Independent*, 3 May 2006.
[16] Saijel Kishan, "Pension funds rise copper bets: LME pressed to cut speculation," *Bloomberg News*, 1 May 2006.
[17] Kevin Morrison, "'Ever higher': why commodity bulls are upbeat," *Financial Times*, 22 May 2006.
[18] Alan Beattie, "Fear and greed turn copper price red hot," *Financial Times*, 23 May 2006.

forward contracts prior to taking delivery or use cash-settled OTC contracts that do not permit the buyer (seller) to take (make) delivery.

In response to this objection, supporters of the speculation explanation for the rapid rise in copper prices frequently argue that speculators distorted the market by buying futures and forwards, thereby raising their prices, which made it profitable for others to hold inventory of physical metal and hedge it by selling the futures and forwards at the prices inflated by speculators.

Under either interpretation, however, the speculative-distortion story requires that inventories rise along with *spot* prices. The data are inconsistent with this implication of the speculation hypothesis. During the period of price rises, inventories fell to very low levels. This is what the fundamentals-based model studied in this chapter and the previous one would predict.

Indeed, the set of demand shocks filtered from the price *and* inventory data result in a very close match between the spot and 3-month prices *and* inventories during the period when prices skyrocketed. That is, given these demand shocks, the fundamentals-based model predicts movements in prices *and* stocks that closely mirror the actual data.

In contrast, if speculation were really distorting prices, it should have distorted stocks too. Remember that the importance of prices is that they provide signals that guide the allocation of resources. If prices are distorted, by speculation for instance, the distorted price signals will cause distortions in *quantities*. In the case of copper in the mid-2000s, if speculation were driving prices to levels in excess of that justified by fundamentals, one would not expect to observe inventories to fall.[19]

Put differently, if speculation was distorting prices in the mid-2000s, a fundamentals-based model that is able to fit the path of prices should not fit the path of stocks. And if it is able to fit the path of inventories, it should not fit the path of prices. In the fundamentals-based model studied here, fundamental demand shocks that lead to price rises should also result in declines in inventories. In a speculation-based story, the speculative "demand" that drives up prices should also drive up stocks.

---

[19] The following chapter presents a model that incorporates stochastic fundamentals that shows that there can be periods in a competitive, rational expectations, undistorted market where inventories and prices can increase simultaneously. In the model of this chapter, that seldom happens. Thus, foreshadowing the results of the next chapter, a positive co-movement between inventories and prices does not necessarily imply that the market has been distorted, but a negative comovement is inconsistent (in either model) with the assertion that speculation has distorted prices.

But the fundamentals-driven model can capture the evolution of prices *and* stocks, and quite closely too. This consistency of inventory and price behavior with the predictions of the basic storage model and the inconsistency of this behavior with the speculative distortion story support the former and cast serious doubts on the latter.

This illustrates a more general point about the value of incorporating physical data into any analysis of an alleged price distortion. Because prices guide quantity movements, distortions in prices should be associated with distortions in quantities. Anomalous quantity-price comovements are a more reliable indicator of distortion than price movements alone. In copper in the 2006–2008 period, prices and quantities co-varied exactly as a fundamentals-based storage model predicts that they should, and quite differently than the speculation story implies. Score one for fundamentals.

The ability to extract demand shocks also suggests a method for determining whether these shocks reflect "real" demand from consumers of copper or speculative demand. The Commitment of Traders reports published by the United States' regulator of futures markets, the Commodity Futures Trading Commission, is widely used as a barometer of speculative demand for commodities. Now, there are problems with these reports, including the fact that the "commercial" and "non-commercial" categories to which traders are assigned do not correspond exactly to "hedger" and "speculator": some commercials speculate, for instance. Moreover, in copper in particular, much of the speculative activity takes place on markets (such as the LME) that the reports do not include. Despite these deficiencies, these reports are widely used to measure speculative participation and have formed the basis of various analyses concluding that speculation has indeed distorted prices.

If the CFTC reports are indeed reasonable proxies for speculative activity, and if speculative rather than "real" demand was the main cause of price movements in recent years, then one would expect that the demand shocks the model extracts from the data using the EKF would co-vary closely with the CFTC report-based measure of speculation. Figure 4.14 plots scaled versions of the z_t series and the series of non-commercial net positions as disclosed in the CFTC report for the copper market. There is clearly little visual correspondence between the two series. Speculators were net short at the time that the demand shock reached its peak; but they switched to net long precisely when the filtered demand shock estimate reached a low ebb in early 2009. Moreover, speculator positions exhibited many more oscillations during periods of time when the demand shock was rising or falling steadily.

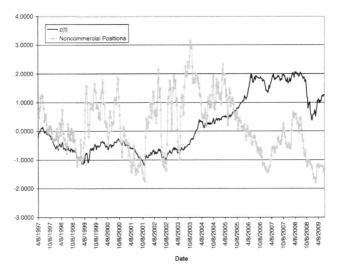

Figure 4.14.

Eyeballs are not a serious diagnostic tool, however, so more rigorous tests are necessary.

One such test is to examine whether these two highly persistent series (each of which has a unit root, based on standard statistics such as the Augmented Dickey-Fuller Test) are cointegrated. One interpretation of co-integration between two series is that they are in a long-run equilibrium relation. If it is believed that speculation exerts an influence over copper demand, one would expect the demand measure and a measure of specula-tive activity to be cointegrated.

In fact, they are not. All major cointegration tests indicate that the z_t and large speculator trading commitments are not cointegrated. Moreover, commercial trader net positions (which are -1 times the sum of net non-commercial and net non-reporting positions) are not cointegrated with the filtered demand shock. This lack of cointegration means that regressions of prices on speculative positions, which are sometimes used to "demonstrate" the effect of speculation on prices, are spurious regressions.

Testing for Granger Causality is another way to determine whether spec-ulative activity affects demand. I have estimated bivariate Granger Causality regressions for z_t and speculative trader commitments and cannot reject the null hypothesis that non-commercial net open interest does not cause z_t in a Granger sense, z_t.[20] It should be noted, though, that this result may

---

[20] See Hamilton (1994) for a clear discussion of the need for caution in interpreting Granger Causality as actual economic causation.

not be all that informative. In an efficient market, information contained in the CFTC reports in 1 week should be reflected in prices immediately, meaning that there should be no lagged response of the demand shock estimate extracted from prices of the type that Granger Causation regressions are designed to detect.

A final straightforward test of the relation between speculation (as measured by the CFTC reports) and demand is to regress changes in one series on contemporaneous changes in the other. Here, the results suggest some relation between non-commercial trading and the filtered-demand measure. Changes in one are positively related, in a statistically significant way, to changes in the other. The correlation between the two series is approximately 50 percent.

This provides tenuous evidence of a speculation-demand link. It is only tenuous, however, because a contemporaneous correlation does not permit unambiguous causal inferences. One interpretation of the results is that hedgers are more desirous to sell (buy) when prices rise (fall) (e.g., producers are more likely to sell to lock in prices when prices are high and rising than when they are low and falling), and this necessitates speculators to buy. In this story, speculators would not be distorting prices, just accommodating the demands of hedgers who are responding to price (and demand) movements.

Moreover, even if prices are responding to changes in speculative trading, and these price changes result in changes in the filtered-demand shock, this does not mean that speculators are necessarily distorting prices. If speculators have information about underlying demand, or anticipated changes in demand, their speculative trades would tend to move prices toward their full-information values, and speculative demand would just be reflecting information about real demand.

Furthermore, although there is a statistically significant short-term association between the filtered-demand shock estimate and changes in non-commercial open interest, the latter cannot explain some dramatic movements in copper prices. For instance, copper prices – and the filtered-demand estimate – rose dramatically in the year-long period 31 May 2005 to 30 May 2006. The demand shock rose from .36 to 1.37 during this period. To determine how much of this rise could be explained by the short-term association between demand movements and speculative trading over this period, I conducted the following "event study." For each week in this period, I calculate the change in the demand shock predicted by the coefficients in a regression of the change in the demand shock on changes in non-commercial net positions and the changes in non-commercial net positions during that week. Then, I add these predicted changes across the

52 weeks in the 31 May 2005–30 May 2006 period to determine a cumulative predicted change in the demand shock; this cumulative predicted change is a measure of how the change in non-commercial open interest, by itself, affected demand during this period.

Because non-commercial positions went from 9,492 contracts long to 6,372 contracts short during this period, the short-term association-based analysis (which finds a positive correlation between non-commercial position changes and changes in z_t) predicts that z_t should have fallen by .0982 rather than rising by 1.01 during May 2005–May 2006, as it did.

Similarly, during the financial crisis from 8 July 2008 to 30 December 2008, the estimated value of z_t fell by 1.15, but the change predicted conditional on (a) the estimated short-term association between changes in z_t and changes in non-commercial net positions, and (b) the observed changes in non-commercial net positions during this period, was only −.16, or about 12 percent of the observed decline.

Finally, during the period in early 2009 (30 December 2008–14 July 2009) when the estimated z_t rose by .62, the predicted rise (conditional on changes in non-commercial positions during this period) was −.004.

In brief, although there is a statistically significant short-term association between a measure of speculation and changes in the estimated demand shock, this short-term association cannot explain changes in the estimated demand shock. Indeed, during periods of steep price rises that spurred the most vocal claims of speculative excess, based on this short-term association, estimated demand for copper (and, hence, prices) should have fallen, if speculation were really driving this demand.

In sum, the data do not support the view that speculation was driving copper prices during its roller-coaster run in the 2005–2009 period. There is no evidence of a long-run, cointegrating-type relationship between the demand shock z_t and a measure of speculation in copper markets. Moreover, current innovations to speculative positions (as measured from CFTC data) do not help forecast future changes in estimated demand. Finally, although there is a contemporaneous positive (and significant) correlation between measured speculation and measured demand changes, this short-term association cannot explain the booms and busts in copper prices in the mid-to-late 2000s. Indeed, estimated demand and the forecast of the change in that estimated demand arising from changes in speculative activity moved in opposite directions.

Thus, the fundamentals-based, two-factor storage model can explain the movements in both prices and inventories, whereas an important implication of the speculation-based story (namely, that inventories should have risen together) is decisively rejected by the data. Moreover, there is little association between the demand shock extracted by the model from the price and inventory data and a commonly employed measure of speculation.

Given that (a) copper was one of many commodities that experienced a price boom in the 2005–2008 time period, and (b) it was widely alleged that speculation drove *all* of these commodities' prices upwards, the data's rejection of the speculative story and their support for the fundamentals-based theory of storage casts doubt on the veracity of these allegations for other commodities as well. This is especially true inasmuch as many of the fundamental factors that plausibly drove copper prices, such as booming Chinese demand, similarly affected the demand for other industrial commodities, including other industrial metals and energy products.

4.6 Summary and Conclusions

The theory of storage is the accepted model of commodity price term structures and price dynamics. Heretofore, the theory has been subjected to limited empirical scrutiny. The extant empirical work has provided only modest support for the theory, but this likely reflects the use of relatively restrictive versions of the model as dictated by the problem's complexity and associated computational costs. This chapter attempts to extend the empirical envelope by examining the performance of the multi-factor model analyzed in Chapter 3 using an EKF methodology and high-frequency data.

For the copper market, the model does an adequate job explaining the behavior of short-to-medium tenor prices, that is, spot prices and forward prices with tenors of 15 months or less. The model does less well on longer-tenor prices (i.e., 27-month forward prices). The calibrated model can generate unconditional variances and correlations for tenors of less than 15 months that mimic those observed in LME copper price data, but simulated unconditional variances and correlations for the 27-month forward are somewhat smaller than those observed in the data. Moreover, the calibrated model generates behaviors in some conditional moments (specifically, the conditional variances of the cash and 3-month prices and the conditional correlation between them) that are broadly similar to those observed empirically; the signs of the coefficients that affect the conditional moments are the same in the simulated and empirical data, but I have not been able to match their magnitudes closely. More specifically, the calibrated model can mimic quite closely the behavior of the conditional variance of the spot price, but it matches the behavior of the 3-month price's conditional variance far less closely. Moreover, even though it does imply that volatility is time varying, the model cannot generate option-implied volatilities as large as those observed in the data during the 1997–2009 period.

The ability of the model to match closely the movements in both spot prices and inventories speaks to the debate that has raged over the role of speculation in the copper market and other commodity markets as well. In particular, the results provide evidence that is consistent with the view that fundamentals were driving prices during the period of alleged speculative excess, but is inconsistent with the assertion that speculation distorted prices.

This chapter extends the existing empirical evidence relating to the theory of storage, but more work remains to be done. In particular, this effort still entails a considerable degree of calibration, rather than estimation, especially of the structural supply-and-demand parameters. Further advances are constrained by computational considerations and the curse of dimensionality, but Moore's Law will continuously relax these constraints. This chapter also suggests that as this proceeds, the methods set out herein – notably the combination of dynamic programming methods and Kalman filtering techniques – are a fruitful way to explore the empirical performance of the theory of storage. On a theoretical level, the results also suggest the need to incorporate stochastic fundamental volatility, as I do in the following chapter.

FIVE

Stochastic Fundamental Volatility, Speculation, and Commodity Storage

5.1 Introduction

The previous chapter showed that the traditional commodity storage model cannot capture some features of the behavior of continuously produced commodity prices, in particular the behavior of price volatility. Although the standard model can generate time variation in spot and forward volatility that matches some features documented in empirical data, it cannot generate volatility levels that reach those observed in actual prices. Moreover, it cannot generate in forward price-implied volatilities similar to those observed in the data.

In the model studied in the earlier chapters, variations in price volatilities resulted from variations in the degree of supply-demand tightness in the market. Volatility peaks in these models when stocks are low and/or demand is high. That is, volatility is a consequence of supply-and-demand fundamentals in this model. These results suggest that to generate richer volatility behavior, it is necessary to introduce another factor related to volatility that is not driven completely by the y and z shocks.

An obvious way to do this is to make the variability of the fundamental net demand shocks stochastic – that is, to introduce stochastic fundamental volatility.

The introduction of this factor is not ad hoc because there is considerable independent basis to believe that the supply and demand for commodities exhibit stochastic volatility. For instance, for industrial commodities such as copper, demand is affected by macroeconomic factors. Moreover, (a) stock prices also reflect macroeconomic fundamentals, and (b) stock prices exhibit stochastic volatility. This last point is illustrated in Figure 5.1, which depicts the VIX volatility index, a measure of the volatility of the S&P 500 stock index. Note that the VIX exhibits considerable variability over

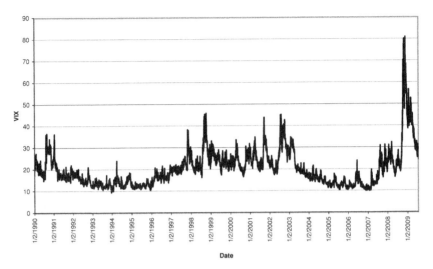

Figure 5.1. VIX 1990–2009.

time. This is consistent with variability in the volatility of fundamental macroeconomic volatility that reasonably contributes to variations in the volatility for the demand. Figure 5.2 presents additional suggestive evidence. It depicts the variance of the daily percentage changes in the Baltic Freight Index, by month, for 1985–2009. This index is widely used by practitioners as a measure of fundamental commodity demand, the idea being that high commodity demand translates into high demand for shipping and high shipping prices.[1] Note that the variability of the index exhibits variability over time.

Commodity supply also plausibly exhibits stochastic volatility. For instance, hurricanes disrupt oil production in the Gulf of Mexico, and there can be considerable uncertainty about the frequency and severity of hurricanes and the path that any particular hurricane can take. Moreover, this uncertainty can vary over time; there is more such uncertainty during hurricane seasons than at other times. In addition, some hurricane seasons (such as 2005) can be more intense than others (such as 2009). Similarly, wars in oil-producing regions can affect supply, meaning that there is more uncertainty about supply fundamentals in times of tension in the Middle East, for example, than when this region is (relatively) quiescent. Finally, the evidence from Chapter 4, namely, (a) the heteroscedasticity of the filtered demand shocks, and (b) the inability of the model with homoscedastic

---

[1]   Killian (2009) uses this variable as a measure of world industrial demand for oil.

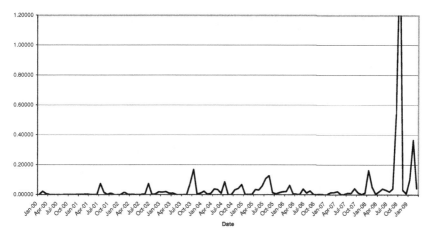

Figure 5.2. Baltic Freight Index Variance.

shocks to generate filtered implied volatilities that approximate observed ones, suggests that stochastic fundamental volatility is present in the commodity markets.

Thus, there are reasons to believe that the demand and supply for commodities vary, and the amplitude of these variations can change unpredictably over time. This motivates the introduction of stochastic volatility into the standard model.

There is another reason to explore this extension of the model. The recent boom in commodity prices has triggered an avalanche of allegations that sharp increases in the prices of oil, industrial metals, and agricultural products have been driven by excessive speculation. Such claims are not new. Indeed, they are hardy perennials, appearing whenever commodity prices spike or plummet. Indeed, to get a sense of the enduring nature of these complaints, consider that Adam Smith devoted a considerable portion of Chapter V of *The Wealth of Nations* to an analysis of assertions made over the centuries before 1776 that "forestalling" (i.e., speculation) distorted prices. Smith compared fears of speculation to "popular terrors and suspicions of witchcraft." Literal witch hunts are now a historical relic, but the same cannot be said of anti-speculative fervor.

It is difficult to evaluate these assertions regarding the destabilizing effects of speculation because they are almost never framed as refutable hypotheses that lead to empirically testable implications that distinguish the effects of excessive speculation from the effects of the normal operation of rational, competitive markets. In recent years, however, various commentators have identified one anomaly that allegedly distinguishes a market driven by irrational speculation from one that responds efficiently to supply and demand shocks. Specifically, during the 2005–2006 period, rising prices for oil were accompanied by increases in the amount of oil inventories. In contrast, historically, inventories and prices have varied inversely, with price rises being associated with drawdowns of inventory and price declines with stock builds. During this period, prices were high given the level of inventories and the historical relationship between prices and inventories. Moreover, this was a period of increasing levels of speculative activity in the oil markets. Critics of commodity speculation have asserted that this provides convincing evidence that speculation has broken the normal relationship between price and fundamentals.

A static simple supply-demand framework suggests that this conjecture is at least plausible. If speculators are driving prices above the competitive level, this would tend to encourage production and discourage consumption, thereby leading to accumulation of inventories – in the hands of the speculators, it should be added.

There are some plausible historical examples of this phenomenon. Beginning in the 1950s, the International Tin Council (ITC) attempted to prop up the price of the metal by purchasing and holding large quantities of it. Eventually the cost of accumulating the supplies necessary to maintain the price became unsustainable, and the ITC abandoned its operation, causing the tin price to collapse (Baldwin 1983; Anderson and Gilbert 1988). As another example, the Hunt brothers bought and held huge quantities of silver, either as part of a manipulative scheme or because they believed the price of silver was too low. Regardless of their motivation, the duo took delivery of and held massive quantities of the metal. They, too, were unable to bear the expense of this for long, and prices collapsed when their inventories were dumped onto the market (Williams 1996). As a final example, governments around the world have supported prices of agricultural products by purchasing and holding massive quantities of grain and cheese. Thus, attempts to drive prices above the competitive level can lead to both high prices and high inventories.

However, because the commodity storage problem is inherently dynamic, claims that positive comovements between inventories and prices *necessarily* indicate speculative distortion should be evaluated in a dynamic rational expectations model like that studied in this book. Moreover, it should be noted that "relationships" between endogenous variables such as inventories and prices can shift in response to structural shocks. Failure to condition on such structural shocks can lead one to attribute mistakenly such a shift to market irrationality, when in fact a rational market response to a structural shock caused it.

Indeed, during the purportedly anomalous period in the oil market mentioned earlier, there was a variety of events that plausibly affected both prices and inventory decisions. In particular, this was a period of increased supply uncertainty. The alleged anomalies began in the aftermath of the devastating Gulf hurricanes of 2005 and predictions of increasing hurricane activity in a major oil-producing region. Moreover, during this period, American difficulties in Iraq mounted; there was increasing concern about American and Israeli response to the Iranian nuclear program; there was a war in Lebanon that posed the risk of spreading to elsewhere in the Middle East; production disruptions occurred with increasing frequency in Nigeria; political uncertainty increased in Russia in the aftermath of the Khodorkovsky/Yukos affair; and conflict increased between the Chavez government in Venezuela and international oil companies. In brief, the 2005–2006 period was one of pronounced uncertainty about supply and demand during a time of already tight supply and demand – a volatility spike, if you will.

An increase in uncertainty plausibly affects incentives to hold inventory and, through the inventory channel, prices. The primary reason to hold inventory is to smooth the price impact of supply and demand shocks. Inventory can be accumulated during periods of relatively abundant supply, and stocks can be drawn down in response to bullish supply or demand shocks. An increase in the volatility of fundamental shocks therefore plausibly induces agents to increase the desired level of inventory. Given current supply and demand shocks, the only way to accumulate additional stocks is to bid up prices to encourage production and discourage consumption.

This chapter investigates this possibility, and the implications of stochastic fundamental volatility more generally, making stochastic the volatility of the fundamental net demand shock. Because of the curse of dimensionality, this comes at a cost: it is only practical to have one net demand shock rather than two. Nonetheless, the exercise is rewarding because it demonstrates that (a) stochastic fundamental volatility can, indeed, affect storage behavior, prices, and the variability of prices; and (b) the augmented model generates outcomes like those conjectured earlier. A positive shock to the variance of the fundamental shock leads rational, forward-looking agents to increase inventory holdings by bidding up prices. Particularly if variance shocks are persistent, a positive variance shock leads to a shift in the relationship between prices and inventories. Indeed, if variance shocks are sufficiently volatile, the price–inventory relationship is very unstable, meaning that it is not even reasonable to characterize it as a relationship, let alone one that is a reliable metric for evaluating the efficiency of a commodity market.

The remainder of this chapter is organized as follows. Section 5.2 presents the evidence on price and inventory comovements during 2005–2006 that led numerous analysts and policy makers to conclude that the oil market had become unmoored from fundamentals. Section 5.3 outlines the model of the storage economy. Section 5.4 characterizes the equilibrium of this economy. Section 5.5 describes the solution of the model. Section 5.6 examines the implications of the model for price and inventory behavior and the behavior of forward curves. Section 5.7 analyzes whether the addition of stochastic fundamental variability can address some of the empirical deficiencies of the storage model studied in Chapters 3 and 4. Section 5.8 uses the theoretical results to motivate an extension of Killian's (2009) study of oil price dynamics. Section 5.9 summarizes the chapter.

5.2 Speculation and Oil Prices

In the 2005–2008 period, the intensity of criticism of speculation in oil markets rose with the commodity's price. In 2006, Citigroup opined that "We believe the hike in speculative positions has been a key driver for the latest surge in commodity prices." This view was echoed by Goldman Sachs: "Unlike natural gas we estimate that the impact of speculators on oil prices is roughly equivalent in magnitude to the impact of shifts in supply and demand fundamentals (as reflected in stocks)." In 2007, OPEC's chairman Al Badri (hardly an unbiased source), chimed in as well: "Inventory data continues to demonstrate that crude stocks are ample. US crude stocks are now at nine-year highs. Inadequate refinery capacity, ongoing glitches in US refinery operations, geopolitical tensions and increased speculation in the futures market are, however, driving high oil prices."

The gravamen of these views is that *controlling for inventories,* oil prices were high in 2005–2007. This view was fleshed out in greatest detail by a study by the Senate Permanent Subcommittee on Investigations in 2006. The report stated:

[Figure 5.3] shows the relationship between U.S. crude oil inventories and prices over the past 8 years, and how the relationship between physical supply and price has fundamentally changed since 2004. For the period from 1998 through 2003, the chart shows that the price-inventory relationship generally centered around a line sloping from the middle-left of the chart down to the lower right, meaning that low inventories were accompanied by high prices, and high inventories were

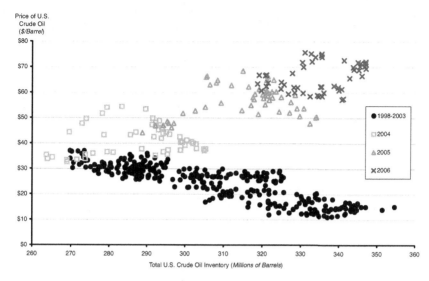

Figure 5.3. Crude Oil Prices Versus Total U.S. Stocks.

accompanied by low prices. For 2004, 2005, and through May 2006, which is the most recently available data, the inventory-price relationships fall nowhere near this downward sloping line; if anything, the points seem to go in the opposite direction, such that higher inventories seem to be correlated with higher prices. [Figure 5.3] clearly indicates that there has been a fundamental change in the oil industry, such that the previous relationship between price and inventory no longer applies. (U.S. Senate 2006)

The report continues:

One reason underlying this change is the influx of billions of dollars of speculative investment in the crude oil and natural gas futures markets. As energy prices have not only increased but become more volatile, energy commodities have become an attractive investment for financial institutions, hedge funds, pension funds, commodity pools, and other large investors. One oil economist has calculated that over the past few years more than $60 billion has been spent on oil futures in the NYMEX market alone . . . this frenzy of speculative buying has created additional demand for oil futures, thereby pushing up the price of those futures. The increases in the price of oil futures have provided financial incentives for companies to buy even more oil and put it into storage for future use, resulting in high prices despite ample inventories. (U.S. Senate 2006)

In brief, it is a widely held view in the oil markets that speculation has caused prices to be artificially high, and that the main evidence for this opinion is that by historical standards, prices are high after controlling for the abundant stocks in the market. Relatedly, the contango in price relationships observed at the time was historically anomalous. The oil market is typically in backwardation (about 80 percent of the time since the advent of oil futures trading in the early 1980s), and the few periods of contango have occurred when prices were very low (e.g., the late 1990s, post the Asian financial crisis). The 2005–2007 period was unusual in that contango occurred when prices were historically high (in nominal terms).

Are these anomalies sufficient to conclude that speculation distorted prices? The crucial issue is whether (a) shifts in price–inventory relationships, and (b) contango price structure when prices are high, are consistent with the operation of a competitive, efficient, and undistorted market. That is, can a rational expectations equilibrium model of the endogenous determination of inventories and prices reproduce the price–inventory and price–contango relations observed in 2005–2008?

To explore this question, the next section presents a modification of the standard rational expectations dynamic storage model studied in previous chapters. The model expands on the traditional one by permitting the variability of the random demand shock to vary stochastically. The basic idea is that agents hold inventory to smooth consumption and production in the face of demand shocks. When these demand shocks become more volatile, agents will plausibly hold more inventory because a bigger inventory cushion is required to smooth output and consumption in the face of more variable shocks. Adding inventory requires an increase in prices to stimulate production and discourage consumption. Therefore, a volatility shock that induces an increase in inventories also induces an increase in price. That is, a shock to demand variability should cause a shift in the relationship between inventories and prices.

5.3 The Storage Economy

To understand how stochastic volatility affects storage behavior and prices, consider a commodity, such as oil or copper, that is produced and consumed continuously and that is not subject to pronounced seasonality in supply or demand. The flow demand for the commodity is a one-shock version of the standard model employed throughout this book:

$$P(q_t) = \Phi e^{z_t} q_t^{\beta}$$

where P_t is the spot price of the commodity at time t, q_t is the consumption of the commodity at t, z_t is a stochastic demand shock, and Φ and β are parameters.

The innovation of this chapter is to make the variance of the demand shock stochastic. The demand shock z_t is characterized by the following mean-reverting stochastic process:

$$dz_t = -\mu_z z_t dt + V_t^{.5} dW_t$$

where V_t is a (stochastic) variance process, W_t is a Brownian motion and μ_z is a parameter. In particular, μ_z gives the speed with which z_t reverts to its mean of 0. Note the time subscript on the demand variance V_t; this means that this variance can change randomly.

The variance process is:

$$dV_t = \mu_v(\theta - V_t)dt + \sigma_V V_t^{\gamma} dB_t$$

where B_t is a Brownian motion and μ_v, θ, σ_V, and γ are parameters. Specifically, μ_v is the speed of variance mean reversion; θ is the level to which variance reverts; and σ_V is the volatility of the variance. B_t and W_t may be correlated, with correlation coefficient ρ.

In brief, in this economy, demand is stochastic and the variability of the demand shock is itself stochastic.

Producers of the commodity are competitive. The commodity is produced subject to strict decreasing returns and a binding capacity constraint. Specifically, the flow supply of the commodity is our familiar:

$$MC_t = A + \frac{v}{(\bar{q} - q_t)^{\psi}}$$

In this expression, MC_t is the marginal cost of producing q_t units of the commodity. $\bar{q} < \infty$ is the flow capacity constraint.

The commodity is storable. Storers forego the possibility of earning an interest rate r on the funds they use to purchase the commodity.[2]

There is a competitive, frictionless forward market for the commodity. This market trades forward contracts for delivery 1 day hence, as well as for maturities in excess of 1 day. There is also a frictionless spot market for the commodity where buyers and sellers can contract for immediate delivery of the commodity.

In addition to producers and consumers, there is a population of price-taking agents who can engage in speculative storage. For simplicity, I assume that the speculators are risk neutral. Hence, the market prices of z_t and V_t risk are zero in equilibrium. The problem is readily modified to incorporate

---

[2] It is straightforward to extend the analysis to include proportional and per-unit storage charges.

risk-averse speculators by incorporating non-zero market prices of risk into the drifts of the processes for the demand and variance shocks. In this case, for the purposes of pricing forwards on the commodity, these market prices of risk would be used to derive an equivalent probability measure.

5.4 Equilibrium Competitive Storage

As in previous chapters, I assume that production, consumption, and storage decisions are made daily. Competitive storers buy the spot commodity, store it, and sell forwards if the 1-day forward price of the commodity exceeds the spot price of the commodity plus the cost of storing it for 1 day. Conversely, they sell the spot commodity out of inventory (to the extent possible implied by the existing level of stocks) and buy forwards if the 1-day forward price is less than the spot price plus the cost of holding inventory. Thus, in equilibrium, if inventories are positive, the 1-day forward price equals the spot price plus the cost of holding inventory for a day.

Moreover, as always, it is possible for there to be a stockout in equilibrium. In this case, inventories are drawn to zero and the spot price plus storage costs exceeds the 1-day forward price of the commodity.

Optimal storage decisions maximize the expected present value of the economy's net surplus, subject to the constraint that inventories are non-negative. Formally, define net surplus at t, the difference between consumer and producer surplus, as:

$$S(q_t^s, q_t^d, z) = \int_0^{q_t^d} P(q_t^d, z) dq_t^d - \int_0^{q_t^s} MC(q_t^s) dq_t^s$$

where q_t^s is the quantity produced at t, and q_t^d is the quantity consumed at t.

Then, given initial inventories X_0, total value is:

$$V(X_0, z_0, V_0) = \sup_{\{q_t^s, q_t^d\}} E_0 \sum_{t=0}^{\infty} \frac{S(q_t^s, q_t^d, z)}{(1+r)^t} \tag{5.1}$$

subject to:

$$X_t = X_{t-1} + q_t^s - q_t^d$$

and:

$$X_t \geq 0 \ \forall t \geq 0$$

The expectation in (5.1) is taken conditional on z_0 and V_0. For any $t \geq 0$, this problem can be re-expressed as:

$$\Lambda(X_t, z_t, V_t) = \sup_{q_t^s, q_t^d} [S(q_t^s, q_t^d) + E_t \frac{\Lambda(X_{t+1}, z_{t+1}, V_{t+1})}{1 + r}]$$

subject to:

$$X_{t+1} = X_t + q_t^s - q_t^d$$

and:

$$X_t \geq 0 \; t \geq 0$$

The expectation E_t is taken conditional on z_t and V_t.

Because the economy is perfectly competitive and there are no externalities, the Second Welfare Theorem ensures that the competitive equilibrium maximizes $\Lambda(X_t, z_t, V_t)$. Thus, defining the 1-day forward price at t as $F(X_{t+1}, z_t, V_t)$ and denoting the spot price at t as $\mathcal{P}(X_t, z_t, V_t)$, if X_{t+1} is the optimal carry-out at t, in equilibrium[3]:

$$\mathcal{P}(X_t, z_t, V_t) = \frac{F(X_{t+1}, z_t, V_t)}{1 + r} \tag{5.2}$$

if $X_{t+1} > 0$, and:

$$\mathcal{P}(X_t, z_t, V_t) > \frac{F(0, z_t, V_t)}{1 + r} \tag{5.3}$$

otherwise.

Finally, given the risk neutrality of the speculators, the 1-day forward price is the expectation of the next day's spot price[4]:

$$F(X_{t+1}, z_t, V_t) = E_t \mathcal{P}(X_{t+1}, z_{t+1}, V_{t+1})$$

5.5 Solution of the Storage Problem

The solution strategy should by now be familiar. I initially posit a spot price function $\mathcal{P}(X, z, V)$. I then solve for the forward price function $F(.)$ using the PDEs approach. Given the forward price function, carry-in X_t, and the current demand and variance shocks z_t and V_t, it is possible to

---

[3] At t, carry-out and, hence, the carry-in $t + 1$ are known. That is, the forward price is a function of time t carry-out or, equivalently, time $t + 1$ carry-in.

[4] If speculators are risk averse, the demand shock and variance shock risks are priced, and this expectation is taken with respect to the equivalent measure.

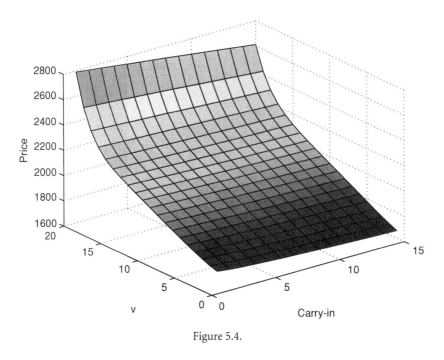

Figure 5.4.

solve for equilibrium (and optimal) carry-out using the forward price function and the demand and supply curves for the commodity. This optimal carry-out (if positive) sets the spot price equal to the present value of the forward price; if equation of the spot and the discounted forward price implies a negative carry-out, agents consume the entire inventory, carry-out is zero, and the equilibrium spot price exceeds the discounted forward price. This problem is repeated recursively until the spot price function converges.

5.6   Results: Storage, Prices, and Spreads

Given that the model is solved numerically, its properties are best understood through figures and simulations. Figure 5.4 depicts the relation between the spot price (on the vertical axis), carry-in, and the volatility shock when the demand shock is at its long-run mean of zero. Note that prices are strongly increasing in the variance shock. Figure 5.5 illustrates the channel through which this price effect occurs. It depicts the relation between inventory and the volatility shock, given that demand is at its mean of zero and carry-in is at its long-run average (derived from long simulations discussed later).

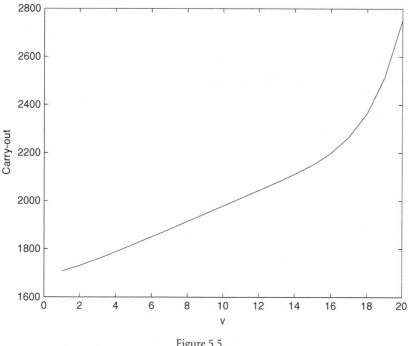

Figure 5.5.

Note that given carry-in, carry-out is increasing in the variance shock. Thus, as variance increases, speculative (or precautionary) stocks increase. Increasing stocks requires stimulation of production and a reduction in consumption; this requires, in turn, an increase in price. Thus, the model generates the comparative statics conjectured in the introduction to the chapter.

These forces also affect the relation between spot-futures spreads and variance. This is illustrated in Figure 5.6, which depicts the relation between the difference among the 3-month forward price (discounted back to the present) and the spot price (on the vertical axis), the variance shock, and the demand shock. The figure has a plateau at zero, due to the fact that the discounted forward price can never exceed the spot price. Most important, the figure illustrates that spreads do vary with volatility away from the plateau.

Figure 5.7 presents a simulation of the behavior of this model over a period of 5,000 days – approximately 20 years of trading days. The simulation is carried out as follows. The SDEs for z_t and V_t are used to simulate 5,000 daily observations for these variables, starting from $z_0 = 0$ and $V_0 = \theta$. The

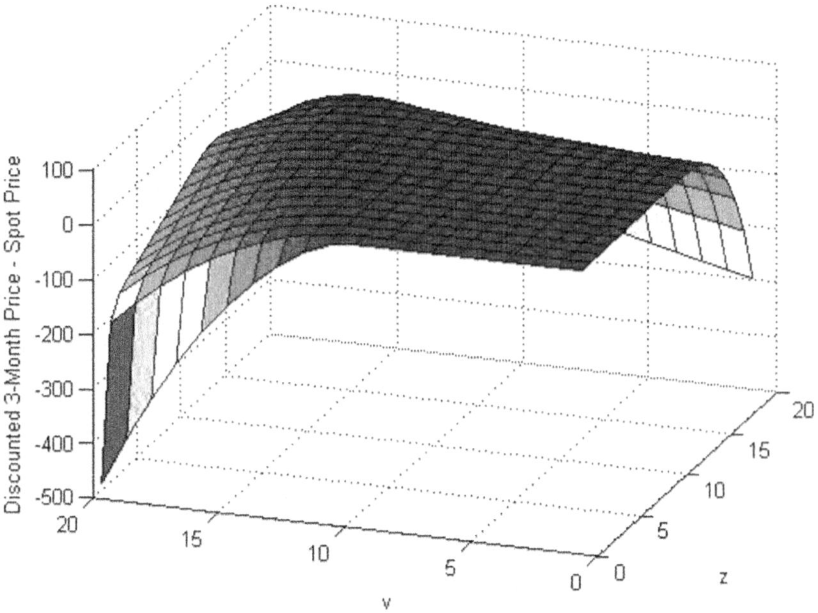

Figure 5.6.

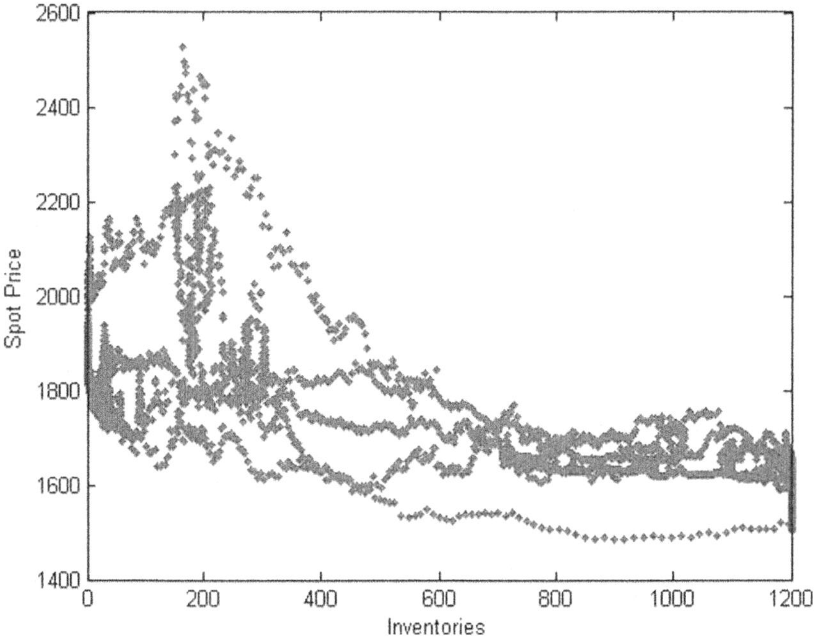

Figure 5.7.

initial inventory is set at 1 month's productive capacity. Given X_0, z_0, and V_0, the optimal carry-out X_1 and the resulting equilibrium spot price $\mathcal{P}_1$ are determined. Given this X_1 and the simulated z_1 and V_1, X_2 and $\mathcal{P}_2$ are solved for, and so on, for the 5,000 simulated days.

Figure 5.7 is a scatter plot of simulated values of inventories and prices and is comparable to the scatter plot based on real data in Figure 5.3. The horizontal axis measures inventories, and the vertical axis measures the spot price. This graph (which is for one simulation, but which is representative of the many I ran) demonstrates that in this model, there is no stable relation between inventories and prices. There are periods of time during which there is a negative relation between these variables (low prices being associated with high inventories), but this relation can shift over time, with a given level of inventory being associated with very different price levels at different points in time. Moreover, there are extended periods during which inventories and prices increase together. These episodes are associated with increases in the variance V_t.

Regression analysis demonstrates a similar point. I regress the simulated price changes against changes in the simulated values of z_t, V_t, and X_t. Similarly, I regress changes in inventory against the changes in the demand and variance state variables. The coefficient on the change in the variance is positive in each of these regressions, meaning that conditioning on the demand shock, higher variance is associated with higher prices and higher inventories.

In sum, the stochastic dynamic programming model in which net demand variance is stochastic implies that there is no stable relation between inventory levels and prices. As conjectured earlier, competitive storers respond to increases (decreases) in the variance of demand (holding demand constant) by increasing (decreasing) inventory. The only way to increase inventory holdings is to discourage consumption and encourage production. These, in turn, require an increase in price. Thus, when net demand variance is stochastic, precautionary inventory holdings vary positively with demand variance. This, in turn, implies that the relations between (a) inventory and the level of demand, and (b) inventory and prices shift randomly in response to variance shocks. Consequently, increases in inventories in response to higher prices are not *necessarily* symptomatic of speculative distortion of the market. Instead, they can reflect the salutary effect of speculative storage on resource allocation. By adjusting stocks in response to changes in risk, speculative storers optimize the time path of production and consumption.

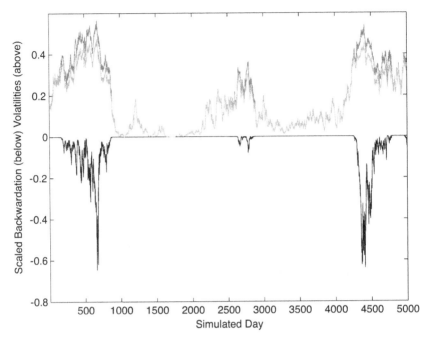

Figure 5.8.

5.7 Results: The Time Series Behavior of Prices, Stocks, and Volatility

Recall some of the empirical deficiencies of the homoscedastic-shock storage model. Specifically, it cannot generate volatilities as high as observed in practice for copper, and forward volatilities tend to exhibit little time variation and do not spike to anywhere near the same degree as spot volatilities. Can the stochastic fundamental volatility model address these deficiencies while maintaining other desirable features of the storage model, namely, the tendency of volatilities to peak when the market goes into backwardation?

The answer is a qualified yes. Figure 5.8 depicts the simulated behavior of key variables in a model with a half-life of a z shock of 2 years, a long-run mean level of fundamental variance of .0625, a volatility of variance of 20 percent and, crucially, a correlation between the demand shock and the variance shock of .8 (i.e., $\rho = .8$).

The upper lines in the graph are the volatilities of the spot and 3-month forward prices, calculated as follows. Ito's Lemma implies that:

$$(d\mathcal{P}_t)^2 = (\frac{\partial \mathcal{P}}{\partial z})^2 V_t dt + (\frac{\partial \mathcal{P}}{\partial V})^2 \sigma_V^2 V_t^{2\gamma} dt + 2 \frac{\partial \mathcal{P}}{\partial z} \frac{\partial \mathcal{P}}{\partial V} \rho \sigma_V V_t^{.5+\gamma} dt$$

Dividing this quantity by P_t^2, taking the square root, and annualizing is the instantaneous spot volatility. The same methodology can be used to determine the instantaneous forward volatility. The two lines on the upper part of Figure 5.8 depict spot and 3-month forward price volatilities calculated in this way.

The line in the lower part of the figure is a scaled measure of the deviation of the spot–3-month spread and its full carry value. Specifically, it is:

$$\mathcal{B}_t := \hat{K} \ln \frac{F_{3,t}}{\mathcal{P}_t e^{.25r}}$$

where $\hat{K}$ is a constant that makes the scale of $\mathcal{B}_t$ comparable to that of the volatility numbers. Thus, $\mathcal{B}_t$ is a measure of the slope of the forward curve, taking a value of 0 when the market is at full carry, and negative values that are large in absolute value when the market is in a substantial backwardation.

Several features stand out. First, volatilities tend to peak when backwardation peaks. This is characteristic of data from a variety of commodity markets, as documented by Ng and Pirrong (1994, 1996) and Pirrong (1996).

Second, there are periods when the market is nearly at full carry but volatility experiences an upsurge. There are episodes of this, some of which were discussed earlier, such as the high level of volatility in 2006 at a time the market was in contango. An even more extreme example is the financial crisis of 2008–2009. During this period, commodity volatilities reached extraordinarily high levels at the same time that markets moved into full carry and inventories skyrocketed (to record levels in the futures delivery point in Cushing, Oklahoma). Indeed, in the oil market, volatility was greater than at any time since the commencement of oil futures trading (even exceeding the volatility of the Gulf War period), and the difference between the prices of the first deferred and expiring oil futures prices was the largest observed (in both levels and logs) over the same period. This was indeed a period of substantial fundamental volatility (as illustrated in Figures 5.1 and 5.2). Thus, both the simulated and real-world commodity markets exhibit periods in which volatility can spike even when fundamental conditions are anything but tight.

Third, although spot volatilities are greater than forward volatilities, forward volatilities tend to rise appreciably when spot volatilities do. The gap between spot volatilities and forward volatilities is greatest when volatilities are at their highest levels and is effectively zero when volatility levels are low.

Fourth, volatilities even for 3-month horizons approach the high levels (e.g., close to 50 percent) observed for copper.

All of these features generated by the model are broadly consistent with the high-frequency empirical behavior of commodity prices and address some of the most marked deficiencies of the homoscedastic-shock model in Chapters 3 and 4. Nonetheless, the support for the model is qualified at present. To generate more realistic inventory behavior in the model, it is necessary to choose a relatively small half-life for the demand shock. This, however, means that the ability of the model to match the behavior of longer-tenor forward prices (such as 15-month and 27-month prices) is worse than the two homoscedastic demand shock model where one of the shocks has a much longer half-life. This suggests that a model with two demand shocks that exhibit stochastic variance, where one of the shocks has a very long half-life and the other has much less persistence, may be able to capture the salient dynamics: the highly persistent shock to fit the behavior of the longer-tenor prices; the less persistent shock to capture inventory dynamics; and the stochastic variances to generate more realistic volatility dynamics and volatility term structures. Such a model, alas, is cursed by dimensionality.

Nonetheless, the results of this chapter, combined with those of the earlier chapters, are promising and suggest that it is possible to specify a storage model of suitable dimension that can accurately describe the high-frequency behavior of continuously produced commodity prices. The results of this chapter in particular demonstrate that stochastic fundamental volatility is likely to be an important component of such a model. Moreover, as discussed earlier, stochastic fundamental volatility (a) is theoretically plausible, (b) has empirical support, and (c) can help explain seeming anomalies that have led some to conclude that speculation has distorted prices.

The main conceptual issue that remains is to justify a high correlation between variance shocks and fundamental shocks. Such a high correlation is necessary to generate in the model the covariation between the slope of the forward curve (i.e., the amount of backwardation) and price volatility. The fundamental economic considerations that could produce such a correlation are not immediately obvious, however. I am aware of no model that suggests that fundamental uncertainty should be greatest when demand is high.

5.8 Some Other Empirical Evidence

The model in this chapter provides a rigorous justification for a conjecture to explain important empirical results about the behavior of oil prices. Killian (2009) demonstrates that in a vector autoregression (VAR) framework, an "oil-specific" shock is necessary to explain the dynamics of oil prices; supply shocks and demand shocks are insufficient to do so. Killian asserts that this oil-specific shock is due to changes in the demand for precautionary inventories. Prices rise when the demand for such inventories increases. But this raises the question: What drives variations in the demand for precautionary inventories if supply and demand shocks do not? The model of this chapter provides an answer: variations in fundamental risk.

Killian's identification of the oil-specific shock with variations in the demand for precautionary inventories therefore has a firm theoretical foundation. But this is not the same as evidence. The model does suggest a route for a rigorous test, however: namely, to incorporate a measure of fundamental uncertainty into Killian's VAR framework.

I have attempted just that. First, using a slightly different measure of fundamental demand, I have replicated Killian's main results over a somewhat different time period.[5] Second, I create a measure of fundamental demand variability. Specifically, because in the model, ocean shipping rates are a proxy for the level of demand, I use the variance of ocean shipping rates as a proxy for the variability in demand. Inclusion of this variable means that any "oil-specific shock" is attributable to something other than changes in precautionary inventories resulting from changes in the volatility of demand.

I modify Killian's identification assumptions to reflect the inclusion of the new variable. I assume that oil supply does not respond in the same month to demand shocks, demand variance shocks, or oil-specific shocks; that demand shocks do not respond to demand variance shocks or oil-specific shocks in the same month; and that demand variance shocks do not respond to oil-specific shocks intra-month.

The empirical results do not provide support for demand variability (with the associated effect on precautionary inventory holdings) as the source of the oil-specific shock. In the estimates over the 1985–2009 period, shocks to demand variance do not appreciably affect oil prices; indeed, the relevant impulse response functions imply that an increase in demand variance leads to a price decline rather than a price decrease. Moreover,

---

[5] Killian's sample is from 1975 to 2006. Mine is from 1985 to 2009. Killian uses a hand-collected data set on shipping prices as his proxy for commodity demand. I use the Baltic Freight Index instead. Nonetheless, Killian's main results hold. Supply shocks have little effect on prices; demand shocks have a greater effect; and an oil-specific shock has a large effect on price movements.

despite the inclusion of demand variance, an oil-specific shock still exerts a large influence on oil price changes.

These results do not support the Killian conjecture or the model in this chapter that provides a rigorous justification for it. It is my sense, however, that this is likely a problem of measurement. Shipping rates are a crude proxy for oil demand, and the second moment of shipping rates is an even cruder proxy for demand uncertainty. Moreover, the model includes no measure of supply uncertainty. What is more, it is difficult to conceive of a cardinal measure that captures all of the sources of supply uncertainty that affect oil prices. These include, among others, war risks, political risks (e.g., political struggles over Venezuela's national oil company that could result in a drastic decline in output, or attacks on oil facilities in Nigeria), and weather risks (e.g., hurricanes). Thus, the absence of a plausible measure for fundamental uncertainty and its arguable unmeasurability preclude a rigorous test of the importance of precautionary inventories on oil prices. Nonetheless, the tantalizing empirical result that some "oil-specific" factor drives oil prices, the theory presented in this chapter that demonstrates that stochastic fundamental variability can lead to precautionary inventory changes and price changes, and the ability of such a model to capture salient features of commodity price dynamics combine to suggest that random variations in fundamental uncertainty may be important drivers of commodity prices.

This factor has largely been ignored in the heated controversies over commodity prices that have raged in recent years, meaning that these debates are seriously incomplete and therefore provide a very dubious basis for major policy changes such as Draconian limits on speculative activity in commodity markets, especially energy markets. These policy changes are in the offing as I write this book. Most notably, the recently enacted Dodd-Frank bill mandates the imposition of speculative position limits on energy exchange traded and OTC derivatives.

5.9 Conclusions

The amount of uncertainty in real economies is itself uncertain. The financial crisis of 2008–2009 forcefully illustrates that fact.

This chapter explores the implications of stochastic fundamental uncertainty. It demonstrates that incorporating such a feature into the standard storage model can redress many of the empirical deficiencies noted in Chapter 4. In particular, this feature results in forward volatilities that vary more extensively than in the homoscedastic demand models in Chapters 3 and 4. It can also result in higher levels of volatility than the homoscedastic demand model, while retaining the strong covariation between backwardation and volatility that is such a salient feature of actual commodity prices.

Moreover, the model can generate price and inventory comovements that the homoscedastic model seldom does: simultaneous increases in prices and inventories. Simultaneous increases in "supply" and price have been seized on as evidence of the distorting effects of speculation and have served as the empirical basis for calls to constrain speculation in commodity markets. All else being equal, speculation that causes the spot price of a commodity to rise above its competitive level should be associated with the accumulation of stocks in the hands of speculators. Speculators willing to pay more than a commodity is worth bid it away from producers and consumers and therefore end up holding large and increasing stocks. Thus – again, all else being equal – simultaneous increases in prices and inventories are indicia of speculative distortion.

But all is not equal. Storage in a rational-expectations economy where speculators stabilize rather than distort is an efficient response to the risk of demand fluctuations. Speculative storers accumulate inventories when demand – and prices – are low and draw down on these stocks when demand – and prices – are high. The optimal pattern of inventory buildup and drawdown depend on the amount of uncertainty. When there is considerable demand volatility, it is desirable to store more than is optimal in low-uncertainty environments.

When demand variability is itself stochastic, shocks to this variability influence optimal storage decisions given the level of demand. The model examined in this chapter implies that a positive shock to demand variance optimally induces competitive storers to increase inventory holdings. Because enhancing storage requires speculators to bid the commodity away from producers and consumers, increasing inventory in response to a variance shock requires an increase in price to encourage production and discourage consumption. In equilibrium, in this economy, one observes periods of time when inventories and prices are both increasing. One also observes periods when these variables are moving in opposite directions; holding demand variance constant, for instance, an increase in demand leads to an increase in price and a reduction in inventory.

Thus, disparate comovements in inventories and prices – including positive covariation between these variables – is completely consistent with an efficient, rational expectations equilibrium. Those searching for evidence

of speculative excess need look elsewhere than the price–inventory relation. Moreover, in addition to shedding light on the contentious debate
over speculation, the results of this chapter demonstrate that incorporating stochastic fundamental variance into the standard rational expectations
theory of storage framework can improve the theory's ability to capture the
high-frequency dynamics of storable commodity prices.

SIX

The Pricing of Seasonal Commodities

6.1 Introduction

The previous chapters have explored various structural models of continuously produced commodities. This chapter examines a different, important category of commodities: seasonally produced ones, such as corn or soybeans.

These commodities are important in their own right. But, as the results of this chapter demonstrate, an examination of seasonal commodities, and the ability of structural models to explain the high-frequency behavior of their spot and forward prices, points out some serious deficiencies in the storage model.

Specifically, I analyze a two-factor model of a commodity that is produced seasonally. One of the risk factors is the by-now-familiar highly persistent demand shock. The other is an output shock. The commodity is produced once a year, and the size of the harvest is random because of factors such as weather and insect infestations. Moreover, information about the size of the next harvest accumulates throughout the year. I solve the model using the techniques employed throughout the book and then examine particular implications of the model. These implications include the sensitivities of spot prices and futures prices with different expiration dates to demand and harvest shocks, and the correlations between spot and futures prices. I then compare these predictions to the empirical behavior of the spot and futures prices for several important seasonally produced commodities.

The analysis focuses on what are commonly referred to as "old-crop" and "new-crop" prices. An old-crop price is the price on any contract calling for delivery before the next harvest. A new-crop price is the price on any contract calling for delivery after the next harvest. For instance, in the United States, in June 2009, the July 2009 corn futures price is an old-crop price.

In contrast, in June 2009, the corn futures price for delivery in December 2009 is a new-crop price.

The solution of the seasonal storage model has several strong implications regarding the relations between new-crop and old-crop prices. Specifically, the model implies that late in the crop year, frequently old-crop prices should respond far less strongly than the new-crop price to revelation of new information about the size of the impending harvest (a "harvest shock"); only when carryover is very large (as may occur when demand is low and the previous harvest was large) and/or when the impending harvest is expected to be very small do old-crop and new-crop prices move by similar amounts in response to the arrival of news about the size of the next harvest. Moreover, the model implies that late in the crop, there should often be a very low correlation (on the order of .3 in simulations) between old-crop and new-crop prices and that correlations typically should decline through the crop year, with values close to 1 right after the harvest and values well below 1 right before the next harvest.

The intuition behind these results is readily understood. Because of the seasonal nature of production, supply increases discontinuously at harvest time. It is not always optimal to hold inventory from the period immediately before the harvest to the harvest period because the additional supply tends to depress prices. As a result, prices exhibit a sawtooth pattern, rising (on average) at the rate of interest from the time of the harvest until the time of the next harvest, and then falling as the new crop arrives. But the frequent absence of storage across crop years means that storage does not connect new-crop and old-crop prices. In turn, this means that although news about the size of the next harvest definitely affects the new-crop price, because storage does not connect the new-crop and old-crop prices, it has little affect on the old-crop price.

Put differently, harvest shocks do not affect the consumption in the old crop year because (a) the amount available depends only on the past harvest and past storage decisions; and (b) frequently, that entire amount available will be consumed before the next harvest. Because harvest shocks do not affect consumption in the old crop year, they do not affect old-crop prices. Furthermore, the fact that harvest shocks have an important effect on new-crop prices, but not on old-crop prices, tends to reduce the correlation between these prices. Although persistent demand shocks affect both new-crop and old-crop prices, this is not sufficient to generate high correlations between them when harvest shocks are sufficiently large.

These predictions, as it turns out, are at odds with the behavior of actual seasonal commodity prices. The empirical evidence shows that both old-crop and new-crop prices move about the same amount on days when the U.S. government releases crop forecasts. Moreover, both new-crop and old-crop prices are exceptionally volatile on these days, indicating that the government crop forecasts embody new information not previously available to the market. Furthermore, late in the crop year, old-crop and new-crop prices routinely exhibit high correlations; these correlations typically vary between .8 and .95.

The explicit incorporation of seasonality in production into the analysis serves several valuable purposes. First, the empirical shortcomings highlight deficiencies in the received theory of storage that motivate refinements and extensions of the theory. Second, the focus on the high-frequency dynamics of old-crop and new-crop prices proves decisively that highly autocorrelated demand is *not* sufficient to explain the high autocorrelation in low-frequency commodity price series, as conjectured by Deaton and Laroque (1995, 1996).

In a nutshell, the stark contrast between the implications of the seasonal storage model for high-frequency price behavior and the actual behavior of prices demonstrates that there *must* be something other than storage or demand autocorrelation to link prices over time. This recognition spurs an inquiry into just what that connection might be.

One plausible source of intertemporal connection is intertemporal substitution. I show that incorporating such an effect in a fairly ad hoc way can dramatically raise the sensitivity of old-crop prices to harvest shocks and thus raise the correlation between old-crop and new-crop prices.

This approach is less than satisfying, however. A more fully structural explanation would be preferable. Here, the curse of dimensionality precludes a definitive answer, but I discuss some promising possibilities. In particular, a multi-storable commodity general equilibrium approach (contrasting to the partial equilibrium framework of the standard storage model) with multiple storable commodities seems most profitable. A harvest shock affects the anticipated future demand for other storable commodities and, hence, the futures prices for those commodities. The storage channel for these other commodities means that the future demand shocks for them affects the current demand for these goods, and importantly, the current demand for the seasonally produced commodity. Thus, the main lesson of the empirical shortcomings of the seasonal storage model is that to understand more fully commodity price dynamics, it is necessary to go beyond partial equilibrium approaches and embrace a general equilibrium framework that captures more fully the intertemporal connections in the economy.

The remainder of this chapter is organized as follows. Section 6.2 presents the seasonal storage model and describes the solution methodology.

Section 6.3 discusses the implications of the model, including implications based on simulations. Section 6.4 presents some empirical evidence on high-frequency seasonal futures prices. Section 6.5 discusses briefly an extension of the model that incorporates intertemporal substitution and describes the implications of that model. Section 6.5 also discusses alternative structural approaches that could improve the empirical performance of the storage model to explain seasonal commodity price behaviors, paying special attention to general equilibrium approaches. Section 6.6 briefly summarizes.

6.2 The Model

In this section, I explore a dynamic, rational expectations model with periodic production. Chambers and Bailey (1996) prove that there is a unique solution to the model studied here. Pirrong (1999) and Osborne (2004) analyze analogs of this model in some detail, and both use the model to study old crop–new crop price relations.

Consider a commodity with flow demand:

$$D(q_t, z_t) = \Phi e^{z_t} q_t^\beta$$

where z_t is a demand shock that evolves according to the now-familiar:

$$dz_t = -\kappa_z z_t + \sigma_z dW_{zt}$$

where W_{zt} is a Brownian motion, and κ_z and σ_z are constants.

The commodity is produced periodically, at times $t = \{\tau, 2\tau, \ldots, K\tau, \ldots\}$, where K is any integer. Output ("the harvest") at time $K\tau - H_{K\tau}$ – is stochastic, with:

$$H_{K\tau} = \bar{H} e^{y_{K\tau, K\tau}}$$

where $y_{t, K\tau}$ is a supply shock that has the following characteristics:

$$y_{t, K\tau} = 0 \qquad t \leq (K - 1)\tau \tag{6.1}$$

$$\frac{dy_{t, K\tau}}{y_{t, K\tau}} = \sigma_y dW_{yt} \tag{6.2}$$

where σ_y is a constant and W_{yt} is a Brownian motion with $W_{yt'} = 0$ for $t' = (K - 1)\tau$.

The y variable can be interpreted (as in Pirrong 1999 and Osborne 2004) as "news" about the size of the impending harvest. Expression (1) means that at the time of the current harvest (and before), agents have no information about the size of the next harvest. Expression (2) means that information about the size of the next harvest arrives diffusively; the information variable y follows a geometric Brownian motion. This means that information is persistent and Markovian: these are properties that "news" should possess.

This specification assumes that the rate of information flow (parameterized by σ) is constant throughout the production period (which I will assume is a year in length). It is straightforward to modify the model to permit the rate of information flow to vary with the time of year by specifying σ_y to be a function of time $\sigma_y(t)$. In actual commodities, for instance, there are periods of the year, such as pollination time, that are particularly important in determining the size of the final harvest and, hence, information about weather during these periods has a bigger impact on output forecasts than during other periods. Together, (6.1) and (6.2) imply that at the time of this year's harvest, the expected harvest next year is:

$$E(H_{K\tau}) = \bar{H}e^{.5\sigma_y^2\tau}$$

The assumption that there is no information about next year's harvest at the time of this year's is unrealistic, but not extremely so, for crops such as corn and soybeans where factors that affect output in one year (e.g., a drought) are unlikely to persist into the following one. This assumption would not be appropriate for tree crops, where a shock that reduces output, such as a freeze, damages the trees and impairs future productivity. In this case, information about this year's harvest has ramifications for harvests in subsequent years. This can be incorporated in the model by positing that the y shock corresponding to the next harvest is not zero at the time of the current harvest; instead, at $(K-1)\tau$, the value of the $K\tau$ harvest shock depends on the $(K-1)\tau$ harvest shock value.[1]

Finally, I assume that the demand and harvest shocks are uncorrelated. This is plausible because in a modern economy agricultural output represents a small fraction of income; hence, shocks to the harvest have little impact on demand. Moreover, demand changes (within the harvest year) have little or no impact on output.

---

[1] The results reported herein do not change materially if $H_{t,K\tau}$ is drawn from some distribution at $t = (K-1)\tau$ and then evolves according to (6.1) and (6.2). The availability of information about the harvest at $K\tau$ prior to $(K-1)\tau$ that is not subsumed in the information about the size of the harvest at $(K-1)\tau$ increases the dimensionality of the problem. It is reasonable to abstract from this consideration for non-tree crops. For one thing, as noted in the text, at the time of the harvest, information about the size of the next harvest is very diffuse. For another, because it is often not optimal to carry over inventory across crop years, information about the next crop is likely to have little effect on optimal storage decisions today.

As should now be familiar, I posit that the spot price is a function of the demand and harvest shocks. Importantly, because the problem is no longer time homogeneous in the way that the continuous-production storage problem is, the spot price is also a function of the time of year. That is, the spot price function is $P(z_t, y_{t,K\tau}, t)$. Moreover, the forward price for delivery at some $t', t \le t' \le K\tau$, $F_{t'}(z_t, y_{t,K\tau}, t)$ must satisfy a second-order parabolic PDE:

$$0 = \frac{\partial F_{t'}}{\partial t} - \kappa_z \frac{\partial F_{t'}}{\partial z} + \frac{1}{2}\frac{\partial^2 F_{t'}}{\partial z^2}\sigma_z^2 + \frac{1}{2}\frac{\partial^2 F_{t'}}{\partial y^2}\sigma_y^2 y_{t,K\tau}^2 \qquad (6.3)$$

The solution technique should be familiar as well. I first discretize the problem in t, y, z, and the carry-in x. The time discretization deserves some discussion. As just noted, the problem is not homogeneous. For given z, y, and x, optimal decisions will depend on the time of the year. Given the values of the shocks and inventory, agents will make different consumption decisions depending on whether the next harvest is imminent or will not occur for some time. Thus, it is necessary to solve for a different spot price function (and storage function) for each different time of year. This effectively increases the dimensionality of the problem in a way that influences the choice of fineness of the time grid.

I assume that agents can make storage decisions on a weekly basis. Therefore, in the time discretization, I choose $\delta t = 1/52$. Moreover, the harvest occurs in "week 1" of the time grid. Week 52 is the week immediately preceding the harvest.

The non-homogeneity also affects the choice of the carry-in grid. It is not efficient to choose the same carry-in grid for every week of the year: carry-ins will be larger soon after the harvest than right before the next one. I therefore choose a different carry-in grid for every week of the year, with a wider range of values between the minimum and maximum of the grid for weeks early in the year than for later in the year.

Given these choices, the algorithm proceeds as follows:

- Make an initial guess for the price function at some "week" of the year. I choose week 52 and make the simple assumption that agents consume all of the carry-in.
- Proceed to week 51. For each value of x, y, and z in the respective grids, solve the PDE (6.3), subject to the terminal boundary condition that the forward price in week 52 is the spot price in that week. This produces a function $F_{52}(z, y, x_1, 51)$.

- Given carry-in $\hat{x}$, find the value of consumption q that equates the spot price $\Phi e^z q^\beta$ to the discounted value of the forward price:

$$e^{-r/52} F_{52}(z, y, \hat{x} - q, 51)$$

where r is an (annualized, continuously compounded) interest rate. This determines the spot price function for week 51 for each point in the grid. If $q > \hat{x}$, set $q = \hat{x}$ to ensure that carry-out is non-negative.

- Using the week 51 spot price function as the terminal boundary condition, solve (6.3) to determine the week 51 forward price as of week 50. Given this forward price function for each shock value and carry-in value, determine the consumption that sets the spot price equal to the discounted forward price. Calculate the spot price function.

- Proceed in this fashion until week 52 is reached again. Check to see whether the week 52 spot price function has converged. If so, stop. If not, continue the recursion for another "year."

Once convergence is achieved, this process creates an array of spot price functions and carry-out functions. The array is of dimension $N_z \times N_y \times N_x \times 52$, where N_z, N_y, and N_x represent the number of points in the demand shock, harvest shock, and carry-in grids, respectively.

Once the spot price array is complete, it can be used to determine forward prices. For instance, one can solve (6.3) to determine the forward price function, as of week 45, for delivery at the time of the next harvest (i.e., week 1 of the following crop year) by using the week 1 spot price function as the terminal boundary condition. This is a new crop futures price.

6.3 Results

In this section, I explore the implications of the storage model for the relations between old-crop and new-crop futures prices. Making predictions about these relations is very useful because there are many futures markets for seasonally produced commodities, and the data from these markets can be used to test these predictions. Moreover, although much of the storage literature (especially the articles by Deaton and Laroque) focuses on autocorrelations of spot prices averaged over some time intervals (e.g., a year), the results can be sensitive to the (inherently arbitrary) averaging period (Osborne 2004). Therefore, examining the implications of the model for new crop–old crop price relations permits a more thorough test of the model that exploits an abundant source of high-quality data.

Several results deserve special attention.

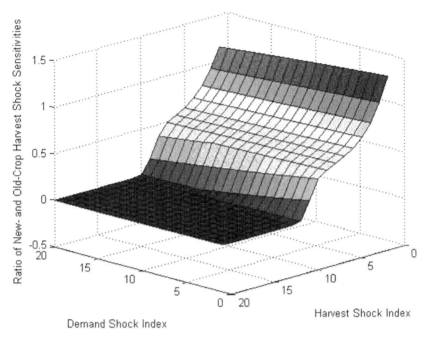

Figure 6.1.

First, given the spot price functions and the new-crop forward price functions for some $(K-1)\tau < t < K\tau$, it is possible to determine the sensitivity of the spot price (an old-crop price) to a harvest shock:

$$\frac{\partial P(z, y, x, t)}{\partial y}$$

and the sensitivity of the new-crop futures price to a harvest shock:

$$\frac{\partial F_{K\tau}(z, y, x, t)}{\partial y}$$

Of particular interest is the ratio between these partial derivatives: this ratio quantifies the relative sensitivity of the old-crop price and new-crop price to a harvest shock. Figure 6.1 depicts this ratio for week 45. One axis represents z, the other represents y. The graph assumes that carry-in is at the average value observed in simulations (which are described later).

Note that this ratio is typically quite small, meaning that a shock to the expected harvest has a much bigger impact on the new-crop price than on the old-crop price. The ratio is decreasing in y and usually increasing in z. When the anticipated harvest is small, it is likely that it will prove optimal to carry inventory from the old-crop to the new-crop year. In this case, storage connects the new-crop and old-crop prices, which means that both prices respond similarly to information about the size of the harvest. However, when the anticipated harvest is large, carryover is not optimal, storage does not link prices, and old-crop prices do not respond to harvest shocks.

The lack of carry-over across crop years means that storage, and the resulting cash-and-carry arbitrage link, often does not connect old-crop and new-crop prices. Thus, a shock to the expected harvest does not affect the derived demand for the old-crop supplies; the same amount will be consumed, regardless of the value of the harvest shock. Only if a harvest shock affects the optimal storage decision can it affect the old-crop price.

When carry-in is very large and/or the expected harvest is very small, it may be optimal to store across the crop year. Under these conditions, current supplies are abundant and future supplies are scarce, and it makes sense to store. Therefore, under these conditions, storage links old-crop and new-crop prices, leading them to respond similarly to supply shocks.

Second, it is possible to calculate the sensitivities of old- and new-crop prices to demand shocks and to use the demand shock and harvest shock sensitivities to calculate the instantaneous correlation between old-crop and new-crop price changes. Specifically, using Ito's Lemma to calculate dP and $dF_{K\tau}$, and multiplying, produces:

$$cov(dP, dF_{K\tau}) = \frac{\partial P}{\partial y} \frac{\partial F_{K\tau}}{\partial y} \sigma_y^2 y^2 dt + \frac{\partial P}{\partial z} \frac{\partial F_{K\tau}}{\partial z} \sigma_z^2 dt$$

where $cov(dP, dF_{K\tau})$ is the instantaneous covariance between the old-crop and new-crop price changes. Variance functions can be similarly derived, and dividing the covariance function by the square root of the product of the variance functions produces an instantaneous correlation function.

Figure 6.2 illustrates the old-crop–new-crop correlation for week 45, again as a function of the harvest shock and z, for the average level of week 45 carry-in obtained from long simulations.

The correlation exhibits an interesting, backwards-S–shaped pattern. The correlation is near 1.0 for very low values of y. As y increases, the correlation changes little; then, for intermediate values of y, it plunges to quite low levels of around .3 and then remains at this level as y increases. This transition from high to low correlation occurs at values of z and y such that for slightly larger values of y (i.e., a bigger expected harvest) or slightly higher values of z (i.e., slightly higher values of demand), it would be optimal to carry

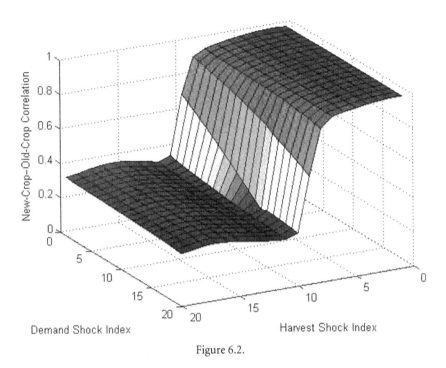

Figure 6.2.

out nothing; but for slightly smaller values of these variables, it would be optimal to carry out a positive amount.[2]

The reasons for this behavior are as follows. When the harvest is expected to be small, it is almost certain that it will be optimal to carry over some inventory. Thus, storage serves to link old-crop and new-crop prices, and the correlation is very high. As the size of the expected crop increases, the likelihood of carry-out declines, making it less likely that storage will link new- and old-crop prices; this reduces correlation. As the size of the anticipated harvest rises to very large levels, the probability of carryover declines to zero.

Figures 6.1 and 6.2 demonstrate that the relative sensitivities and correlations are dependent on the state variables and that they can be close to 1 or far below it. To compare the results of the model to the data, it is necessary to run simulations that make it possible to determine the relative frequency of combinations of state variables that produce high and low values.

---

[2]   Osborne (2004) also shows that correlations between a pre-harvest and post-harvest price are small in her seasonal storage model.

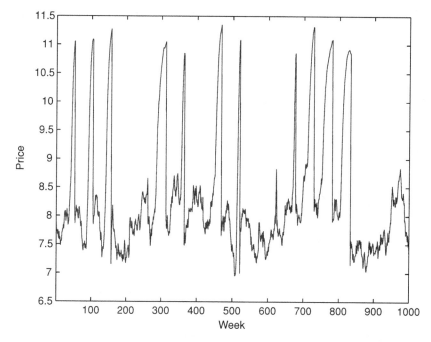

Figure 6.3.

For the simulations, I generate 100 years' worth (5,200 values) of the z and y shocks. Using the old-crop price, new-crop price, and carry-out arrays already solved for, given these shocks, I then simulate the paths of old-crop and new-crop prices and of inventories.

Figures 6.3 through 6.6 depict some salient simulation results. Figure 6.3 shows the spot prices for the last 20 simulated years. Each point in the figure is a spot price for a different week. Note that the prices exhibit a sawtooth pattern. They tend to rise through the crop year, and then fall as the new crop is harvested in week 1 of each simulated year.

This price behavior explains the inventory (carry-out) behavior depicted in Figure 6.4. Note that carry-out also exhibits a sawtooth pattern. Inventories are largest right after the harvest and then decline through the year as the good is consumed. Significantly, for most years, carry-out reaches zero in week 52. In fewer than half of the simulated years is there carry-over across crop years. Because there is no carry-over in most years, the non-negativity constraint on storage binds, meaning that the spot price right before the harvest is above the discounted new-crop futures price. This results in the

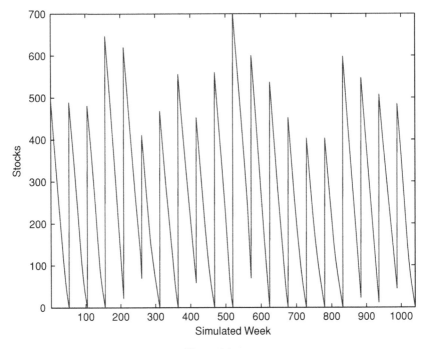

Figure 6.4.

spot price at the harvest also exceeding the spot price during the harvest week in those years when there is no carryover.

Figure 6.5 is a histogram of the values of:

$$\frac{\partial P/\partial y}{\partial F/\partial y}$$

across the 100 simulated years. This ratio is calculated as of week 45 of each year, using the futures price for delivery on week 1 of the following year. For corn in the United States, for instance, this would correspond roughly to a spot price in August and an October forward price. Note that the distribution is bimodal and that the leftmost modal value is less than .05. That is, the single most likely outcome is for the sensitivity of the old-crop price to the harvest shock is between 0 and .05. The second most common value for the sensitivity ratio is 1.

To facilitate comparison of the results to the empirical analysis to follow, I estimate a coefficient of the regression of the percentage change in the old-crop price against a constant and the percentage change in the new-crop price. The observations in the regression are weeks 40–52 from all

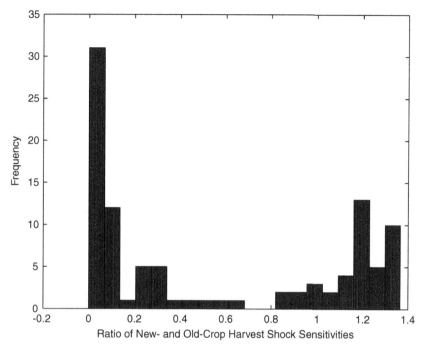

Figure 6.5.

the simulations. This corresponds to the 3 months prior to the harvest and hence is analogous to the July–September period for corn.

The slope coefficient in this regression is .4, meaning that across the sample, a 1 percent change in the new-crop price on a date during these weeks when information about the harvest is released is associated with a .4 percent change in the old-crop price.

Figure 6.6 is a histogram of the values of the instantaneous correlation between the spot price and the new-crop futures price (for delivery in the following week 1) as of week 45 of each simulated year. Again, the distribution of correlations is bimodal. The largest number of observations are between .95 and 1.00, but a large number of values (about a third) fall below .4.

Again, to facilitate comparison with the empirical analysis, I also calculate, by simulated year, the correlation between the new-crop and old-crop prices in weeks 40–52. Figure 6.7 is a histogram of these 100 correlations. In this particular simulation, sixteen of the correlations are negative, the median correlation is .42, and the mean correlation is .46.

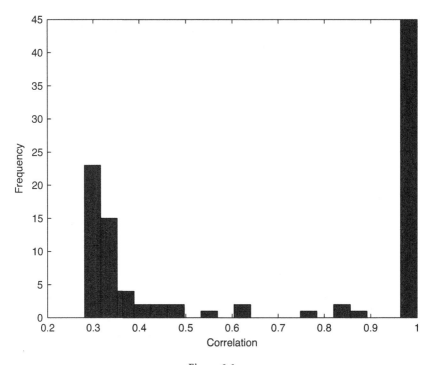

Figure 6.6.

There is also a distinctive pattern in the correlations. New-crop–old-crop correlations decline systematically through the year. In weeks 14–26 (which would correspond to the spring months for corn or soybeans), the median correlation across the 100 simulations is .99 and the mean correlation is .93. Thus, the correlation in the spring is roughly double the correlation in the weeks immediately preceding the harvest.

Figure 6.8 graphs the weekly values of the instantaneous correlations for 10 randomly selected years. The horizontal axis is the week of the year (between 1 and 52), and the horizontal axis measures the instantaneous correlation for that week. Note that for most of the years, the correlations start near 1 and then decline throughout the year.

In sum, the solution to the storage model has distinctive implications for the behavior of old-crop and new-crop prices. New-crop prices are typically far more sensitive to information about the size of the next-harvest old-crop prices. Quite frequently, old-crop prices do not respond at all to harvest shocks late in the crop year. Moreover, the correlations between old-crop and new-crop prices are often far below 1 late in the crop year, but close

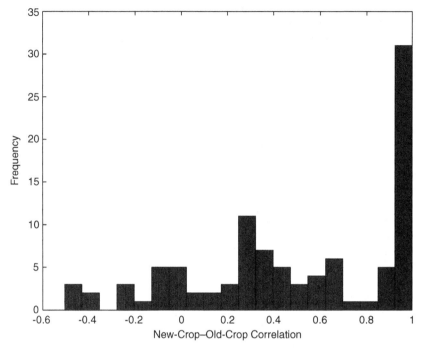

Figure 6.7.

to 1 early in the crop year. The next section examines futures prices to see whether these patterns are found in practice.

6.4 Empirical Evidence

To test the foregoing implications, I examine the behavior of the prices of new-crop and old-crop prices for corn, soybeans, oats, cotton, and three varieties of wheat (soft red winter, hard red winter, and spring wheat).

I first examine correlations between new-crop and old-crop futures prices in the second quarter of the crop year (e.g., January–March for corn) and in the fourth quarter of the crop year (e.g., July–September for corn). For each commodity, each year, and each of these two quarters of the crop year, I estimate the correlation between the daily percentage change in a new-crop price and the percentage change in an old-crop price. Table 6.1 lists the new-crop and old-crop futures used in the analysis.

Note that the correlations, which are reported in Table 6.2, are typically quite high. In particular, in the fourth quarter, correlations are almost always

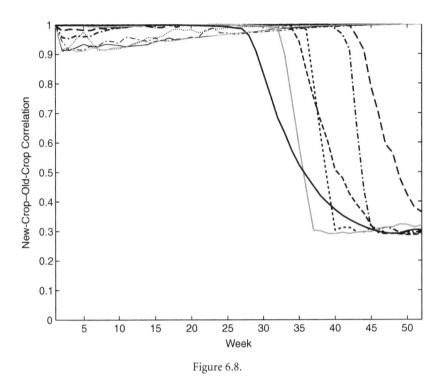

Figure 6.8.

above .9, never fall to levels routinely observed in the simulations, and are never negative. Moreover, there is no pronounced difference between the correlations between the two quarters studied, and for two of the commodities (oats and canola), the average correlation is actually slightly higher in the fourth quarter than the first quarter. For the other three commodities, the decline in correlation between the first and fourth quarters averaged less than .025. These empirical results are quite different from the simulated ones.

Table 6.1. *Commodities Included in Correlation Analysis*

Commodity	Symbol	Old-Crop Month	New-Crop Month
Corn	CN	September	December
Oats	OA	September	December
Soybeans	SY	September	November
Hard Spring Wheat	MW	September	December
Canola	WC	September	November
Cotton	CT	July	October

Table 6.2. *Panel A: New-Crop–Old-Crop Correlations in First Quarter of Crop Year*

Year	CN	OA	SY	MW	WC	CT
1981	0.969	0.942	0.985	0.862	0.959	0.890
1982	0.969	0.955	0.976	0.935	0.937	0.931
1983	0.933	0.974	0.987	0.937	0.937	0.838
1984	0.885	0.943	0.900	0.905	0.731	0.862
1985	0.934	0.865	0.976	0.617	0.837	0.755
1986	0.938	0.983	0.990	0.968	0.987	0.032
1987	0.936	0.979	0.987	0.898	0.991	0.936
1988	0.963	0.980	0.986	0.838	0.976	0.752
1989	0.930	0.987	0.971	0.911	0.989	0.845
1990	0.958	0.987	0.982	0.836	0.957	0.731
1991	0.974	0.988	0.985	0.975	0.937	0.819
1992	0.977	0.988	0.988	0.962	0.975	0.935
1993	0.973	0.984	0.979	0.906	0.859	0.934
1994	0.969	0.987	0.993	0.953	0.897	0.779
1995	0.978	0.954	0.988	0.949	0.948	0.702
1996	0.862	0.993	0.979	0.978	0.953	0.789
1997	0.982	0.940	0.906	0.982	0.909	0.918
1998	0.985	0.973	0.984	0.940	0.875	0.968
1999	0.979	0.942	0.985	0.943	0.906	0.868
2000	0.992	0.948	0.995	0.969	0.949	0.939
2001	0.995	0.934	0.990	0.976	0.816	0.892
2002	0.990	0.837	0.979	0.969	0.777	0.986
2003	0.978	0.774	0.952	0.979	0.844	0.949
2004	0.988	0.951	0.965	0.982	0.825	0.919
2005	0.965	0.733	0.964	0.984	0.969	0.957
2006	0.990	0.701	0.976	0.983	0.915	0.950
2007	0.977	0.777	0.992	0.962	0.943	0.929
2008	0.990	0.982	0.979	0.986	0.992	0.990
2009	0.998	0.995	0.987	0.993	0.935	0.992

Cotton represents a partial exception to the foregoing generalization. There are a few years in which the new-crop–old-crop correlations for this commodity are quite low, and 1 year (1999) in which the fourth-quarter correlation is negative. But even though the differences between fourth-quarter and first-quarter correlations are more likely to be negative for cotton than other crops, even this commodity does not exhibit the pronounced tendency for correlation declines found in the simulations.

I next examine the relative responsiveness of the new-crop and old-crop prices to release of information about the size of the harvest. To do this, I focus on price movements for corn, soybeans, oats, and spring wheat

Table 6.2. Panel B: New-Crop–Old-Crop Correlations in Fourth Quarter of Crop Year

Year	CN	OA	SY	MW	WC	CT
1981	0.952	0.873	0.970	0.912	0.968	0.706
1982	0.868	0.894	0.957	0.914	0.986	0.985
1983	0.898	0.980	0.996	0.915	0.992	0.933
1984	0.794	0.906	0.978	0.910	0.934	0.878
1985	0.832	0.939	0.981	0.919	0.820	0.829
1986	0.859	0.876	0.915	0.887	0.991	0.453
1987	0.910	0.937	0.958	0.893	0.959	0.716
1988	0.992	0.976	0.993	0.970	0.992	0.575
1989	0.966	0.977	0.972	0.916	0.993	0.612
1990	0.929	0.978	0.987	0.943	0.986	0.825
1991	0.988	0.965	0.992	0.961	0.983	0.737
1992	0.910	0.943	0.966	0.954	0.926	0.314
1993	0.951	0.964	0.991	0.825	0.957	0.488
1994	0.848	0.871	0.956	0.902	0.782	0.890
1995	0.942	0.969	0.993	0.892	0.938	0.001
1996	0.855	0.949	0.954	0.896	0.944	0.872
1997	0.972	0.926	0.844	0.910	0.946	0.883
1998	0.985	0.942	0.955	0.902	0.888	0.797
1999	0.976	0.915	0.995	0.931	0.967	−0.281
2000	0.993	0.949	0.994	0.883	0.872	0.994
2001	0.996	0.932	0.987	0.928	0.815	0.895
2002	0.994	0.910	0.969	0.926	0.694	0.966
2003	0.959	0.924	0.949	0.921	0.886	0.949
2004	0.976	0.875	0.965	0.894	0.656	0.461
2005	0.992	0.896	0.995	0.810	0.961	0.802
2006	0.996	0.840	0.989	0.972	0.966	0.945
2007	0.993	0.900	0.996	0.952	0.934	0.569
2008	0.998	0.991	0.756	0.970	0.870	0.966
2009	0.993	0.996	0.963	0.990	0.974	0.993

on days in June–September when the USDA releases its crop reports, as it does once each month during this period. For each commodity, I use the September futures price as the old-crop price. For corn and oats, December is the new-crop price; for soybeans, it is November. The sample period begins in 1981 and ends in 2008.[3]

---

[3] Prior to 1996, the USDA released its reports after the market close. In 1996 and the following years, the USDA released its reports during the trading day. Therefore, prior to 1996, I use the price change from the close on the announcement day to the open on the following day to measure the price response to the report. After 1996, I use the price change from the close on the day prior to the report to the close to measure the price impact.

Table 6.3. *Price Variances on USDA Announcement Days and Non-Announcement Days*

Commodity	Announcement Day Variance	Non-Announcement Day Variance	Brown-Forsythe Statistic
New-Crop SY	1235.1	136.3	16.1
Old-Crop SY	1335.0	22.1	16.9
New-Crop CN	230.4	21.5	19.6
Old-Crop CN	219.3	21.8	18.4
New-Crop MW	330.7	70.3	9.7
Old-Crop MW	334.8	67.8	9.9
New-Crop OA	138.6	11.8	18.4
Old-Crop OA	132.1	10.8	18.7

First, to verify that these crop reports are indeed informative, I compare the variance of percentage price changes on the release days to the variance on non-release days in the same months and carry out a Brown-Forsythe test to determine whether price dispersion is higher on release days than on days when no releases are made. The relevant results are reported in Table 6.3. For each commodity and for both new-crop and old-crop prices, the variances are substantially higher on USDA report dates than on other days in the same months. Moreover, for each commodity, for both new-crop and old-crop prices, the dispersions on announcement dates are statistically different from variances on non-announcement dates at a high level of confidence.[4] Thus, the data support the hypothesis that the USDA reports are highly informative, and because these reports are about the size of the harvest, they further support the use of price movements on these days as responses to harvest shocks.

I then regress the percentage change in the old-crop price on USDA report dates against the percentage change in the new-crop price on these dates (and a constant). Table 6.4 reports the regression results. Note that the coefficients are very close to 1. Indeed, for corn and oats, one cannot reject (at the 5 percent level) that the coefficient is 1. For spring wheat and soybeans, one can reject the null that the coefficient is 1, but the coefficients

---

[4] The Brown-Forsythe test statistic has a t-distribution, with the number of degrees of freedom equal to the total number of observations minus 2. The p-values on all of the test statistics in Table 6.3 are essentially zero. I have also conducted F-tests to test the null hypothesis of equal variances. These tests also reject the null with very low p-values for each of the four commodities. The Brown-Forsythe test is preferable because it is less sensitive to deviations from normality.

Table 6.4. *Regression of Old-Crop Price Change Versus New-Crop Price Change on USDA Announcement Days*
$$(\Delta F_{O,t} = \alpha + \beta \Delta F_{N,t} + \epsilon_t)$$

Commodity	β	t–statistic $\beta = 0$	t–statistic $\beta = 1$	p–value $\beta = 1$
SY	0.94	79.91	4.69	1.00
CN	0.98	49.95	1.04	0.85
MW	0.97	74.91	2.04	0.98
OA	1.00	66.34	0.16	0.56

for these commodities are still well above .9 and more than double the values derived from the simulations.

In sum, actual new-crop and old-crop futures prices behave quite differently from the prices produced by solution of a storage model for a seasonally produced commodity. Generally, actual new-crop and old-crop futures prices co-move much more closely than their simulated model counterparts. Moreover, actual old-crop and new-crop prices move much more closely together in response to the release of information about the size of the harvest than do the model prices.

This really is not news. Referring to work he published in 1933, Holbrook Working wrote:

It was regarded as clear that, in the presence of a current relative scarcity of wheat, prospects for an abundant harvest in the following summer would have no significant bearing on the prices paid for existing supplies.

Statistical studies published in 1933, supplemented by further evidence later, showed this belief to be untrue. What happens in fact is that any change in price of a distant, new-crop, wheat future tends to be accompanied by an equal change in prices paid for wheat from currently available supplies. . . . In effect, then, the spot price is determined as the sum of the [new-crop] futures price determined primarily on expectations, plus a premium dependent on the shortage of currently available supplies.

Although Working's conjecture in the last quoted sentence is a realistic characterization of an empirical regularity, it is not based in a rigorous theory. The theoretical analysis shows that the structural storage model – a rigorous, internally consistent theory – cannot produce this same regularity.

These empirical results showing that prices are highly correlated across crop years are also consistent with the findings of Deaton-Laroque, who show that annual average spot prices are highly autocorrelated for all of the commodities they study, including seasonally produced commodities. Both the strong covariation between new-crop and old-crop prices and the high annual autocorrelation in prices mean that there is something that connects prices over time.

One advantage of looking at seasonally produced commodities is that this permits the untangling of supply and demand shocks. This makes it possible to determine more precisely what can – or, as it turns out, cannot – explain the high intertemporal correlations in commodity prices.

In the seasonal model, storage cannot explain the high degree of correlation over time. This is true because in the model, storage frequently does not occur across crop years; as a result, new-crop and old-crop prices can exhibit very low correlations in that model. The correlations are low because in the absence of storage, there is no mechanism to communicate shocks to the size of the coming harvest to old-crop prices. When agents perceive that it is highly unlikely that it will be optimal to carry over inventory into the new-crop year, shocks to the size of the new harvest have no implications for consumption throughout the remainder of the old-crop year. Because shocks to the harvest have a large impact on new-crop prices, this makes correlations low.

The seasonal commodity model also shows that the Deaton-Laroque explanation for high correlations cannot be right either. They find that in a model with independent net demand shocks, storage can generate some autocorrelation in prices, but not the high correlation observed in the actual time series. To generate such high autocorrelations, they have to assume that the net demand shock is highly persistent; in their view, this high net demand autocorrelation, rather than storage, is what ties prices together over time. Moreover, because for agricultural products there is little autocorrelation in output, Deaton and Laroque conclude that highly persistent demand shocks cause the high autocorrelation observed in commodity prices.

But the seasonal storage model throws cold water on that explanation. The numerical results are based on very persistent demand shocks, but new-crop–old-crop correlations are often very low. This is because in the model for seasonally produced commodities, stockouts occur quite regularly, and these stockouts prevent information about the size of the impending harvest from affecting old-crop prices. Because for such commodities it is undeniable that information about the size of the harvest has a large impact on prices (as the extremely high variability of prices on the days of USDA crop reports attests), demand persistence alone is inadequate to explain co-movements between prices across crop years. Only when supply shocks are an unimportant source of price variability can demand persistence generate high-price persistence across crop years. In this case, we have essentially a one-shock model and commensurately high correlations. This is not plausible for agricultural commodities such as wheat or corn. Therefore, the Deaton-Laroque conjecture founders too.

So what might explain the high correlations between new-crop and old-crop prices and the very high sensitivity of old-crop prices to information about the harvest? The next section explores some possibilities.

6.5 Alternative Explanations for the Empirical Regularities

Because storage and persistent demand cannot explain the high-frequency behavior of seasonal commodity prices, explanations must lie elsewhere. Here, I consider three preferences, inventories as a factor of production, and general equilibrium effects.

6.5.1 Preferences

First consider preferences. One potential source of connection between current and future prices that future prices affect the current willingness to pay for the commodity. One potential mechanism that could create such a linkage is intertemporal substitution. If current and future consumption are substitutes, an increase in expected future availability will induce individuals to want to substitute future consumption for current consumption. This will reduce the demand for the spot commodity and could depress prices.

This possibility can be incorporated into the standard storage model in a straightforward but admittedly ad hoc way. For instance, the spot demand function could be changed as follows:

$$D(q_t, z_t) = \Phi^* F_{t+\delta t}^{\nu} e^{z_t} q_t^{\beta}$$

where $F_{t+\delta t}$ is a forward price, as of time t, for delivery at $t + \delta t$ and $\nu > 0$ is a parameter that reflects the substitutability of current and future consumption.

This model is straightforward to implement using the standard machinery and, indeed, it generates closer connections between old-crop and new-crop prices, but its arbitrary nature is not wholly satisfactory; it comes dangerously close to assuming the result.

It is preferable instead to start from a specification of preferences directly. One natural approach would be recursive preferences along the lines of Kreps and Porteus (1978) or Epstein and Zin (1989). Kreps-Porteus and Epstein-Zin preferences allow separation of risk aversion and intertemporal substitution effects.

A little formal analysis demonstrates, however, that these preferences cannot resolve the puzzle. Consider a generalization of an Epstein-Zin model with multiple commodities. There is a representative consumer who has preferences over two goods: a continuously produced good C and a seasonally produced good S. There are assets ("trees") that produce a stochastic amount of this good. At time t, output of the continuously produced good is $Q_t = C_0 e^{z_t}$, where:

$$dz_t = -\mu_z dt + \sigma_z dW_{tz}$$

The production of S is described by the same model as analyzed earlier in this chapter.

S is storable, but, crucially, C is not. The importance of this assumption will be evident shortly. It is made here to ensure that intertemporal linkages are due solely to preferences and the storability of S, and not the storability of C.

À la Epstein-Zin, preferences are recursive:

$$U_t = \lim_{\Delta t \to 0} W(V(C_t, S_t), E U_{t+\Delta t}(x_t))$$

where S_t and C_t are the consumptions of the seasonal and continuously produced goods at t and x_t' is the amount of the seasonal good carried out as inventory at t, and where $W(.,.)$ is an aggregator function that incorporates intertemporal consumption and risk preference effects. The flow utility at t is:

$$V(C, S) = A[S^\rho + C^\rho]^{\frac{1}{\rho}}$$

In a decentralized economy in which the continuous good is the numeraire, a consumer who owns x_t units of the seasonal good and, as a result of ownership of an asset that produces the continuous good, receives a dividend of q_{ct} units of that good, chooses C_t and S_t to maximize:

$$W(V(C_t, S_t), E U_{t+dt}(x_t)) + \lambda(P x_t + q_{ct} - P S_t - e^{-rdt} F x_t' - C_t)$$

where P is the spot price of the seasonal good (in terms of the numeraire), F is the forward price of the seasonal good, and λ is the Lagrangian multiplier on the agent's budget constraint.

The first-order conditions for a maximum imply that:

$$P = \frac{W_1 V_S}{W_1 V_C} = \frac{V_S}{V_C}$$

Now consider the effect of a shock to the expected future harvest on the spot price. Inspection of the expression for price makes it plain that this shock can only affect the spot price through its effect on the consumption of S or C. Because the continuously produced good is not storable, the harvest shock cannot affect how much of it is consumed. Therefore, the only way a harvest shock can affect the spot price is through its effect on the consumption of S.

But this means that just as in the standard storage model, here harvest shocks will not affect the spot price with some regularity. Quite frequently, it will be optimal to consume all inventories of the seasonal commodity before the next harvest. For instance, if the next harvest is expected to be large, it is not optimal to carry inventory across crop years.[5] In this situation, a positive harvest shock will not affect current consumption of the seasonal good, meaning that the price of the seasonal good will not change in response to the harvest shock.

In brief, the explicit incorporation of intertemporal substitution into preferences does not overturn the counterfactual implication of the standard storage model: namely, the prediction that spot prices should not respond to harvest shocks when there is a high probability that there will be no carryover across crop years. This occurs because in both this model and the standard one, there is only one margin along which consumers may adjust: their consumption of the seasonal good (or, equivalently, their choice of inventory of that commodity). Because of the fundamental nature of the economy with the seasonal good, with some regularity, carry-out across crop years will be zero, meaning that it is not optimal to adjust consumption in response to news about the size of the next harvest. Because prices in a competitive economy induce agents to undertake the optimal decision, this means that prices need not adjust in response to news about the next harvest, intertemporal substitution or no.

Numerical solution of this model validates this reasoning. Optimal storage decisions do vary with the degree of intertemporal substitution, but spot prices generally exhibit substantially less sensitivity to harvest shocks than do new-crop futures prices, and these sensitivities vary through the (simulated) crop year in ways not observed in the actual data. In brief, the numerical results for correlations and the relative sensitivities of old-crop prices to harvest shocks are nearly the same in this model as in the standard storage model analyzed earlier in the chapter.

---

[5] Any model of a seasonal commodity that does not have this feature would be objectionable and empirically falsified because it would not exhibit the backwardation across crop years regularly observed in seasonal commodity markets. As it turns out, numerical solution of the Epstein-Zin model exhibits this regularity.

Altering preferences, in sum, is not a promising way to correct the deficiencies of the standard storage model.

6.5.2 Inventories as a Factor of Production

Ramey (1989) posits that inventories can be viewed as a factor of production. Drawing on this insight, Carter and Revoredo (2005) and Revoredo (2000) derive a storage model in which the demand for a commodity by processors depends not just on the current spot price but also on the expected future price. This linkage between current quantity demanded and the future price is the kind of linkage that could communicate information about future harvests (that affect future prices) into current consumption decisions and, hence, pre-harvest spot prices. Although this seems promising, as will soon be seen, this approach is ad hoc and unrealistic in the extreme.

Formally, drawing on Ramey, Carter, and Revoredo, posit that production of a finished (processed good), Q_t, depends on inventories of the raw commodity, I_t:

$$Q_t = \min\{\frac{I_t}{\lambda}, \ f(K_t)\}$$

where K_t is another productive input (e.g., capital or labor) and λ is a parameter. Carter-Revoredo assume that $f^{-1}(Q) = Q(\ln Q - 1)$. Given this technology, they show that in a discrete time competitive industry:

$$Q_t = \exp\{\frac{P_t - \lambda(1 + r)[(p_t + k) - E(p_{t+1})]}{w}\}$$

and

$$I_t = \lambda Q_t$$

where P_t is the price of the processed good at t, p_t is the price of the raw commodity at t, and w is the price of the other productive input.

Note the presence of the expected future spot price of the raw commodity in the inventory expression. If the price of the raw material in the future is expected to be low (for instance, because of the anticipation of a large impending harvest), processors hold low inventories. This reduces the demand for the raw commodity and correspondingly reduces the spot price. This basically reflects the nature of the Ramey model from which this model is derived. The difference between the spot and expected future prices is a rental rate on inventory, which is a form of capital in these models. If the future price is expected to be low, the rental rate is high, leading processors to economize on the use of this form of capital. In this way, the model rationalizes a link between future prices and spot prices by which news about the harvest can affect current demand and, hence, spot prices.

Mystery solved? Alas, no. This model does not provide a satisfactory resolution of the issue because of the magical role of inventories in the model, a role that corresponds not at all to their function in reality.

I say "magical" quite deliberately. In this model, larger inventories result in larger production *but they are never actually consumed.* In the model, just having more raw material inventory sitting around improves productivity. A processor with 2,000 units of the raw commodity on hand is more productive than one with 1,000 units. But if he starts out with 2,000 units, he ends up with 2,000 units. In this sense, the inventory is literally rented, but never consumed. Commodity processors never actually process the commodity. In the model, a soybean processor buys soybeans and at the end has soybean oil and soybean meal – and the same quantity of soybeans with which he started. Magical indeed.

In reality, of course, the raw commodity is used up in processing. A soybean crusher who buys 500,000 bushels of soybeans and processes them ends up with soybean oil and meal, but no soybeans.

Thus, the inventories as a factor of production approach is not a reasonable way to forge a link between future and current prices. Because, as Carter-Revoredo demonstrate, "convenience yield" models like those of Miranda and Rui (1996) are special cases of their model, the convenience yield approach is not reasonable either.

A more realistic interpretation of raw material inventories held by processors would reflect rigidities in processing. For instance, because of the time involved in transporting a commodity and preparing it for processing, processors may have to purchase raw material inputs before the realization of demand for the final product.

Incorporating this type of friction into the storage model necessarily increases the dimensionality of the storage problem, for now there are two stock variables that need to be accounted for: the amount of the raw commodity that processors have purchased in the past for processing today and in the future, and the amount of the commodity held by "speculators" and not yet committed to processors.[6] Moreover, because processed output (e.g.,

---

[6] Processor inventories and speculative inventories are not fungible. Most processor facilities have the ability to load in raw materials, but not load them out again. As an illustration of this, a grain trader told me of a story that during a soybean manipulation during the late 1970s, his company's mills blasted holes in their storage bins so their beans could be loaded

soybean meal and oil) is itself storable, a realistic model would incorporate processed inventories as well.

Unfortunately, this expansion in the number of state variables makes the problem numerically intractable. But this is unlikely to be a serious loss, because the "time to process" rigidity that gives rise to holding inventories does not fundamentally transform the storage problem in a way that is likely to resolve the old-crop–new-crop puzzle. This rigidity can indeed result in inventories being carried over between the old- and new-crop years, for instance, if inventory must be ordered 2 weeks before it is processed, to be able to have the final good available for sale in the first week of the new-crop year, it is necessary to hold inventory from the week before the harvest to the week after. But this very rigidity means that the new crop is not a substitute for the in-process inventories held over the crop year. A processor cannot increase output in the early part of the new-crop year by avoiding purchases of old-crop supplies and using new-crop supplies instead. Not purchasing the old-crop supplies means that he is unable to produce anything early in the new-crop year because of the time-to-process constraint. The fact that new-crop supplies are not substitutes for old-crop supplies in processing means that the inventories of the old crop carried over the crop year cannot provide a linkage between new- and old-crop prices and hence cannot be a channel by which news about the harvest affects old-crop prices. So this too is a dead end.

6.5.3 Multiple Storable Commodities

The third alternative avenue to explore is a general equilibrium model with multiple storable commodities. The basic idea is that there are two commodities that are substitutes in consumption, both storable, with one produced seasonally and the other produced continuously. Storage of the continuously produced commodity provides another intertemporal connection that can cause future harvest shocks to affect old-crop prices.

For instance, consider the effect of a favorable y shock that occurs late in the crop year. This increase in the size of the expected harvest effectively leads to an increase in the future demand for the continuously produced good: there will be more of the seasonal good to trade for it. This provides

---

onto trucks for shipment to the futures delivery point to take advantage of the distorted price. They had to do this because the bins were designed only to load in soybeans, not load them out. Moreover, shipping inventories from a processor to another consumer entails another transportation cost.

an incentive to store additional units of the continuously produced good. Given the stocks of this good, this requires a reduction in consumption. This in turn requires its spot price to rise relative to the price of the seasonally produced good. If the continuously produced good is the numeraire, this is equivalent to a fall in the price of the seasonally produced good.

To consider these ideas more formally, consider the following model, which is analogous to the one discussed earlier in the context of the Epstein-Zin model with one crucial difference. There is a representative consumer who has preferences over two goods: a continuously produced good C and a seasonally produced good S. The consumer's preferences are given by a constant elasticity of substitution form:

$$U(C, S) = A[S^\rho + C^\rho]^{\frac{1}{\rho}}$$

Production of C takes place continuously; there is an asset that produces a stochastic amount of this good. At time t, output of the continuously produced good is $Q_t = C_0 e^{z_t}$, where:

$$dz_t = -\mu_z dt + \sigma_z dW_{tz}$$

The production of S is described by the same model as analyzed earlier in this chapter.

In this model, *both* S and C are storable. Call inventories of the continuously produced good at t x_{ct} and the inventories of the seasonally produced good x_{st}. The (annual) discount rate is r.

Use the continuously produced good as the numeraire and define the spot price of the seasonal good in terms of this numeraire as P. In a competitive market, this spot price equals the ratio of marginal utilities:

$$P = \frac{U_S(C_t, S_t)}{U_C(C_t, S_t)}$$

where C_t and S_t are consumptions of the continuously and seasonally produced goods, respectively, at t.

Given the availability of both goods, agents choose their consumptions C_t and S_t to maximize their expected discounted utility:

$$V = \max_{C_t, S_t} E \int_0^\infty e^{-rt} U(C_t, S_t) dt$$

The availability of the continuously produced good is carry-in plus production, $x_{ct} + Q_t$. The availability of the seasonal good is $x_{st} + H_t$.

Optimal allocation of the goods over time (as will occur in a competitive market) equates expected marginal utilities over time:

$$U_C(Q_t + x_{ct} - C_t, H_t + x_{st} - S_t) \geq e^{-rdt} E U_C(C_{t+dt}, S_{t+dt})$$

$$U_S(Q_t + x_{ct} - C_t, H_t + x_{st} - S_t) \geq e^{-rdt} E U_S(C_{t+dt}, S_{t+dt})$$

where a relation holds as an equality if the corresponding non-negativity constraint on inventory for the corresponding good is not binding at t, and where it holds as a strict inequality if the constraint is binding. For instance, if carry-out of the continuously produced good is zero, the marginal utility of that good at t will exceed its discounted expected value at time $t + dt$, but if its carry-out is positive, the marginal utility of C will equal its discounted expected value.

The crucial feature of this model is the response of the marginal utility of one good – notably, the continuously produced one – to an increase in consumption of the other. Note that:

$$U_C = A[C^\rho + S^\rho]^{\frac{1-\rho}{\rho}} C^{1-\rho}$$

and

$$U_{CS} = A(1 - \rho)[C^\rho + S^\rho]^{\frac{1-2\rho}{\rho}} C^{\rho-1} S^{\rho-1}$$

For $\rho < 1$, $U_{CS} > 0$, meaning that an increase in consumption of the seasonal commodity causes an increase in the marginal utility of the continuously produced one.

Consider the implications of this for the effect of a favorable harvest shock (i.e., a favorable y shock) immediately before the harvest, when prior to the shock, (a) the Euler equation for the continuous good holds as an equality, but (b) the Euler equation for the seasonal good is an inequality, because current availability is low relative to the availability expected after the harvest.[7] In response to the shock, the marginal utility of the continuously produced good is expected to be higher immediately after the harvest because (a) a bigger harvest results in an increase in the consumption of the seasonal good then; and (b) the marginal utility of C is increasing in the consumption of the seasonal good. But because before the shock, the marginal utility of the continuously produced good was (by assumption) equal to its discounted expected post-harvest value when evaluated at the

---

[7] The equality in the continuous-good Euler equation means that inventories of this good are positive.

consumptions optimal prior to the shock, after the shock this equality cannot hold. The current marginal utility is less than the expected future utility. To restore the equality, it is necessary to reduce current consumption and increase future consumption. This requires agents to increase the amount of the continuously produced commodity that they hold in inventory. This tends to drive up the current marginal utility of that good. But, because (a) consumption of the seasonal good and, hence, its marginal utility does not respond to the harvest shock, because if it was not optimal to carry over before the revelation of favorable information, it is not optimal to do so afterwards; and (b) the price of the seasonal good (in terms of the continuous good numeraire) is the ratio of marginal utilities, this rise in the continuous good's marginal utility causes the price of the seasonal good to fall. In this way, a harvest shock is communicated to the old-crop price even though none of this good is stored.

Conceptually, the standard machinery can be employed to solve this problem with some modifications. First, make a grid in the four state variables, z_t, y_t, x_{ct}, and x_{st}, and time; as with the other seasonal problems, I divide time into weekly increments. Next, make a guess for $C_t(z_t, y_t, x_{ct}, x_{st}, t)$ and $S_t(z_t, y_t, x_{ct}, x_{st}, t)$ for some point in the time cycle: as before, I choose the week immediately before the harvest. Then, given this guess, solve the two Euler equations to get consumptions – and, hence, marginal utilities – at the previous time step. As before, by invoking the Feynman-Kac Theorem, it is possible to show that each expected marginal utility (which is equivalent to the forward price in the earlier models) must solve a parabolic, second-order PDE. Given the solution of the consumptions at this date, proceed to the preceding date, solve for the consumptions, and continue stepping backward in time to the date right before the harvest. Check to see whether the marginal utility functions have converged. If so, stop; if not, repeat the process.

Although the recipe for solving the problem is conceptually identical to that employed throughout the book, practically this is a much more difficult and challenging problem. This is due to the fact that allowing for a second storable commodity increases the dimensionality of the problem. Specifically, there is an additional state variable: the inventory of the continuously produced good. This raises computational costs. Moreover, whereas in the standard storage model for each state variable it is necessary to solve one equation in one unknown subject to one constraint, in this problem, it is necessary to solve simultaneously a set of two equations subject to two constraints. This is substantially numerically trickier than the solution of one equation, and it requires the use of linear complementarity methods like those described in Chapter 3.8 of Fackler and Miranda (2002).

As it turns out, these additional complexities have precluded solution of the problem; I have been unable to surmount the curse of dimensionality. Specifically, the algorithm has not achieved convergence even after running 20 days on a fast desktop computer.

Although the numerical solution to the problem has as yet proved impractical, this approach is appealing and represents a promising conceptual extension of the storage model. The seasonal model points out quite clearly some deficiencies in the received, partial equilibrium approach. In that approach, storage is crucial in linking prices over time. The seasonal model makes it abundantly clear that highly autocorrelated demand cannot explain the high degree of linkage observed over time. Nor, as discussed earlier, can preferences or in-process inventories perform this function. Inventories are necessary to communicate the supply shocks that are an important source of uncertainty for seasonal commodities from post-harvest prices to pre-harvest prices. But because of the seasonality of production, it is often optimal to exhaust inventories immediately before the harvest, meaning that it is often the case that inventories *cannot* link new-crop and old-crop prices, and that the model implies that these prices should often become disconnected.

But the data show that these prices are closely connected. This means that, in practice, there must be some other decision margin to allocate goods over time that can affect intertemporal price relations: one storable good is not sufficient to produce the observed intertemporal price connections for that good. An obvious alternative is other storable goods. Agents can alter their consumption – and storage – of other goods in response to a shock that affects the expected production of the seasonal good. If the goods are substitutes, a favorable shock to the expected future supply of the seasonal good tends to induce agents to want to shift their consumption of other goods to the future. Even in situations where carry-over of the seasonal good is not optimal, this shift of consumption of other goods from the present to the future tends to depress the current price of the seasonal good relative to the prices of these other goods.

There is another way to see this. If the impending harvest is expected to be large, agents would like to move the seasonal good from the future to the present, but lacking time machines, this is impossible. So they do the next best thing. They shift the consumption of other goods from the present to the future. The big harvest essentially represents a big future demand for the other goods, and agents respond by storing more of these other goods to meet this large anticipated future demand. This effectively reduces the current demand for the seasonal good, depressing its price.

Although the full solution of the multi-good, general equilibrium problem has as yet proved computationally impractical, this is perhaps not so disappointing. Even a two-good model possesses far fewer intertemporal allocation decision margins than the real economy. As a result, it is highly likely that although the expanded model would exhibit stronger intertemporal price connections than the standard model, it would be unable to match the high intertemporal (e.g., new-crop–old-crop) price covariation observed in practice. The real world presents far more potential to move consumption through time in a way that links prices than would any model remotely capable of being solved computationally even after many years of the continued operation of Moore's Law.

6.6 Summary and Conclusions

The seasonal storage model fails rather spectacularly in characterizing the high-frequency behavior of periodically produced commodities such as corn or soybeans. Actual seasonal commodity new-crop and old-crop prices move together much more closely and respond much more similarly to news about the harvest than do prices from the model. It would be nice to have a model that accurately captures the observed behavior, but this failure is highly instructive.

For one thing, the failure makes it possible to discard some explanations for the high degree of intertemporal covariation of prices. Specifically, the failure of the seasonal model makes it clear that highly autocorrelated demand absolutely cannot explain the observed autocorrelations and the high degree of association between new-crop and old-crop prices. Moreover, and relatedly, the failure demonstrates the essential role of storage in connecting prices over time in the standard model: no storage, no connection. In particular, with no storage across the harvest (as occurs frequently in the model), there is no connection between old-crop prices and the expected size of the new harvest. The contrast between the routine high responsiveness of old-crop prices to harvest-related information in the actual data and the frequent absence of such responsiveness in the model demonstrates strikingly the essential role of storage in connecting prices in the partial equilibrium model. Furthermore, the seasonal model's ability to generate different testable implications for supply and demand shocks makes it possible to rule out definitively the possibility that highly autocorrelated demand accounts for price behavior. This further emphasizes the critical role of storage in linking prices.

For another, the failure shows that it is necessary to search for other things that connect prices over time. Because storage of seasonal commodities or autocorrelated demand is not sufficient to explain the close covariation of new-crop and old-crop prices, there must be something else.

The most promising possibility is to recognize that there are myriad intertemporal decision margins, because there are myriad storable goods in the economy. Even if agents' ability to move one good through time is constrained, they can often circumvent that constraint by moving other goods intertemporally. Such intertemporal movements affect relative prices. This tends to connect prices in ways impossible in the simple storage model and provides a mechanism whereby a shock to the future availability of a commodity that will experience a stockout affects its current price.

Thus, through its failure, the storage model for periodically produced goods points the way to improving our understanding of the ways in which commodity markets work and commodity prices behave. Following this direction, alas, requires the relaxation of another constraint: computational costs. Given the secular improvements in computational power, however, our understanding is sure to improve over time.

SEVEN

The Dynamics of Carbon Markets

7.1 Introduction

Carbon permits issued as part of cap-and-trade systems around the world, and derivatives thereon, are likely to become one of the world's largest commodity markets in the coming years. Virtually every economic activity involving the production or consumption of energy will be affected by cap and trade, and this system for controlling greenhouse gases will therefore entail the purchase and sale of large quantities of carbon permits and derivatives.

This raises the question: How will carbon prices behave? The answer to that question depends on the design of the carbon market, which points to one of the distinctive things about this commodity: its market will be one of our own design. Throughout this book, I have noted that storage decisions and, hence, commodity prices depend on characteristics of the commodity, such as the nature of production (is it seasonally produced or not?) and spatial factors (how easy is it to trade across space?). With most of the commodities we are familiar with, say wheat or copper, some of these factors are outside of human control. Fundamental natural factors make wheat a periodically produced commodity, and nothing humans can do will change that.

Things are quite different with carbon. It is possible to choose – to design – virtually all of the salient features of this commodity. For instance, the frequency of production can be determined by legislative fiat. The author of the laws establishing cap and trade can specify that the permits will be issued yearly, or monthly, or weekly, or whatever. Similarly, the ability to trade across space is subject to legislative choice: legislators can limit the amount of carbon that can be traded across certain jurisdictions, or not. Perhaps most remarkably, for carbon it is possible to circumvent the constraint that has played such an important role in the analysis of "natural" commodities: the constraint that storage is non-negative. Whereas it is impossible to borrow copper produced in the future to consume today, it is possible to design the carbon market so that agents borrow carbon permits to be issued in the future in order to emit the gas today. Thus, the "inventory" of permits can go negative, because obligations to deliver carbon in the future can exceed the currently available supply of permits.

This chapter examines the effects of carbon market design on the behavior of carbon prices. Specifically, I examine the implications of three key design choices: the frequency of issuance of carbon permits; whether or not these permits expire or can be stored indefinitely; and whether it is possible to borrow permits to be issued in the future to allow agents to emit today.

The results should be quite understandable to someone who has read the book to this point. First consider the effects of the expiration of permits – that is, what happens when permits are issued annually, say, and can only be utilized in a given calendar year. Here, storage is precluded across "permit years" or "vintages." As the expiration date nears, agents will have a good idea of the likely demand for the expiring permits over their remaining life. Any permits left over at the end of the year will be worthless because they cannot be held for use in future years; thus, if the supply of permits is close to the quantity that would be demanded if the price is close to zero, the price will be very low. Conversely, if the supply is relatively low, prices will have to be very high in order to ration the remaining amount. Thus, one expects substantial volatility in prices of permits near expiration, as prices will plummet to nearly zero (if it is likely that supply is sufficient to satisfy the maximum amount that can be utilized in the remainder of the year) or skyrocket (if supplies are small).

Next, consider the effects of allowing storage of permits across years, but varying the frequency of issue. If certificates are issued annually, say, carbon will resemble an agricultural commodity, and the price patterns will resemble those of corn or wheat. That is, they will exhibit a sawtooth pattern, rising from the time immediately after issuance until the time of a new issuance, when under most circumstances prices will fall. As with a seasonally produced agricultural commodity, sometimes it will be optimal to carry over old permits for use after new permits are issued, but usually the prospect of a predictable influx of supply will make it optimal to consume the entire outstanding stock immediately before the new issuance. Conversely, if permits are issued more frequently, say, weekly or monthly, the commodity will resemble more closely a continuously produced commodity such as copper and, hence, will exhibit less of a sawtooth pattern, and the timing of stockouts will become less periodic.

Finally, consider borrowing. Borrowing relaxes the non-negativity constraint on storage, but most proposals that permit borrowing impose a constraint nonetheless. For instance, the ACES bill in the United States (more commonly known as the Waxman-Markey bill) limits the amount of the commodity that can be borrowed to 15 percent of the allocation. Thus, there is still a constraint, and the market does not perform that much differently from one in which borrowing is not allowed (holding the frequency of issue constant).

The remainder of this chapter is organized as follows. Section 7.2 sets out the model and briefly recaps the solution method. Section 7.3 presents simulation results that compare and contrast the behavior of carbon prices under alternative market designs. Section 7.4 summarizes.

7.2 The Model

In the model, there is a single industry that produces carbon as a byproduct. Each unit of output that the industry produces generates one unit of carbon. The commodity is produced and consumed continuously, which is not subject to pronounced seasonality in supply or demand. Moreover, the commodity itself is not storable.[1]

The flow demand for the commodity is our standard:

$$D(q_t, z_t) = \Phi e^{z_t} q_t^{\beta}$$

where $D(q_t, z_t)$ is the spot price of the commodity at time t, q_t is the consumption of the commodity at t, z_t is a stochastic demand shock, and Φ and β are parameters.

Producers of the commodity are competitive. The commodity is produced subject to strict decreasing returns and a binding capacity constraint. Specifically, the flow supply of the commodity is:

$$MC_t = A + \frac{v}{(\bar{q} - q_t)^{\psi}}$$

In this expression, MC_t is the marginal cost of producing q_t units of the commodity. $\bar{q} < \infty$ is the flow capacity constraint.

---

[1] Allowing storability of the commodity would introduce an additional state variable and inflict the curse of dimensionality. Note that the output of one of the main producers of CO_2, electricity generation, is effectively non-storable.

The government limits the total amount of carbon that can be emitted and requires each producer to obtain one permit per unit of output of the commodity (equivalently, of carbon). The permits are issued every τ years, and the number of permits issued is a fraction of the industry's expected output in the absence of a cap-and-trade system. Specifically, assume that the unconditional expectation of industry output at time t is $\hat{q}_t$. The number of permits issued at t' is:

$$K = \alpha \int_{t'}^{t'+\tau} \hat{q}_t dt$$

where $\alpha < 1$.

The demand for carbon permits is a derived demand. The value of being able to produce an additional unit of output in a competitive market is the difference between the marginal value of the commodity at that output and the marginal cost of producing that output. Competitive suppliers (or equivalently, competitive buyers) would be willing to pay that difference in order to obtain the right to produce (or consume) the marginal unit. Thus, if industry output is q and the realization of the demand shock is z, the competitive price of a carbon permit is[2]:

$$P(q) = \max[\Phi e^z q^\beta - (A + \frac{v}{(\bar{q} - q)^\psi}), 0]$$

The demand shock dynamics are somewhat different from those considered elsewhere in the book. There are two shocks of differing persistence. There is a permanent demand shock y_t that follows a Brownian motion with drift:

$$dy_t = \mu dt + \sigma_y dW_{yt}$$

where W_{yt} is a Brownian motion and μ and σ_y are constants. The actual demand shock is an Ornstein-Uhlenbeck process that reverts to the value of the permanent demand shock:

$$dz_t = \kappa_z[z_t - y_t] + \sigma_z dW_{zt}$$

where W_{zt} is a Brownian motion, $\kappa_z < 0$ is a constant speed of mean reversion, and σ_z is a constant.

The basic motivation for this specification is that demand for the good is driven in part by overall economic activity, which is highly persistent: the y shock essentially represents the contribution of overall economic

---

[2] Because carbon permits are freely disposable, their price can never fall below zero.

activity to the demand for the commodity.[3] In addition, there is a transitory component to demand. This specification captures salient aspects of some industries that are major carbon producers, such as electricity generation. Aggregate economic activity affects the demand for electricity, but other highly transitory factors, such as weather, also affect demand.[4]

The market for carbon permits is perfectly competitive, and there are risk-neutral agents who can engage in speculative storage of these permits.

I consider a variety of different policies relating to expiration, the frequency of issue, and the storability of permits:

- Permits are issued annually and expire at the end of a calendar year.
- Permits are issued annually but can be stored indefinitely. No borrowing of permits to be issued in the future is permitted.
- Permits are issued annually, can be stored indefinitely, and can be borrowed. Moreover, the quantity of certificates that can be borrowed is limited to kK, and borrowers must pay interest in the form of certificates on each certificate borrowed. An agent who borrows a certificate for t' years must return $1 + t' R$ of them.
- Permits are issued weekly and can be stored indefinitely. No borrowing is permitted.
- Permits are issued weekly, can be stored indefinitely, and can be borrowed, with borrowing limited to a maximum of kK permits and an interest rate on borrowings of R annualized.

Solution of the model varies slightly depending on the market rules. As always, the problem is discretized in the state variables (z, y, the amount of permits X) and time.[5] In the numerical solutions reported here, I use a weekly time step.

With permits that expire annually and no carry-over, solution is straightforward. If agents hold Q permits at expiration, the price of the permit is equal to:

$$P(q) = \max[\Phi e^z q^\beta - (A + \frac{\nu}{(\bar{q} - Q)^\psi}), 0]$$

---

[3] There is a long-running debate about whether GDP has a unit root; that is, whether GDP shocks are permanent.

[4] The transitory factors in the demand for electricity have a seasonal component to them. This could be incorporated in the analysis along the lines of the seasonal model of Chapter 4, but in the interest of simplicity I abstract from it here.

[5] If permits are issued at intervals greater than the time step, it is desirable to have different discretizations in X for each time step, as in the seasonal commodity model.

This expression holds because agents either consume the entire amount of permits available (because they cannot carry them over for use in the future) or consume enough to drive the price of a permit to zero and dispose of the rest.

Given the prices at expiration, it is possible to determine the forward price for delivery for each value of carry-in at the expiration of the permits at the time step prior to that expiration date. As usual, for carry-in X_0, the competitive amount of permits carried out X_1 equates the spot price of the permits $P(X_0 - X_1)$ to the present value of the forward price for carry-in X_1, if that carry-out is positive.[6] Given this spot price function for one period prior to permit expiration, solve for the forward price function for two steps prior to permit expiration; determine optimal carry-out and the spot price function; and continue this backward induction process until the most recent permit issue date. No recursion is required here.

When the interval between issuance of permits exceeds the size of the time step (e.g., permits are issued annually and the time step is a week), recursive methods like those used in the seasonal model of Chapter 4 are appropriate. Begin with a guess for the spot price function (and, hence, consumption and carry-out) at some date, such as the period immediately prior to issuance. Because some periods involve increases in supply and some do not, each period has a distinct spot price function. Determine the forward price (for delivery at that initial date) as of the previous time step. For each possible combination of state variables in the grid, find the consumption (equivalently, the carry-out) that equates the present value of the forward price to the spot price. Given this spot price function, proceed to the preceding time step and repeat the process. Continue this until the time step prior to the most recent permit issuance is reached. Check to see whether the new spot price function has converged. If it has, stop; if it has not, continue the process again.

The ability to borrow affects the solution of this problem. If no borrowing is allowed, if the consumption that equates the discounted forward price to the spot price requires a negative carry-out, the optimal solution involves a stockout. If borrowing is permitted, if the consumption that equates the discounted forward price to the spot price requires a carry-out of less than $\hat{X}_1 = kK/(1 + \delta t R)$, optimal carry-out is $\hat{X}_1$.[7] This is the equivalent to a stockout in the conventional model.

---

[6] Given the assumed demand function, where price goes to infinity if consumption is zero, carry-out will always be positive.

[7] Because of the in-kind interest on permit borrowings, if carry-out is less than $\hat{X}$, the borrowing constraint would be violated on the next time step.

When the interval between permit issuances is the same as the time step, the problem is no longer analogous to the seasonal commodity one but is instead similar to the continuous production problem. Here, every period is effectively identical, and the algorithm involves making an initial guess of a (single) spot price function; solving the forward price function for every state variable combination in the grid; solving for the optimal carry-out by equating the discounted forward price to the spot price, and setting carry-out to the minimum possible level if this solution entails a violation of the relevant lower bound on carry-out; checking for convergence of the spot price function; and continuing this process until convergence. The relevant lower bound for carry-out depends on whether borrowing is allowed. If it is not, this lower bound is zero. If it is, the lower bound is $\hat{X}$.

7.3 Results

The effects of market design are best illustrated using simulations. For each design, I simulate 100 years of weekly z and y shocks and then simulate prices and stocks given these shocks. So that the figures and statistics calculated are directly comparable, for each market design I utilize the same set of shocks.

The behavior of prices and inventories in the various market designs is illustrated in several figures. To ease interpretation, the graphs illustrate simulated prices for only a fraction of the simulations.

Figure 7.1 shows the behavior of prices when there is no ability to "store" emissions permits across years. Unlike the charts that follow, this chart depicts several lines, each corresponding to the evolution of simulated prices over a different year (for a total of 20 years). Moreover, to ease interpretation, it depicts the ratio for the price in a given week to the price on the first week of the respective year. This adjusts for the fact that the week 1 price depends on the level of the demand shock, which differs across years. The most noticeable feature of the price behavior is that prices are relatively stable early in the year and then as the end of the year approaches. Thus, as the permits near expiration, prices either spike to very high levels or plunge to levels substantially lower than observed at the beginning of the year.

Moreover, examination of the figure suggests that the volatility of prices increases as the year progresses and the permits approach their expiration. This is indeed the case, as illustrated in Figure 7.2, which depicts the standard deviation of the percentage change in the emissions spot price by week of the year. This is calculated by calculating the price changes observed in a given

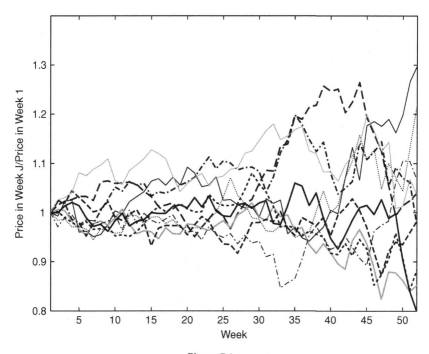

Figure 7.1.

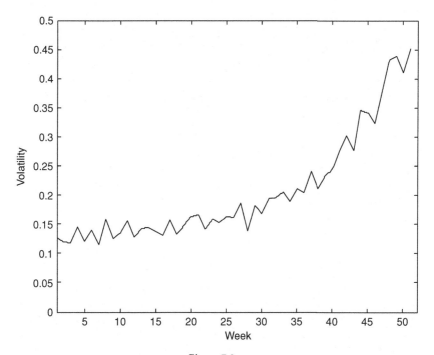

Figure 7.2.

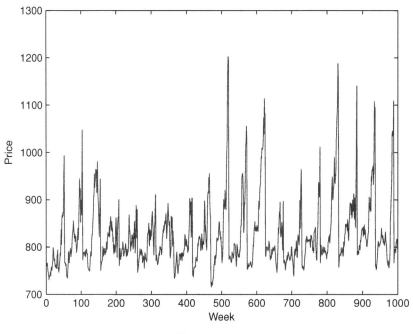

Figure 7.3.

week (e.g., week 25) of each year and then taking the standard deviation of the 100 price changes. This is done for weeks 2 through 52 because in week 1, prices jump because of the combined effect of the expiration of the old vintage of permits and the issue of new ones. These standard deviations are annualized by multiplying by $\sqrt{52}$. Note that as Figure 7.1 suggests, volatility indeed rises continuously, and at an increasing rate, as the year progresses and expiration nears.

Although not depicted, inventories of permits exhibit a sawtooth pattern, declining relatively smoothly throughout the year.

Figure 7.3 depicts the evolution of prices over 1,000 simulated weeks when carry-over is allowed but permits cannot be borrowed. Note that prices exhibit a sawtooth pattern, very similar to spot prices of agricultural prices, and for the same reason. Prices must rise on average throughout the year to provide an incentive to store permits to allow production until more permits are issued.

As with agricultural commodities, the periodic "production" of permits also affects volatility. This is illustrated in Figure 7.4, which like Figure 7.2 depicts the standard deviation of percentage price changes, by week of the year, across the 100 simulated years. Note that the volatility tends to increase,

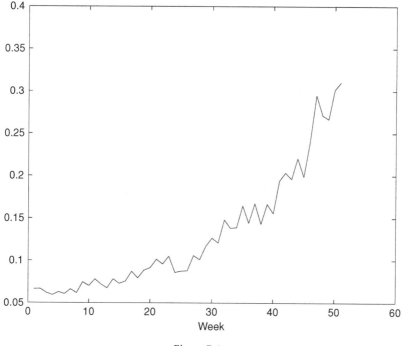

Figure 7.4.

and at an increasing rate, as the year progresses and the time of issuance of new certificates nears.

This reflects rational storage behavior under this market design. Agents draw down on inventories of permits as the year progresses. Moreover, under most circumstances, it is rational to exhaust inventories immediately before the new permits are issued. Thus, as the year ends, supplies of permits tend to fall to low levels, meaning that prices, rather than inventory adjustments, must bear the bulk of the burden of response to demand shocks. This makes prices more volatile at the end of the year.

Similar behaviors are manifest when borrowing is allowed, as illustrated in Figures 7.5 and 7.6. There are the same seasonal patterns in price levels and price volatilities, and for the same reasons. Borrowing does affect prices over time and inventory behavior. In the simulations, certificates are typically borrowed. In the simulations, agents are net borrowers of permits immediately before the new issue date in more than 80 percent of the years. Only when demand is very low do agents not borrow, and in those circumstances, they typically carry over positive amounts to the following period.

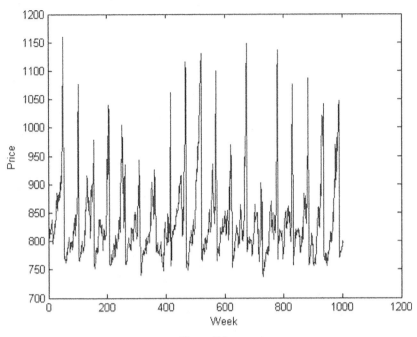

Figure 7.5.

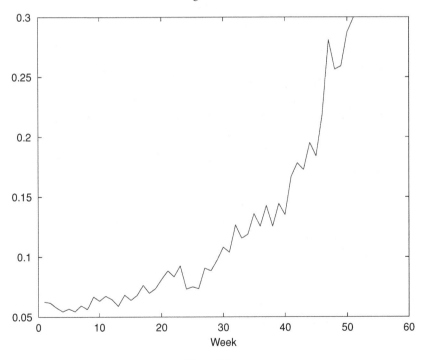

Figure 7.6.

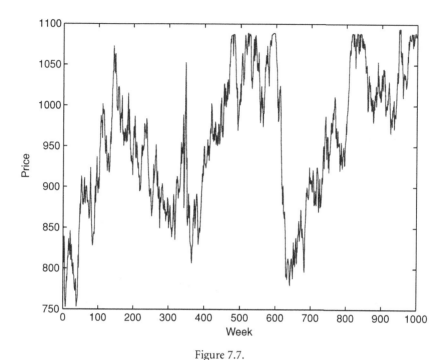

Figure 7.7.

The reason for borrowing is straightforward: it facilitates the smoothing of consumption over time. Agents desire to smooth production and consumption over time, but the periodic "production" of permits impedes that smoothing. Put differently, in the absence of borrowing, the non-negativity constraint on storage is costly and, as the model without borrowing demonstrates, this constraint usually binds except when demand is very low. Thus, agents derive benefits from the ability to relax this constraint and do so under most circumstances.

Finally, consider price and inventory behavior when permits are issued weekly. Figure 7.7 depicts the 100 years of simulated weekly prices when borrowing is precluded. Note that the sawtooth pattern apparent in prices when permits are issued annually is absent. Prices behave nearly like a random walk, with very slight evidence of mean reversion. A regression of the change in the log spot price on a constant and the lagged level of the log spot price produces a coefficient on the lagged log price of $-.0032$, indicating that the half-life of a price shock is 216 weeks – or more than 4 years.

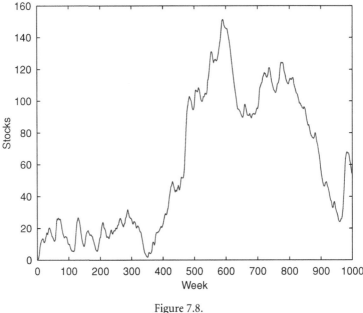

Figure 7.8.

Figure 7.8 depicts 100 years of simulated weekly inventories of permits. Note that like prices and like inventories of continuously produced commodities such as copper, these inventories also exhibit substantial persistence. Moreover, they do not exhibit the sawtooth, periodic pattern as is the case when permits are issued annually.

Figure 7.9 depicts the simulated prices when borrowing is permitted. Again, they exhibit no seasonality and are very persistent; the half-life of a price shock is again about 216 weeks.

The volatilities of permit prices are virtually identical when borrowing is allowed and when it is not. In each instance, the annualized standard deviation of percentage price changes is 14.64 percent.

Figure 7.10 displays the simulated inventories when borrowing is allowed. The timing of the peaks and troughs in the inventory series when borrowing is allowed matches those observed in Figure 7.8 when it is not, but note that agents frequently exercise their option to borrow.

The numerical simulation also allows welfare comparisons. Specifically, along the simulated path, I calculate output of the commodity q_t,[8] which

---

[8] Given the price of a permit, output is such that the marginal willingness to pay given that output minus the marginal cost of producing it.

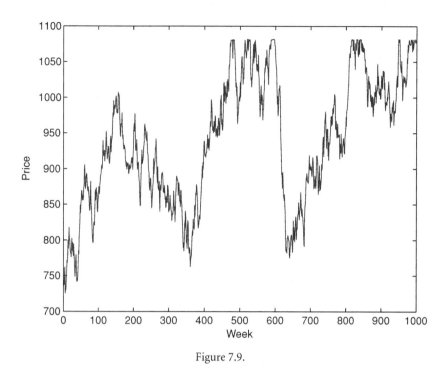

Figure 7.9.

implies a total surplus (consumer surplus net of cost) of:

$$\mathcal{S}_t = \int_0^{q_t} [\Phi e^{z_t} q^\beta - A - \frac{v}{(\bar{q} - q)^\psi}] dq$$

I then discount $\mathcal{S}_t$ back to the commencement of the simulation and sum these discounted surpluses to obtain the present value of the surplus.

There is an ordering of the surplus amounts. The no carry-over market design delivers the lowest surplus. Weekly creation of permits generates higher surplus than with annual issue and no carry-over; with this frequency of issue, surplus is slightly higher when borrowing is permitted than when it is not. Surplus is highest with annual issue and carry-over; with this basic design, surplus is greatest when borrowing is allowed. Borrowing generates a larger increase in surplus when permits are issued annually than when they are issued weekly.

Some of these results are readily explained. The no-carry-over market design imposes the most restrictive constraint and generates the lowest surplus. The difference between surplus when borrowing is allowed and when it is not, when permits are issued more frequently than annually,

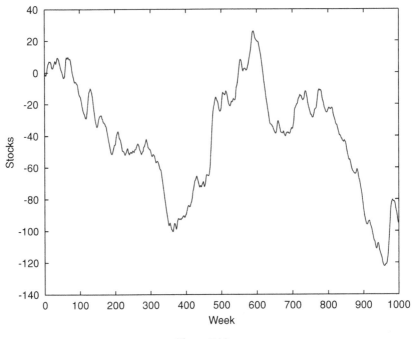

Figure 7.10.

is small because the more frequent issuance of permits reduces the discontinuities in availability that make borrowing valuable. In contrast, the markedly greater benefit from borrowing when permits are issued annually arises from the pronounced discontinuities in availability under this market design.

The difference in surplus between annual issuance and weekly issuance is more subtle. It arises from the fact that the variability of output in the simulations is greater with weekly issuance than with annual issuance. This, combined with the fact that the surplus function is concave, produces the result. Specifically, the standard deviation of simulated output in the weekly issue simulations is about .5, whereas it is about 10 percent less, or .45, in the annual issue case.

7.4 Summary

Certificates granting the right to emit a given amount of greenhouse gases could well become the largest commodity traded in the world in coming decades. Unlike other, more traditional commodities, these certificates are human creations, and their characteristics can be established by legislation or regulation. In particular, the salient characteristics that have been the focus of analysis in this book, such as the frequency of production and storability, are design choices.

This chapter has explored the pricing of CO_2 certificates using the standard storage machinery, focusing on the implications of certificate design for price behavior and economic welfare. The analysis demonstrates that price behavior is very sensitive to the frequency of issuance in particular and to constraints on the inventorying and borrowing of certificates as well. When certificates are issued relatively infrequently (e.g., annually) and expire after a new vintage is issued, prices tend to rise dramatically or fall to zero as expiration approaches. When certificates are issued relatively infrequently, but can be stored, their prices tend to behave like those of seasonal commodities such as corn. They exhibit sawtooth patterns, typically rising as the next issuance date approaches, then falling at the time of the next issuance. Frequently, it is efficient to utilize the last of the outstanding certificates immediately before new ones are issued, but sometimes it is optimal to carry over inventories of certificates across an issuance date. When certificates are issued frequently (e.g., weekly), their prices behave like those of continuously produced commodities (e.g., copper). The ability to borrow certificates from the future (something that is impossible in physical commodity markets) affects prices, but generally prices behave similarly when borrowing is or is not allowed.

As international efforts to control CO_2 emissions evolve, different nations will receive different allocations of certificates. Differences in these endowments, and differences in economic conditions across nations, will create opportunities to trade certificates between nations. Some proposed greenhouse gas regulation regimes contemplate restrictions on such trade (e.g., a given nation will only be able to cover a given percentage of its carbon emissions with certificates purchased from other nations). These restrictions will result in differential pricing across jurisdictions. Conceptually, the storage model is capable of characterizing the behavior of prices in different markets, the relations between prices in different markets, and how these prices depend on demand conditions and endowments across jurisdictions. However, incorporating such features into the storage model necessarily increases the dimensionality of the problem (e.g., with N jurisdictions, it is necessary to have N state variables corresponding to the inventories of each country's certificates). Moreover, the constraints on trade that motivate the problem pose acute challenges to the determination of the optimal allocation of certificates. Thus, at present, computational constraints preclude using the storage model to study the implications of trade and constraints on trade for the pricing of carbon certificates.

Nonetheless, the results of this chapter provide numerous insights into how carbon prices are likely to behave and how these behaviors depend on key carbon market design parameters.

EIGHT

The Structural Modeling of Non-Storables: Electricity

8.1 Introduction

I now turn attention from storable commodities to non-storable ones. There are many important non-storable commodities, including electricity, weather, and shipping, that are actively traded on spot, forward, and derivatives markets.[1]

By their very nature, non-storable commodities present fewer modeling challenges than storable ones. The very fact that they are not storable breaks the intertemporal linkages that necessitate the use of computationally intensive recursive techniques such as those utilized in the previous chapters. Storability means that every decision today must be made with an eye on tomorrow, and the tomorrow after that, and ad infinitum. In contrast, non-storable commodities can be modeled myopically, instant by instant, because in the absence of storage, current decisions do not affect tomorrow's economic opportunities. This lack of the need to look forward and consider the implications of current decisions on decision makers' future opportunity sets dramatically reduces the complexity of the modeler's task.

Structural models are eminently feasible for some commodities and, indeed, not only can these models be used to derive testable implications

---

[1] Some may object to calling weather or shipping *commodities*. They are widely considered such in industry and are traded on commodity desks. They are also closely related to things that are without dispute commodities. For instance, there is a close relationship between weather variables such as temperature and electricity or natural gas prices. Similarly, shipping is an important part of the commodity value chain connecting, say, the producers of oil and the consumers thereof. The modeling tools discussed in this chapter can also be used to value contingent claims with payoffs tied to weather or shipping prices, so at the very least they are metaphorically commodities, and exploiting the metaphor can facilitate their pricing.

about the behavior of the prices of such commodities, they can also be used to price derivatives. In particular, two commodities with very transparent fundamentals – electricity and weather – are very well suited to structural models. Other non-storable commodities, notably shipping, can be modeled structurally, but the inputs necessary to calibrate these models and to use them for real-world derivatives pricing are not readily observable, as is the case for weather and power.

Consider electricity. The main drivers of electricity prices are demand (measured by load; i.e., the amount of electricity consumed in any instant) and fuel prices (Eydeland and Wolyniec 2002). Particularly in modern, centrally dispatched electricity markets (e.g., the PJM or NYISO markets in the United States), load is observable on a near real-time basis, and there is extensive historical data on load that make it possible to understand how it behaves over time. Moreover, important fuels, such as natural gas and coal, are traded in transparent markets, so their prices are observable. Finally, electricity price data are available and, in many markets (e.g., PJM again), data on supply curves that indicate the price at which generators will produce a given quantity of electricity are available. This information can be used to create a structural model of electricity prices that can be used to characterize the behavior of spot prices and price electricity derivatives. The modeler essentially knows demand at every instant of time, the time series properties of demand, and the supply curve at any instant of time. Intersection of demand and supply in a textbook fashion instant by instant determines prices; given this, the dynamics of supply and demand determine the dynamics of price. This information can be used to price electricity derivatives.

Similar considerations hold for weather. Weather derivatives (e.g., derivatives on temperature in a particular city) have payoffs that are given by a function of observable weather variables. Moreover, vast amounts of historical weather data can be used to estimate models of the dynamic behavior of the payoff-relevant weather variables. Using standard derivatives pricing tools, this information can be combined to determine the prices of weather derivatives.

The remainder of this chapter presents a structural model of electricity prices and shows how it can be used to price electricity derivatives. I then proceed to explore the implications of this model for the pricing of electricity derivatives. Specifically, Section 8.2 provides a brief overview of modern electricity markets. Section 8.3 shows how reduced form models cannot capture the behavior of power prices and uses this to motivate a structural modeling approach. Section 8.4 discusses some implementation details.

Section 8.5 describes the basic electricity options traded in the marketplace. Section 8.6 shows how the model can be used to price these options; Section 8.7 presents results showing how the prices of these instruments depend on fundamentals. Section 8.8 shows how to handle additional structural features of a market, such as random outages of physical generating capacity. Section 8.9 summarizes and discusses extensions – including the integration of structural models for storable and non-storable commodities to characterize electricity price behavior in markets where hydropower is important.

8.2 Electricity Markets

In the United States and most other developed economies, electricity was traditionally supplied by vertically integrated utilities subject to price or rate-of-return regulation, or by state monopolies. These entities generated power, transmitted it over distances via high-voltage lines, and distributed it to customers in monopoly geographic service territories. Starting in the 1980s, and progressing rapidly in the 1990s, electricity production, transmission, and distribution have been restructured. Although the details of this restructuring vary by country and among regions in the United States, several salient features are found in most restructuring regimes. First, vertical integration has been scaled back sharply and, in some instances, vertically integrated firms have been replaced by separate generating, transmission, and distribution firms. Service territory monopolies have been eroded. Second, and relatedly, whereas wholesale and retail markets were unnecessary in vertically integrated electricity sectors, they are essential in restructured settings. Thus, most restructured electricity sectors have wholesale markets in which independent generators of electricity compete to supply load-serving entities and industrial and large commercial consumers of power. Moreover, some jurisdictions (such as Texas in the United States) have implemented competition at the retail level. In these cases, retail consumers have some choice over their household electricity supplier.

There are many variations in the designs of competitive wholesale power markets. Some markets are largely bilateral, OTC markets. In these markets, owners of generation independently decide how to operate their assets and enter into bilateral contracts with electricity users. Others markets are more formal and centralized. For instance, the PJM market in the United States operates centralized day-ahead and real-time markets for electricity. Owners of generation submit offers specifying the prices at which they are willing to generate various quantities of electricity, and load servers similarly specify bids at which they are willing to buy varying quantities. The market operator assembles the offers into supply curves and the bids into demand curves, determines the intersection of these curves to establish the market clearing price, and uses the generators' offers to dispatch the generation so as to minimize the cost of serving the realized (stochastic) load.

Restructuring has never been a smooth process anywhere – with California being the poster child for what can go wrong. These difficulties are attributable to the nature of electricity as a commodity. For practical purposes, electricity is not storable in large quantities.[2] Moreover, lack of electricity supply in real time leads to blackouts, which can cause massive economic losses. Because supplies of electricity cannot be stored for use when demand surges or generating units go offline, markets must be designed to ensure adequate generation supply at every instant of time. Electricity is also a highly localized commodity; constraints in transmission mean that power prices in proximate locations can differ substantially and that these price differences can change dramatically over short periods of time.

Non-storability also means that inventories cannot be utilized to soften the impact of supply-and-demand shocks, as is the case for other commodities – including other energy commodities such as oil and natural gas. Because power demand can fluctuate substantially with variations in weather, and because power supply can also fluctuate as a result of mechanical failures at generating or transmission assets, the inability to use inventories as a shock absorber means that power prices can fluctuate wildly in response to random supply-and-demand changes.

The extreme movements in power prices (illustrated and discussed in more detail in the next section) create substantial risks for market participants. Moreover, many market players – including generators and load-serving entities – are subject to quantity risks. These risks create a need for hedging tools, and such tools have evolved in the wake of restructuring. Hedging tools include standard forward contracts and a variety of options. Some forward contracts are for very short delivery periods and are entered into very shortly before the delivery period – for instance, there are many day-ahead and even hour-ahead contracts in power markets. Other forward contracts are for blocks of power delivered over longer periods of time and entered into well in advance of the delivery period. For example, contracts calling for delivery of power rateably over the peak hours of an entire month are quite common. There are also a variety of options contracts in power markets; I defer discussion of these instruments until

---

[2] Hydro generation incorporates an element of storability into power markets.

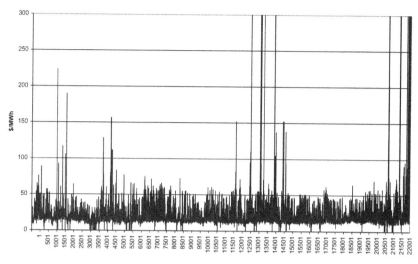

Figure 8.1.

Section 8.5. Most power derivatives are traded OTC, although there are some exchange-traded instruments available.

Although the derivative contracts traded in power are superficially quite similar to those traded in other energy derivatives markets, power's distinctive characteristics and price behaviors mean that valuation methods that work well for other commodities are problematic in the extreme for electricity. The next section explores electricity price behavior in more detail and discusses the challenges inherent in applying traditional valuation approaches to pricing power forwards and options.

8.3 A Structural Model for Pricing Electricity Derivatives

The traditional approach in derivatives pricing is to write down a stochastic process for the price of the asset or commodity underlying the contingent claim. This approach poses difficulties in the power market because of the extreme non-linearities and seasonalities in the price of power. These features make it impractical to write down a "reduced-form" power price process that is tractable and that captures the salient features of power price dynamics.

Figure 8.1 depicts hourly power prices for the PJM market for 2001–2003. An examination of this figure illustrates the characteristics that any power price dynamics model must solve. Linear diffusion models of the type underlying the Black-Scholes model clearly cannot capture the behavior depicted in the figure; there is no tendency of prices to wander as a traditional random-walk model implies. Prices tend to vibrate around a particular level (approximately $20 per megawatt hour) but sometimes jump upward, at times reaching levels of $1,000/MWh.

To address the inherent non-linearities in power prices illustrated in Figure 8.1, some researchers have proposed models that include a jump component in power prices. This presents other difficulties. For example, a simple jump model like that proposed by Merton (1973) is inadequate because in that model, the effect of a jump is permanent, whereas Figure 8.1 shows that jumps in electricity prices reverse themselves rapidly.

Moreover, the traditional jump model implies that prices can jump either up or down, whereas in electricity markets, prices jump up and then decline soon after. Johnson and Barz (1999) incorporate mean reversion and exponentially distributed (and hence positive) jumps to address these difficulties. However, this model presumes that big shocks to power prices damp out at the same rate as small price moves. This is implausible in some power markets. Geman and Roncoroni (2006) present a model that eases this constraint, but in which, conditional on the price spiking upward beyond a threshold level, (a) the magnitude of the succeeding down jump is independent of the magnitude of the preceding up jump, and (b) the next jump is necessarily a down jump (i.e., successive up jumps are precluded once the price breaches the threshold). Moreover, in this model, the intensity of the jump process does not depend on whether a jump has recently occurred. These are all problematic features.

Barone-Adesi and Gigli (2002) attempt to capture power spot price behavior using a regime-shifting model. However, this model does not permit successive up jumps, and constraining down jumps to follow up jumps makes the model non-Markovian. Villaplana (2004) eases the constraint by specifying a price process that is the sum of two processes, one continuous, the other with jumps, that exhibit different speeds of mean reversion. The resulting price process is non-Markovian, which makes it difficult to use for contingent claim valuation.

Estimation of jump-type models also poses difficulties. In particular, a reasonable jump model should allow for seasonality in prices and a jump intensity and magnitude that are also seasonal, with large jumps more likely when demand is high than when demand is low. Given the nature of demand in the United States, for instance, this implies that large jumps are most likely to occur during the summer months. Estimating such a model on the limited time series data available presents extreme challenges.

Geman and Roncoroni (2006) allow such a feature, but most other models do not; furthermore, because of the computational intensity of the problem, even Geman-Roncoroni must specify the parameters of the non-homogeneous jump intensity function based on a priori considerations instead of estimating it from the data. Fitting regime-shifting models is also problematic, especially if they are non-Markovian, as is necessary to make them a realistic characterization of power prices (Geman 2005). Moreover, changes in capacity and demand growth will affect the jump intensity and magnitude. None of the extant models take this into account.

Even if jump models can accurately characterize the behavior of electricity prices under the physical measure,[3] they pose acute difficulties as the basis for the valuation of power contingent claims. Jump risk is not hedgeable; hence, the power market is incomplete.[4] A realistic jump model that allows for multiple jump magnitudes (and preferably a continuum of jump sizes) requires multiple market risk prices for valuation purposes; a continuum of jump sizes necessitates a continuum of risk price functions to determine the equivalent measure that is relevant for valuation purposes. Moreover, these functions may be time varying. The high dimensionality of the resulting valuation problem vastly complicates the pricing of power-contingent claims. Indeed, the more sophisticated the spot price model (with Geman-Roncoroni being the richest), the more complicated the task of determining the market price of risk functions.

The traditional valuation approach is also very difficult to apply to some important power valuation problems, notably those where quantity as well as price affect the payoff. Although most financial power contracts do not possess this feature, many physical contracts (such as load-serving transactions) do. Pricing volume-sensitive claims in the traditional framework requires grafting a quantity process to an already complicated price process; such a Frankenstein's monster–like model is complex and cannot realistically capture the state dependence of the load-price relation.

Given these difficulties, it is desirable to take an alternative approach to valuing power derivatives. Fortunately, such an alternative exists. This approach exploits the fact that the fundamentals that drive power prices are very transparent – a situation that contrasts starkly with that which prevails in currency, equity, or fixed-income markets.

---

[3] Recall the discussion of the distinction between the physical measure and equivalent measures in Chapter 2.

[4] The market would be incomplete even if power prices were continuous (as is possible in the model presented later) because power is non-storable. Non-storability makes it impossible to hold a hedging "position" in spot power.

Specifically, a structural model based on the fundamentals of electricity production and consumption can capture the salient features of power prices and the relations between fundamental variables (such as demand) and prices. The model assumes that prices are determined by the intersection of a supply curve (that fluctuates randomly because of changes in fuel prices) and a (randomly fluctuating) demand curve.

In this approach, power prices in the physical measure are a function of two state variables. These two state variables capture the major drivers of electricity prices, are readily observed because of the transparency of fundamentals in the power market, and result in a model of sufficiently low dimension to be tractable.

The first state variable is a demand variable: load. Load is the amount of electricity consumed. Because load depends heavily on temperature, it is also possible to use temperature as a state variable.

Analysis of the dynamics of load from many markets reveals that this variable is very well behaved. Load is seasonal, with peaks in the summer and winter for most U.S. power markets. Moreover, load for each of the various regions is nearly homoscedastic, and there is little evidence of jumps in load. Finally, load exhibits strong mean reversion; random deviations of load from its seasonally varying mean tend to reverse fairly rapidly.

I treat load as a controlled process. The concept of a controlled process is a technical one, but it has a natural application in this power pricing problem. Every electricity system has some sort of central control; in modern, centralized markets, independent system operators perform this function. Knowing that the power system becomes unstable if the amount generated or consumed violates the capacity and transmission constraints in the system, these controllers can intervene to ensure stability. For instance, if consumption becomes dangerously high, the controllers can "shed load"; in essence, they can shut off the power of certain consumers.

The idea that system operators can control load to ensure that system constraints are not violated can be expressed mathematically. Defining load as q_t, note that $q_t \leq X$, where X is physical capacity of the generating and transmission system.[5] If load exceeds this system capacity, the system

---

[5] This characterization implicitly assumes that physical capacity is constant. Investment in new capacity, planned maintenance, and random generation and transmission outages cause variations in capacity. This framework is readily adapted to address this issue by interpreting q_t as capacity utilization and setting $X = 1$. Capacity utilization can vary in response to changes in load and changes in capacity. This approach incorporates the effect of outages, demand changes, and secular capacity growth on prices. The only

may fail, imposing substantial costs on power users. The operators of electric power systems monitor load and intervene to reduce power usage when load approaches levels that threaten the reliability of the system. Under certain technical conditions (assumed to hold herein), the arguments of Harrison and Taksar (1983) imply that under these circumstances, the controlled load process is a reflected Brownian motion. Formally in the physical measure $\mathcal{P}$, the load solves the following stochastic differential equation (Skorokhod Equation):

$$dq_t = \alpha_q(q_t, t)q_t dt + \sigma_q q_t dB_t - dL_t^u \qquad (8.1)$$

where B_t is a standard Brownian motion and L_t^u is the so-called local time of the load on the capacity boundary. The process L_t^u is increasing (i.e., $dL_t^u > 0$) if and only if $q_t = X$, with $dL_t = 0$ otherwise. That is, q_t is reflected at X.

The dependence of the drift term $\alpha_q(q_t, t)$ on calendar time t reflects the fact that output drift varies systematically both seasonally and within the day. Moreover, the dependence of the drift on q_t allows for mean reversion. One specification that captures these features is:

$$\alpha_q(q_t, t) = \mu(t) + k[\ln q_t - \theta_q(t)] \qquad (8.2)$$

In this expression, $\ln q_t$ reverts to a time-varying mean $\theta_q(t)$. The parameter $k \leq 0$ measures the speed of mean reversion; the larger $|k|$, the more rapid the reversal of load shocks. The function $\mu(t) = d\theta_q(t)/dt$ represents the portion of load drift that depends only on time (particularly time of day). For instance, given $\ln q_t - \theta_q(t)$, load tends to rise from around 3 AM to 5 PM and then fall from 5 PM to 3 AM on summer days. The load volatility σ_q in (8.1) is represented as a constant, but it can depend on q_t and t. There is some empirical evidence of slight seasonality in the variance of q_t.

The second state variable is a fuel price. For some regions of the country, natural gas is the marginal fuel. In other regions, coal is the marginal fuel. In some regions, natural gas is the marginal fuel sometimes and coal is the marginal fuel at others. We abstract from these complications and specify

obstacle to implementation of this approach is that data on capacity availability are not readily accessible. One approach that I have implemented is to apply Bayesian econometric techniques to extract information about the capacity process from observed real-time prices and load. Later, I sketch an approach using readily available data on generation outage probabilities that can be incorporated into the PDE-based framework explored here.

the following $\mathcal{P}$ process for the marginal fuel price:

$$\frac{df_{t,T}}{f_{t,T}} = \alpha_f(f_{t,T}, t) + \sigma_f(f_{t,T}, t)dz_t \qquad (8.3)$$

where $f_{t,T}$ is the price of fuel for delivery on date T as of t and z_t is a Brownian motion. Note that $f_{T,T}$ is the spot price of fuel on date T.

The processes $\{q_t, f_{t,T}, t \geq 0\}$ solve (8.1) and (8.3) under the physical probability measure $\mathcal{P}$. To price power-contingent claims, we need to find an equivalent measure $\mathcal{Q}$ under which deflated prices for claims with payoffs that depend on q_t and $f_{t,T}$ are martingales. Because $\mathcal{P}$ and $\mathcal{Q}$ must share sets of measure 0, q_t must reflect at X under $\mathcal{Q}$ as it does under $\mathcal{P}$. Therefore, under $\mathcal{Q}$, q_t solves the SDE:

$$dq_t = [\alpha_q(q_t, t) - \sigma_q\lambda(q_t, t)]q_t dt + \sigma_q q_t d\hat{B}_t - d\hat{L}_t^u$$

In this expression, $\lambda(q_t, t)$ is the market price of risk function, $\hat{B}_t$ is a $\mathcal{Q}$ martingale, and $\hat{L}_t^u$ is the local time process under $\mathcal{Q}$.[6] Because fuel is a traded asset, under the equivalent measure $df_{t,T}/f_{t,T} = \sigma_f d\hat{z}_t$, where $\hat{z}_t$ is a $\mathcal{Q}$ martingale.

Define the discount factor $Y_t = \exp(-\int_0^t r_s ds)$, where r_s is the (assumed deterministic) interest rate at time s. (Later, we assume that the interest rate is a constant r.) Under $\mathcal{Q}$, the evolution of a deflated power-price-contingent claim C is:

$$Y_t C_t = Y_0 C_0 + \int_0^t C_s dY_s + \int_0^t Y_s dC_s$$

In this expression, C_s indicates the value of the derivative at time s and Y_s denotes the value of 1 dollar received at time s as of time 0. Using Ito's

---

[6] The local time process changes with the measure. Intuitively, if the q_t process drifts up more rapidly under the equivalent measure than under the physical measure, it will hit the upper boundary more frequently under the equivalent measure. Because the local time measures the amount that the controller "pushes" on the process to keep it within the boundary, more pushing is required under the equivalent measure than under the physical measure, so the local times will be different under the two processes. However, the SDE for the process under the equivalent measure must include a local time term if the physical measure process does, and both processes must reflect at the same boundaries. This is true because the physical and equivalent measures must share sets of measure zero. Under the physical measure, the probability that load exceeds capacity is zero, so this probability must also be zero under the equivalent measure. Thus, both processes must reflect at the same boundary.

Lemma, this can be rewritten as:

$$Y_t C_t = C_0 + \int_0^t Y_s (\mathcal{A}C + \frac{\partial C}{\partial s} - r_s C_s) ds$$

$$+ \int_0^t [\frac{\partial C}{\partial q} d\hat{B}_t + \frac{\partial C}{\partial f} d\hat{z}_s] - \int_0^t Y_s \frac{\partial C}{\partial q} d\hat{L}_s^u$$

where $\mathcal{A}$ is an operator such that:

$$\mathcal{A}C = \frac{\partial C}{\partial q_t}[\alpha_q(q_t, t) - \sigma_q \lambda(q_t, t)]q_t + \frac{1}{2}\frac{\partial^2 C}{\partial q_t^2}\sigma_q^2 q_t^2$$

$$+ \frac{1}{2}\frac{\partial^2 C}{\partial f_{t,T}^2}\sigma_f^2 f_{t,T}^2 + \frac{\partial^2 C}{\partial q_t \partial f_{t,T}}\sigma_f \sigma_q \rho_{qf} q_t f_{t,T} \qquad (8.4)$$

For the deflated price of the power contingent claim to be a Q martingale, it must be the case that:

$$E^Q[\int_0^t Y_s (\mathcal{A}C + \frac{\partial C}{\partial s} - r_s C_s) ds] = 0$$

and

$$E^Q[\int_0^t Y_s \frac{\partial C}{\partial q} d\hat{L}_s^u] = 0$$

for all t. Because $Y_t > 0$, and $d\hat{L}_t^u > 0$ only when $q_t = X$, with a constant interest rate r, we can rewrite these conditions as:

$$\mathcal{A}C + \frac{\partial C}{\partial t} - rC = 0 \qquad (8.5)$$

and

$$\frac{\partial C}{\partial q} = 0 \text{ when } q_t = X \qquad (8.6)$$

Expression (8.5) can be rewritten as the fundamental valuation PDE[7]:

$$rC = \frac{\partial C}{\partial t} + \frac{\partial C}{\partial q_t}[\alpha_q(q_t, t) - \sigma_q \lambda(q_t, t)]q_t + \frac{1}{2}\frac{\partial^2 C}{\partial q_t^2}\sigma_q^2 q_t^2$$

$$+ \frac{1}{2}\frac{\partial^2 C}{\partial f_{t,T}^2}\sigma_f^2 f_{t,T}^2 + \frac{\partial^2 C}{\partial q_t \partial f_{t,T}}\sigma_f \sigma_q \rho_{qf} q_t f_{t,T} \qquad (8.7)$$

---

[7] Through a change of variables (to natural logarithms of the state variables), this equation can be transformed to one with constant coefficients on the second-order terms, if the volatility parameters are constant.

For a forward contract, after changing the time variable to $\tau = T - t$, the relevant PDE is:

$$\frac{\partial F_{t,T}}{\partial \tau} = \frac{\partial F_{t,T}}{\partial q_t}[\alpha_q(q_t, t) - \sigma_q\lambda(q_t, t)]q_t + \frac{1}{2}\frac{\partial^2_{t,T}}{\partial q_t^2}q_t^2\sigma_q^2$$

$$+ \frac{1}{2}\frac{\partial^2_{t,T}}{\partial f_{t,T}^2}\sigma_f^2 f_{t,T}^2 + \frac{\partial^2_{t,T}}{\partial q_t \partial f_{t,T}}q_t f_{t,T}\sigma_f\sigma_q\rho_{qf} \qquad (8.8)$$

where $F_{t,T}$ is the price at t for delivery of one unit of power at $T > t$.

Expression (8.6) is a Neumann boundary condition. It arises from the reflecting barrier that is inherent in the physical capacity constraints in the power market and has an intuitive interpretation.[8] If load is at the upper boundary, it will fall almost surely. If the derivative of the contingent claim with respect to load is non-zero at the boundary, arbitrage is possible. For instance, if the partial derivative is positive, when load is at the boundary, selling the contingent claim cannot generate a loss and almost surely generates a profit.

In (8.7)–(8.8), there is a market price of risk function $\lambda(q_t, t)$. The valuation PDE *must* contain a market price of risk because load is not a traded claim; hence, load risk is not hedgeable. Accurate valuation of a power-contingent claim (PCC) therefore depends on accurate specification and estimation of the $\lambda(q_t, t)$ function. This function is an adjustment that changes from the physical measure to the equivalent pricing measure. Recall from Chapter 2 that the equivalent measure incorporates information about investor risk preferences, as well as information about the dynamics of the state variable in the physical measure.

The pricing of a PCC also requires specification of initial boundary conditions that link the state variables (load and the fuel price) and power prices at its expiration. Unlike the storage model (see Chapter 2), there are economically motivated, natural boundary conditions in the electricity market structural model.

In most cases, the buyer of a PCC obtains the obligation to purchase a fixed amount of power (e.g., 25 megawatts) over some period, such as every peak hour of a particular business day or every peak hour during a particular month. Similarly, the seller of a PCC is obligated to deliver a fixed

---

[8]   If there is a lower bound on load (a minimum load constraint), there exists another local time process and another Neumann-type boundary condition.

amount of power over some time period. Therefore, the realized payoff to a forward contract at expiration is:

$$\int_{t'}^{t''} \delta(s)[P^*(q(s), f(s), s) - F(0)]ds \qquad (8.9)$$

where $F(0)$ is the forward price, $q(s)$ is load at time s, $f(s)$ is the fuel spot price at s, $\delta(s)$ is a function that equals 1 if the forward contract requires delivery of power at s and 0 otherwise, $P^*(.)$ is a function that gives the instantaneous price of power as a function of load and fuel price, t' is the beginning of the delivery period under the forward contract, and t'' is the end of the delivery period. In words, (8.9) states that the payoff to the forward equals the value of the power, measured by the spot price, net of the agreed-upon forward price, received over the delivery period. For instance, if the forward is a monthly forward contract for the delivery of 1 megawatt of power during each peak hour in the month, $\delta(s)$ will equal 1 if s falls between 6 AM and 10 PM on a weekday during that month and will equal 0 otherwise.

In this equation, $P^*(q(s), f(s), s)$ is the instantaneous electricity supply curve. When depicted in a two-dimensional load-price space, economic considerations suggest that the supply function $P^*(.)$ is increasing and convex in q. As load increases, producers must employ progressively less efficient generating units to service it. Moreover, the curve should shift up as fuel prices rise because it is more costly to generate when fuel prices are high.

This pricing function determines the dynamics of the instantaneous power price. As in previous chapters, it is possible to combine information about the sensitivities of prices to the state variables and the dynamics of these variables, and use Ito's Lemma, to show how the power price evolves under $\mathcal{P}$:

$$dP^* = \Phi(q_t, f_{t,f}, t)dt + P_q^* \sigma_q q_t d B_t + P_f^* \sigma_f f_{t,f} dz_t \qquad (8.10)$$

with

$$\Phi(q_t, f_{t,f}, t) = P_q^* \alpha_q(q_t, t)q_t + P_f^* \alpha_f(f_{t,t}, t) f_{t,t}$$

$$+ \frac{1}{2} P_{qq}^* \sigma_q^2 q_t^2 + \frac{1}{2} P_{ff}^* \sigma_f^2 f_{t,f}^2 + P_{qf}^* q_t f_{t,f} \sigma_q \sigma_f \rho_{qf}$$

where ρ_{qf} is the correlation between q_t and $f_{t,T}$; this correlation may depend on q_t, $f_{t,T}$, and t. Given this equation, as in previous chapters, it is possible to evaluate the behavior of higher moments, such as variance. The variance of the instantaneous price in this setup is time varying because P^* is a convex, increasing function of q:

$$\sigma_P^2(q_t, f_{t,t}, t) = P_q^{*2}\sigma_q^2 q_t^2 + P_f^{*2} f_{t,t}^2 \sigma_f^2 + 2 P_f^* P_q^* q_t f_{t,t} \rho_{qf} \sigma_q \sigma_f \qquad (8.11)$$

Because P_q^* is increasing with q, demand shocks have a bigger impact on the instantaneous price when load is high (i.e., demand is near capacity) than when it is low. In particular, because the price function becomes nearly vertical when demand approaches capacity, small movements in load can cause extreme movements in the instantaneous price. Moreover, given the speed of load mean reversion, the convexity of P^* implies that the speed of price mean reversion is state dependent; prices revert more rapidly when load (and prices) are high than when they are low. These are fundamental features of electricity price dynamics and explain many salient and well-known features of power prices, most notably the "spikes" in prices when demand approaches capacity and the variability of power price volatility.

The model also implies that the correlation between the fuel price and the power price varies. Assuming that $\rho_{qf} = 0$ (which is approximately correct in most markets), then:

$$corr(dP^*, df) = \frac{P_f^* \sigma_f f_{t,T}}{\sqrt{P_q^{*2} q_t^2 \sigma_q^2 + P_f^{*2} f_{t,T}^2 \sigma_f^2}}$$

Note that when load is small, $P_q^* \approx 0$, in which case $corr(dP^*, df) = 1$. Moreover, when load is large, $P_q^* \approx \infty$, in which case $corr(dP^*, df) = 0$. It is also straightforward to show that the correlation declines monotonically with q_t because P_q^* increases monotonically with q_t.[9] Thus, the model can generate rich patterns of correlation between power and fuel prices, and commensurately rich patterns of spark spread behavior.

Thus, as with storable commodities, the structural model of electricity prices can be used to characterize the time-varying dynamics of power prices.

The following sections discuss implementation of this model and describe some of its implications.

8.4 Model Implementation

This model has many moving parts, the operation of which I will only sketch out here. Readers interested in the details can refer to Pirrong and Jermakyan

---

[9] This result can be generalized to $\rho_{qf} \neq 0$.

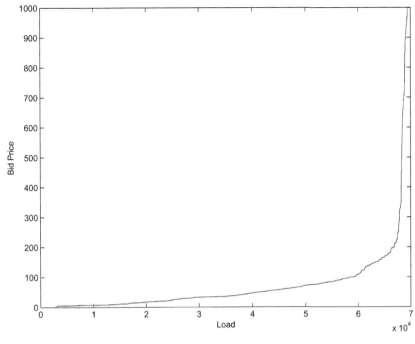

Figure 8.2.

(2008) or Pirrong (2007). One step is to estimate the function that relates the price of power at any instant to the state variables, that is, to specify the supply curve $P^*(q(s), f(s), s)$. One approach is to collect data on prices, loads, and fuel prices and estimate this function econometrically. Because this function is likely to be non-linear, relatively flat for low loads and rising steeply as load reaches capacity, flexible non-parametric techniques are appropriate here (Pirrong and Jermakyan 2008).

Another approach can be employed in some markets. Specifically, where an independent system operator implements markets where generators submit bids indicating the prices at which they are willing to supply a given amount of power, it is possible to combine these bids to construct a supply curve. Pirrong and Jermakyan (2008) provide the details of constructing this supply curve. Figure 8.2 depicts a real-world PJM supply curve derived in this way.

Another step in the analysis is to derive the dynamics of load. This involves two sub-steps.

The first sub-step is to estimate the $\theta_q(t)$ function, that is, the average (log) load as a function of the day of the year and the time of day.

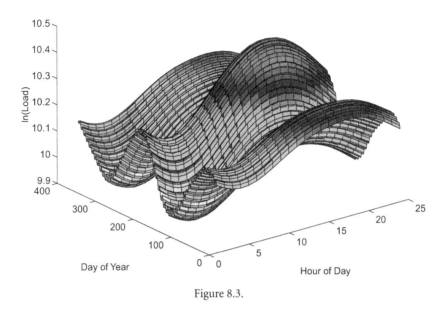

Figure 8.3.

Pirrong-Jermakyan do this using non-parametric techniques (see their article for details); Figure 8.3 illustrates the fitted (log) load surface for PJM.

The second sub-step is to estimate the dynamics of the deviations between load and its (time-varying) mean. This essentially involves estimating the speed of mean reversion of load shocks and the volatility of these shocks. These can be estimated by applying standard time series econometric techniques to the deviation between load and the mean load function.

Once these steps are complete, it is possible to use PDE techniques to price PCCs – if one knows the market price of risk function, $\lambda(q)$. I will discuss the application of PDE methods to the solution of the "direct" problem of estimating a PCC value given an estimate of the market price of risk. The same PDE solution techniques can be applied to the problem of extracting an estimate of the market price of risk function from some observed derivatives prices.

In brief, the earlier equations imply that every derivative on power prices from a particular market should embed the same market price of risk function. Intuitively, therefore, one can "invert" derivatives prices to determine the market price of risk. This is a delicate task, however. First, because there is no closed-form solution for the price of a power derivative, it is necessary to perform this inversion numerically. Second, and more important, these

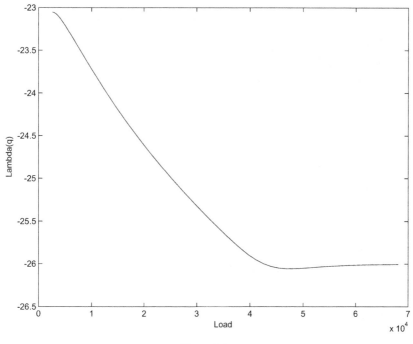

Figure 8.4.

"inverse problems" are ill posed. Put roughly, because one can specify a functional form for $\lambda(q)$ with an arbitrary number of degrees of freedom, and because one has only a limited number of derivatives prices to use in the estimation, it is possible to choose a $\lambda(q)$ function that fits these prices exactly. But an exact fit is a bad fit: more precisely, it is an overfit, and a very slight change in the prices used for the fitting (e.g., using bid prices instead of ask prices) could lead to a radically different estimate of the market price of risk function. Therefore, these inverse problems must be "regularized" to penalize overfitting to get reasonable results. Pirrong and Jermakyan (2008) and Pirrong (2007) provide the details of the application of the regularization methods to the power pricing problem. Figure 8.4 presents a graph of a market price of risk function derived from actual market data using this process.

Once all of these steps are in place, it is possible to use the structural model to solve for the value of any PCC. The next section discusses some power derivatives that are commonly traded, and the subsequent ones show how to solve for the theoretical prices of these derivatives using the PDE approach and the structural model.

8.5 Commonly Traded Power Options

A variety of electricity options are traded (primarily on the OTC market). Among the most common are daily strike options, monthly strike options, and spark spread options. I consider each in turn.

8.5.1 Daily Strike Options

A daily strike option has a payoff that depends on the price of power on a given day. Typically, these options have a payoff that depends on the price of power for delivery during peak hours of a given day.

Daily strike options can be physically settled or cash settled. For a physically settled daily strike call option, on exercise, the owner effectively receives a long position in a daily forward contract that entitles him to receive delivery of a fixed amount of power during the peak hours on that day. On exercise, the owner of a put establishes a short position in a daily forward contract. The option owner must decide to exercise prior to the beginning of the delivery period (e.g., the day before delivery).

A cash-settled daily strike option can be constructed in many ways. For instance, one can have a cash-settled daily strike call in which the owner is paid an amount equal to the maximum of zero or the difference between the relevant daily forward as of some date prior to the delivery period and the strike price. As an example, the call owner's payoff (determined on Tuesday) may depend on Tuesday's forward price for delivery on Wednesday. Alternatively, a daily strike call can pay the difference between the average spot price observed on the pricing date and the strike. For instance, the daily strike call can pay the maximum of zero or the difference between the average spot price observed on Wednesday and the strike price. In a market with a centralized real time market (e.g., PJM), it is eminently feasible to construct options with such a payoff structure.

The option payoff may depend appreciably on how the contract is written. Specifically, as detailed in Section 8.6, variations in realized spot prices driven by highly transitory factors (other than load and fuel prices) would tend to cause the expected payoff to the option that is based on realized spot prices to exceed that for the option that is based on the forward price measured some time prior to the delivery period, which is assumed to depend only on load and the fuel price. That section details some potential solutions to this difficulty, but until then I focus on daily strike options with payoffs that depend on a forward price. For such an option, the call payoff at exercise is $(F_{t',T}(q_{t'},\, f_{t',T}) - K)^+$ and the put payoff is $(K - F_{t',T}(q_{t'},\, f_{t',T}))^+$.

8.5.2 Monthly Strike Options

On exercise, the holder of a monthly strike call receives a long position in a monthly forward contract. For instance, on exercise at the end of June, the holder of a July monthly strike call receives a forward contract for delivery of a fixed amount of power during the peak hours of the coming July. Denoting the forward price as of exercise date t' for delivery of peak power on day j in the option month as $F_{t',j}$, the payoff to the monthly strike call is

$$\left(\frac{\sum_{j \in M} F_{t',j}}{\sum_{j \in M} \delta_j} - K\right)^+$$

where M is the set of delivery dates in the contract month and δ_j is an indicator variable taking a value of 1 when $j \in M$ and zero otherwise.

8.5.3 Spark Spread Options

A spark spread call option has a payoff equal to the maximum of zero or the difference between a forward price and the price of fuel multiplied by a contractually specified heat rate. The heat rate is measured in terms of megawatts (MW) per million British thermal units (mmBTU). The heat rate measures the efficiency of a generating plant. The marginal cost of generating power from that plant equals its heat rate multiplied by its fuel price. Therefore, a spark spread option can be viewed as an option to burn fuel to produce power because its payoff is based on the difference between the price of power and the cost of generating it at a given heat rate. For this reason, power plants are often viewed as bundles of spark spread options, although spark spread options are also traded as stand-alone financial products.

Spark spread options raise some of the same issues relating to the timing of exercise and physical settlement and cash settlement as daily strike options. Specifically, if the spark spread option must be exercised at some time t' prior to the power delivery date T, the call payoff is $(F_{t',T} - f_{t',T} H^*)^+$, where H^* is the contractually specified heat rate, which effectively determines the strike. If the payoff to a cash-settled option is based on realized spot prices over the delivery period, the valuation approach applied herein may underestimate its value because it ignores short-term price fluctuations driven by variables other than load and fuel prices. Again, this issue is discussed in more detail in Section 8.6.

8.6 Valuation Methodology

8.6.1 Daily Strike and Monthly Strike Options

I value daily strike and monthly strike options by solving the PDE (8.7) using the splitting finite difference method already described in Chapter 2 and applied to all of the 2D PDEs studied in earlier chapters.

As should now be familiar, the technique first involves creating a grid in time, the fuel price, and log load. The time increment is δt; given the seasonality in load, it is convenient to use $\delta t = 1/365$. The fuel increment is δf, and the log load increment is δq.

As before, I split the PDE (8.7) into three parts at each time step. The first PDE "split," which captures the effect of the purely q-related terms, is:

$$\frac{rC}{3} = \frac{\partial C}{\partial t} + \frac{\partial C}{\partial q_t}[\alpha_q(q_t, t) - \sigma_q \lambda(q_t, t)] + \frac{1}{2}\sigma_q^2 \frac{\partial^2 C}{\partial q_t^2} \qquad (8.12)$$

The second split handles the cross derivative term:

$$\frac{rC}{3} = \frac{\partial C}{\partial t} + \frac{1}{2}\sigma_f \sigma_q \rho_{qf} f_{t, T} \frac{\partial^2 C}{\partial q_t \partial f_{t, T}} \qquad (8.13)$$

The third PDE split, which handles the purely f-related terms, is:

$$\frac{rC}{3} = \frac{\partial C}{\partial t} + \frac{1}{2}\sigma_f^2 f_{t, T}^2 \frac{\partial^2 C}{\partial f_{t, T}^2} \qquad (8.14)$$

One time step prior to expiry, (8.8) is solved using an implicit method for each different fuel price from the second lowest to the second highest. At each time step, the solution to (8.8) is used as the initial condition in the solution for (8.9), which is again solved implicitly at each load level. Then, the solution for (8.9) is used as the initial condition for (8.10), which is solved implicitly for each log load from highest to lowest. At all time steps but the one immediately preceding expiration, the solution to (8.10) from the prior time step is used as the initial condition for (8.8).

At each step, I use Dirichlet conditions for the fuel boundary and the von Neumann conditions discussed before for the load boundary. For one time step prior to expiration, the option payoff is used as the initial condition. Given the typical high speed of mean reversion, the coefficient on the first-order term in (8.8) is usually large in absolute value. Therefore, although (8.7) is a convection-diffusion equation, the convection effect is more important than is typically the case in parabolic PDEs found in finance settings, and so it is desirable to utilize discretization approaches commonly employed for convection problems. Specifically, I use forward differencing to estimate $\partial C/\partial q$ when the coefficient is negative, and backward differencing when the reverse is true.

For daily strike options, the payoff is determined as follows. It is assumed that the option holder must decide to exercise the option the day prior to the power delivery date; that is, $t' = T - \delta t$.[10] On exercise, for a (log) load q and fuel price f, the holder of the call receives a payment equal to the maximum of zero, or the difference (a) between the day-ahead forward price $F_{t',T}(q, f)$ implied by the solution to the Pirrong-Jermakyan (PJ) model calibrated to the observed curve, and (b) the strike price.[11]

For monthly strike options, the delivery days in the month are first determined. For simplicity, I assume that delivery occurs during the peak hours of each business day of the month. The option is assumed to be exercisable on the business day prior to the first day of the delivery month. On this date, the PJ model forward price for each day of the delivery month is determined for each f and q in the grid.[12] For instance, the prices of forwards expiring on business days falling between 1 July and 31 July are determined as of the expiry date of 30 June. The proceeds to the exercise of the call equal the maximum of zero, or the difference between the average of these forward prices and the option strike price.

8.6.2 Spark Spread Options

In the model, the forward price is a multiplicatively separable function of the fuel forward price and a function of load. In this case, the payoff to the spark spread call can be re-expressed as:

$$(F_{t',T} - f_{t,T}H^*)^+ = (f_{t',T}V(q_{t'}, t', T) - f_{t',T}H^*)^+$$
$$= f_{t',T}(V(q_{t'}, t', T) - H^*)^+$$

Therefore, the payoff to the spark spread option is multiplicatively separable in load and fuel. Consequently, it is possible to utilize the Pirrong and

---

[10] This assumption can be readily modified.
[11] The daily strike put payoff is defined analogously.
[12] The forward is calculated using the market price of risk function calibrated to the forward curve observed on the valuation date.

Jermakyan (2008) decomposition to write the value of the spark spread option as another multiplicatively separable function of the current fuel forward price and current load. Specifically, denoting the spark spread option value as $H(.)$:

$$H(q_t, f_{t,T}, t, T, H^*) = f_{t,T} \Phi(q_t, t, T, H^*)$$

The $\Phi(.)$ function can be determined using a standard implicit solver with $(V(q_{t'}, t', T) - H^*)^+$ as an initial condition.[13]

8.7 Results

The behavior of power options prices implied by this model is best understood through the use of various figures and focusing on a few salient results. The behavior of the "Greeks" in particular sheds light on the economic factors driving the option values. The Greeks, notably Delta and Gamma, are related to the shape of the option price function. Delta measures the slope of the function, Gamma its curvature (i.e., its convexity/concavity). Greeks are of particular interest and importance to options traders.

In this regard, it bears noting that because of the two-dimensional nature of the problem, there is a set of Greeks for each of the state variables. For instance, there is a "load Delta" ($\partial C/\partial q$) and a "load Gamma" ($\partial^2 C/\partial q^2$), a "fuel Delta" ($\partial C/\partial f$), a "fuel Gamma" ($\partial^2 C/\partial f^2$), and a cross-Gamma ($\partial^2 C/\partial f \partial q$). The behavior of the Gammas is of particular interest.

All option values in the figures are based on a calibrated PJ model. The model is calibrated using estimates of load volatility σ_q, mean reversion parameter k, load-fuel correlation ρ, and average log load $\theta_q(t)$ estimated from PJM data for 1 January 2000–31 May 2005; see Pirrong and Jermakyan (2008) for a description of the estimation methodology. The model is calibrated to PJM power forward prices (from the NYMEX ClearPort system) and natural gas forward prices for Texas Eastern Pipeline Zone M-3 observed on 7 June 2005 using the PJ method. The fuel volatility is the implied volatility from the at-the-money NYMEX natural gas futures options with delivery months corresponding to the maturity of the option being analyzed, as observed on 7 June 2005.

The valuation grid has 100 points in the load and fuel dimensions. The minimum fuel price is $1.00 and the maximum is $25.00. The minimum load is the smallest PJM load observed in 1999–2005, and the maximum

---

[13] Because of the multiplicative separability, using the transformation presented in Pirrong and Jermakyan (2008), it is possible to solve for $\Phi(.)$ even when $\rho \neq 0$.

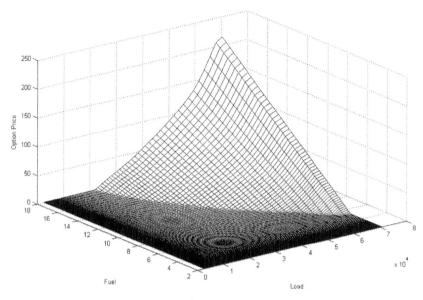

Figure 8.5.

load is the total amount of generation bid into PJM on 15 July 2004 (the date used to determine the payoff function for July forwards in the model calibration – PJM bid data are available only with a 6-month lag).

Figure 8.5 depicts the value of a daily strike call option expiring on 15 July 2005, measured 2 days prior to expiration, as a function of fuel price and load. The strike of this option is $85, which was the ATM strike on 7 June 2005. The horizontal plane dimensions are the fuel price f and the load q (running into the chart from front to back). The option value is increasing in fuel price and load, as would be expected. Thus, load and fuel Deltas are both positive. Note, too, that there is noticeable convexity of the option value in both f and q. That is, both load and fuel Gammas are positive. The load Gamma is noticeably large and positive for high levels of load and for high fuel prices. This reflects (a) the convexity of the load-power price relation when time to expiry is short, and (b) the convexity of the option payoff function.

Figure 8.6 depicts the value of the same option on 7 June 2005, or approximately 38 days prior to expiry. In the figure, the positive fuel Delta and Gamma are readily apparent; the convexity in fuel price is especially evident for intermediate fuel prices (where the option is near-the-money).

However, the option value exhibits little dependence on load. In fact, the load Delta and load Gamma are effectively zero. (When one plots the option

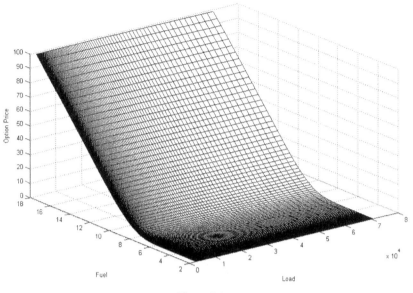

Figure 8.6.

value as a function of load for a given fuel price in MATLAB, the change in the option value across the range of load values is smaller than the minimum increment that can be depicted by the MATLAB plotting function.) Indeed, the zeroing out of the load Delta and Gamma occurs as time maturity falls to as little as 7 or 8 days. Thus, despite the strong dependence of spot power prices on load, daily strike options with maturities of more than a few days exhibit virtually no dependence on load.

This phenomenon reflects the strong mean reversion in load.[14] Because of this strong mean reversion, the distribution of load for future dates conditional on current load converges quite quickly to the unconditional load distribution. Thus, for maturities beyond a few days, variations in current load convey very little information about the distribution of load at expiry; thus, such variations have little impact on the daily strike option value.

This analysis implies that for a week or more prior to daily strike option expiration, such options are effectively options on fuel. Until expiration

---

[14] It is important to remember that this refers to mean reversion in load, not prices. Prices can mean revert due to mean reversion in load, but also because price spikes tend to reverse quickly. In the PJ model, prices spike periodically when load approaches the rapidly increasing portion of the bid stack; this happens with positive probability even when the load process is a diffusive one with no spikes. As an empirical matter, I have analyzed load data from several markets, and there is little evidence of spikes in load.

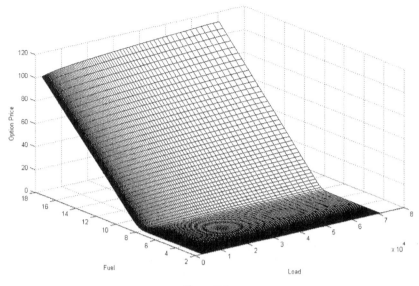

Figure 8.7.

nears, these options can be hedged using fuel forwards (to hedge fuel Delta) and fuel options (to hedge fuel Gamma). In the last few days before expiry, however, the option value exhibits progressively stronger dependence on load (especially when load is high), and hedging requires the use of load-sensitive claims (e.g., a power forward to hedge load Delta, or another load-sensitive option to hedge load Gamma).

The effects of load mean reversion on power option value are especially evident when one examines monthly strike options. Figure 8.7 depicts the value of a July 2005 monthly strike call option 1 day prior to expiry. Even given this short maturity, there is only a slight load Delta and virtually no load Gamma. However, the non-zero fuel Delta and Gamma are evident. The lack of load dependence reflects the fact that the payoff to the monthly strike option depends on forward prices for delivery dates that are half a month on average after option expiry. For all but the forward contracts maturing a few days after the monthly strike option's expiry, load has little impact on the forward price. Hence, variations in load at expiry have little effect on most of the daily forwards included in the monthly bundle.

Mean reversion also affects option time decay. This is most evident for a spark spread option. Note that because of their multiplicative separability in load and fuel (and the separability of the forward price in these variables in the PJ framework), conditional on q spark spread option values are linear in the fuel price and, hence, have a fuel Gamma of zero. Thus, in

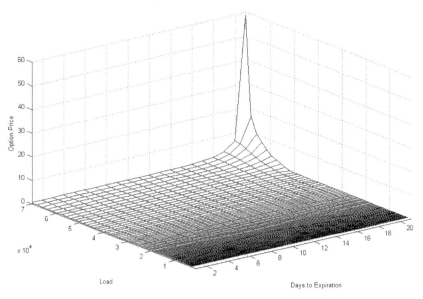

Figure 8.8.

contrast to what is observed for monthly and daily strike options, this implies that there is no time decay attributable to the fuel factor for a spark spread option. Because any time decay for this type of option is attributable to the impact of load, an examination of spark spread options allows isolation of the contribution of load dynamics on time decay.

With this in mind, consider Figure 8.8, which depicts the value of $\Phi(q_t, t, T)$ for a spark spread call option with $H^* = 10$ as a function of time to expiration and load (with the load dimension running into the chart).[15] The maximum time to expiration on the chart is 60 days and, hence, corresponds to a mid-August 2005 expiration date. Note that the option value is virtually constant until a few days short of expiration. Thus, there is very little time decay until very close to expiration. As the option nears expiry, however, for low loads the option value declines precipitously. Conversely, for high loads (especially very high loads), the value of the option increases dramatically.

These characteristics again reflect mean reversion in load. Well before expiry, because of mean reversion the conditional distribution of load (the only payoff-relevant variable for the spark spread claim) changes virtually

---

[15] The spark spread option value is extremely high when load is high close to expiration. Therefore, to highlight the lack of time decay and avoid the impact of option values for very high loads on the scaling of the figure, spark spread option values are presented only for loads that are no more than 15 percent above the mean load.

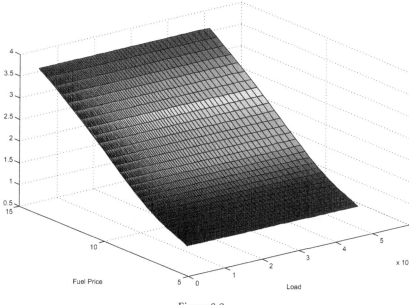

Figure 8.9.

not at all as time passes. This contrasts with the value of an option with a payoff determined by a geometric Brownian motion (GBM), where the dispersion in the conditional distribution of the payoff-relevant variable declines monotonically as time passes. The stationarity of load translates into little time decay.

Similar influences affect time decay for daily and monthly strike options. These options exhibit time decay, but this reflects the dependence of payoffs on a GBM – the fuel price. The dispersion in payoffs declines as time passes for monthly and daily strikes because of the fall in the dispersion of fuel prices at expiry. Holding fuel price at expiry constant, the passage of time does not affect the variability in payoffs attributable to load. That is, $\partial u/\partial t$ is very close to zero when a daily strike option has more than a few days prior to expiry (regardless of the level of load) and is very close to zero immediately prior to expiry even when a monthly strike option is ATM.

The strong mean reversion in load also affects the behavior of implied volatility for power options. Although the Black model is not well suited for pricing power options, practitioners still employ it for that purpose, and option values are often quoted in terms of implied volatilities.

One impact of load mean reversion is to cause implied volatilities for daily strike options to rise systematically as expiration nears. This is depicted in Figures 8.9 and 8.10. Figure 8.9 depicts implied volatility as a function of q and f when a daily strike option (struck at \$85) has a month to expiration.

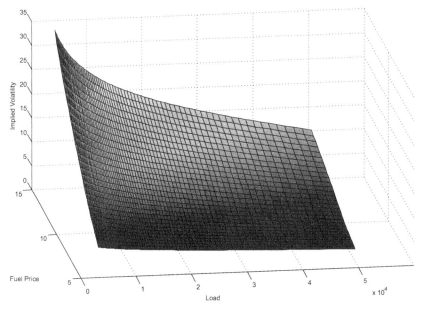

Figure 8.10.

Figure 8.10 presents the implied volatility surface for the same option with only 2 days to expiration. The implied volatilities set the Black formula for an option value with strike $85 and a forward price given by the model for the appropriate q and f equal to the daily strike option value implied by the solution to (8.7) for that q and f.

Note that the implied volatility surface is markedly higher with shorter time to expiration, especially for large values of the fuel price. This again reflects mean reversion. Volatility measures the rate of information flow (Ross 1989). The constant volatility in a GBM process (which underlies the Black model) means that the rate of information flow is constant over time. This is wildly misleading for electricity. Strong mean reversion in load means that a load shock today confers very little information about the distribution of load even a few days hence. That is, one learns little new about the distribution in load in a month based on an observation of current load. Virtually all of the load-related information flow occurs in the last few days prior to expiration (and variations in load explain more than 65 percent of PJM spot power price fluctuations). The Black implied volatility effectively calculates an average rate of information flow. For a power option, the average rate of information flow over a long time prior to expiry is small, whereas the average rate of information flow over a short time leading up to expiry of a daily strike option is large, because virtually all of the information flow occurs in these last few days.

Note that the shape of the implied volatility surface also changes dramatically as one nears expiry. A month prior to expiration, the implied volatility depends on the level of the fuel price (with high fuel prices associated with higher implieds in an S-shaped form), but does not vary with load. With the short-dated option, however, the volatility surface exhibits a strong dependence on load, especially for high fuel prices.

Not surprisingly, the shift in the volatility surface over time is much less pronounced for monthly strike options. As noted earlier, much of the payoff for a monthly strike option is determined by forward prices for forward contracts with more than a few days to maturity. Thus, load shocks that occur even in the days immediately prior to maturity of the monthly strike option confer very little payoff-relevant information. The rate of information flow days before the monthly strike's expiry is therefore not markedly different from the rate weeks before maturity. Indeed, the information flow is almost entirely related to the price of fuel. Under the assumption that the fuel futures price is a GBM, this implies that the implied volatility is effectively the same regardless of time to expiry of the monthly strike option.

Mean reversion also affects the nature of volatility "smiles" and "smirks" in power options. Long-maturity daily strike options exhibit no smile or smirk – the implied volatility does not vary with strike.[16] However, Figure 8.11 demonstrates that (a) implied volatilities smirk for short-dated daily strike options, and (b) the smirk depends on load when time to expiry is small. The figure depicts three smiles for a daily strike option expiring on 15 July with 2 days to expiry. The highest curve is for a load that is 5 percent below the mean value (given by $\theta_q(t)$) on this date. The curve with the next lowest values of implied volatility at the low strike is for a load that is at the mean value on this date. Each of these curves slopes downward from left to right; that is, they smirk. The curve that cuts across the other two and that is U-shaped is for a load that is 5 percent above

---

[16] These options should exhibit smiles if fuel options do, as would be the case when fuel prices exhibit stochastic volatility or jumps. In this case, the power option smile will be related to the smile in fuel options. To see this, rewrite the option value as $C = \int_0^\infty v(f_{t',T}, t, T, K|q_{t'})h(q_{t'}|q_t)dq_{t'}$, where $h(.)$ is the distribution of $q_{t'}$ conditional on q_t and $v(.)$ is the value of a contingent claim with initial condition given by its payoff. For instance, for a call this payoff is $(f_{t',T}V(q_{t'}, t', T) - K)^+$ which is the value of a call on $V(.)$ units of fuel and strike K. In the presence of stochastic volatility or jumps, the $v(.)$ function will exhibit a volatility skew, which will affect the skew of the power claim C.

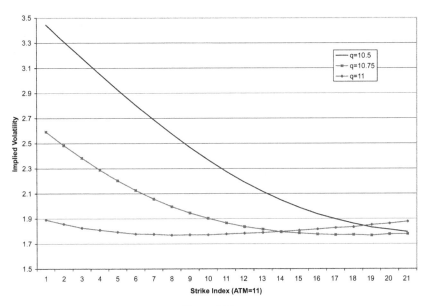

Figure 8.11.

the mean. Each smirk is centered on the ATM strike; because the relevant forward price is different for different load levels this close to expiry, the ATM strike differs across options. The figure is centered at the ATM strike, with $1 increments between strikes. The smile is calculated assuming a fuel price of $7 and a time to expiration of 2 days. Note that the smirk is toward the put wing with loads at or below the mean (i.e., higher volatilities are associated with higher strikes) but that it smiles more symmetrically when the load is well above the mean. It should be noted, however, that the behavior of the smile is also dependent on fuel prices. For some values of fuel price and load, implied volatility can smirk toward the put wing, for instance.

Because of the general lack of load dependence for monthly strike options, even when time to expiration is low, there is no pronounced smile or smirk for these options.

The model implies power options exhibit other features that deserve comment, but are quite intuitive. These include:

- Daily and monthly strike option values are increasing in the volatility of the fuel price σ_f. Because spark spread option prices are linear functions of fuel forward prices, their values do not vary with fuel price volatility.

- Daily and monthly strike and spark spread call option values are increasing in the volatility of load σ_q. The increase is due to two factors. First, an increase in load volatility increases the power forward price due to the effect of Jensen's inequality because the forward payoff is a convex function of load. Second, holding the moneyness of the option constant (by increasing the call strike to offset the impact of the higher volatility on the forward price), the payoff to the option is a convex function of load, so again a Jensen's inequality effect implies that the higher volatility is associated with a higher option value. For puts, the effect of higher load volatility is ambiguous a priori because these two effects work in opposite directions. However, a strike-compensated increase in load volatility increases the put value.

8.8 Complications

As noted earlier, although fuel prices and load are crucial determinants of power prices, electricity spot prices depend on other factors as well. For instance, outages of transmission or generation assets can influence power prices. Such events can have a large impact on option valuations in particular because of the effect of Jensen's inequality. For instance, outages can cause spikes in prices that can appreciably increase the likelihood of positive payoffs for deep-out-of-the-money calls. Because such outages are typically of relatively short duration, they will have the biggest impact on the payoffs to options based on very short-dated forwards or spot electricity prices.

Fortunately, the structural framework outlined here can be augmented to capture the impact of outages (and other structural sources of power price fluctuations unrelated to load and fuel prices). I characterize "forced" outages by a Markov process and a transition probability matrix.[17] Generator i's state is "on" ("state 1") or "off" ("state 2"), and it can transition from on to on, on to off, off to on, and off to off, with associated probabilities given by the matrix:

$$\Pi_i = \begin{pmatrix} p^i_{11} & p^i_{12} \\ p^i_{21} & p^i_{22} \end{pmatrix}$$

Data collected by North American Electric Reliability Corporation (NERC) and reported in the Generating Availability Data System (GADS) database can be used to determine these probabilities. Theoretically, each

---

[17] Planned seasonal outages can also be incorporated into the analysis.

individual generator has a distinctive Π_i, but in practice it is conventional to assume that generation units of a particular type, such as coal units, share a particular Π matrix that differs from that for other types of unit, such as gas or nuclear plants.[18]

Consider a market with N generating units, possibly of different types and hence with different Π_i matrices. Define Ω_t as the N-vector describing the state of the market's generating units at time t. I refer to this as the "generation state." Element i of Ω_t equals 1 if that unit is available at t and equals 0 if it is unavailable because of an outage.

At time t, the generation state is Ω_t. Conditional on this, it is possible to calculate the probability of each possible generation state at $T > t$. If T is only modestly greater than t, these conditional probabilities are very close to the unconditional probabilities.

The probabilities of the generating states in the physical measure are relevant for determining expected prices in this measure, but for the purpose of valuing a power forward contract or option, it is necessary to utilize probabilities produced by an equivalent measure. Because outages represent a non-hedgeable risk, the market is incomplete, and these equivalent-measure generation-state probabilities are not unique.

Spot power prices depend on fuel prices and load, as in the PJ model, but also depend on outages. Specifically, I assume that:

$$P_t = f_{t,t}\phi(q_t, \Omega_t) \tag{8.15}$$

where P_t is the spot price of power at t. In (8.15), $\phi(.)$ is the market heat rate function.

All else being equal, increases in outages at t are associated with higher spot power prices.

Consider valuation of a derivative with a payoff contingent on P_T. Assuming the independence of the generation outage state on the one hand and load and fuel prices on the other, the time t value of this derivative is the expectation under the equivalent measure of the present value of the payoff:

$$V(q_t, f_{t,T}, \Omega_t) = e^{-r(T-t)} \tilde{E}_{q,f} \tilde{E}_\Omega G(f_{T,T}\phi(q_T, \Omega_T)) \tag{8.16}$$

---

[18] There is likely some weak relation between outages and the state variables in the PJ model, most notably load. Breakdowns are somewhat more likely to occur when units are operating intensively, as during high-load periods. Moreover, there may be some path dependence in outages – breakdowns are more likely after extended periods of intensive operation. Nonetheless, the relation between load and outages is sufficiently weak that it is conventional to assume that outage probabilities are independent of fuel prices, load, and temperature. Assuming such independence has great computational benefits.

where $G(.)$ is the payoff function, $\tilde{E}_{q,f}$ indicates the expectation over q and f under the equivalent measure, and $\tilde{E}_\Omega$ is the expectation over the generation state under this measure. The former expectation is conditional on $f_{t,T}$, the T-expiry fuel forward price as of t, and q_t, the time-t load. The latter expectation is conditional on the time-t generation state.

With regard to the payoff function, for a forward contract:

$$G(.) = f_{T,T}\phi(q_T, \Omega_T)$$

whereas for a call option with strike K, it is:

$$G(.) = (f_{T,T}\phi(q_t, \Omega_T) - K)^+$$

Define $\hat{C}(q_T, f_{T,T}) = \tilde{E}_\Omega G(f_{T,T}\phi(q_T, \Omega_T))$; $\hat{C}(.)$ is a function of q_T and $f_{T,T}$ alone because outages are integrated out when taking the expectation. This function can serve as the initial condition in the PDE (8.7).

Thus, incorporating outages into the PJ framework requires only the determination of the relevant $\tilde{E}_\Omega$ expectation. This, in turn, requires determination of (a) the $\phi(.)$ function, and (b) the relevant probabilities under the equivalent measure. Moreover, the expectation must be calculated. These matters are beyond the scope of this book but are discussed in some detail in Pirrong (2006).

Similar modifications can be employed to capture other sources of power price variations in addition to load, fuel prices, and outages. Because of Jensen's inequality, the option holder benefits from these fluctuations, and ignoring them would lead to underestimates of option value. This is of particular importance for power options with payoffs dependent on spot prices or very short-dated forward prices.

Other complications are not so readily handled. For instance, the model valuations depend on the market price of risk function $\lambda(q_t)$. Given a $\lambda(q_t)$ function calibrated to observable derivative price information (e.g., visible forward prices), the solution to the PDE (8.7) solved subject to the appropriate initial condition will give an option value that is consistent with contemporaneous forward prices used for calibration. However, as Joshi (2003) notes, the market chooses $\lambda(q_t)$, and the market can change its mind. For instance, changes in hedging pressure, driven perhaps by financial shocks to market participants, can affect risk premia in the forward market. That is, such shocks may affect $\lambda(q_t)$. As an example, the collapse of Enron and the subsequent deterioration in the financial condition of merchant energy firms plausibly affected the market price of risk. Similarly, Bessembinder and Lemmon (2002) and Pirrong and Jermakyan (2008) note that changes in available generating capacity and the changes in supply of risk-bearing capacity by financial intermediaries can also affect the market price of risk function.

Variations in the market price of risk imply changes in the value of PCCs. Although it is not difficult to calculate the sensitivity in power-claim values to changes in $\lambda(.)$, this is not sufficient to quantify fully the risk of a power option or forward position, because this risk depends on both this sensitivity and the dynamics of $\lambda(.)$. These dynamics are quite difficult to model and estimate because (a) the process for estimating this function is computationally expensive, (b) the function is typically non-linear, and (c) the function is estimated statistically and is hence subject to sampling error. Thus, although the methodology set out here and in Pirrong and Jermakyan (2008) can give consistent valuations of many PCCs at a point in time, it cannot readily quantify all of the risks of power forwards and options. The market chooses the measure, and the market can change its mind; this source of variability is not readily captured in the standard derivatives valuation framework.

8.9 Summary and Conclusions

A structural model, which posits that power prices are a function of load and fuel prices, can be used to price a variety of options on electricity. This chapter demonstrates that the behavior of one of these state variables – notably load – exerts a decisive impact on the pricing of these options. Specifically, load is strongly mean reverting. As a consequence, the conditional distribution of load at option expiration does not vary substantially with contemporaneous load with more than a few days to expiration, even though variations in load are the single most important cause of variations in power spot prices. This causes the prices of daily strike options (i.e., options on the delivery of power on a single day that are exercised shortly before the delivery date) to vary little with load more than a few days to expiration. Monthly strike options (i.e., options on the delivery of power during a month that are exercised shortly before the delivery month) exhibit almost no load dependence even as expiry nears. Mean reversion also affects option time decay; an option with a payoff that is proportional to the fuel price (e.g., a spark spread option) exhibits virtually no time decay until right before expiry.

The model assumes that variations in load and fuel prices explain all variations in power prices. In reality, although these factors are the most important determinants of power price movements, other variables affect power prices as well. Fluctuations in these variables are likely to be highly transitory, so they can be ignored when determining forward prices a few days before contract maturity, or when valuing options with payoffs that depend on the prices of forwards maturing more than a day or two after option expiry. This is not reasonable when valuing options with payoffs that depend on very short-term forward prices (e.g., a hour-ahead forward) or on spot prices. Under certain simplifying assumptions, however, it is possible to modify the initial conditions to the valuation PDE to take into account transitory fluctuations in power prices attributable to factors other than load and fuel prices, such as outages or out-of-merit dispatch driven by transmission constraints and fluctuations in the spatial pattern of load.

The structural model studied in this chapter assumes that electricity is truly non-storable. This means that the dynamic programming problems that required such careful handling in Chapters 2 through 7 are absent here. As a result, price in every instant depends only on current conditions and not on anticipation about future supply and demand conditions. Even in markets where all generation is fossil fueled, this is not exactly right; non-convexities in electricity generation, arising from startup and shutdown costs, for instance, mean that current decisions (e.g., whether to start up a plant) affect future opportunity sets. Nonetheless, from a practical perspective, this is a second-order consideration because even some centrally dispatched markets ignore these considerations for many decisions.

There are circumstances, however, where the non-storability assumption is problematic. In particular, hydro generation introduces an element of storability; although the electricity cannot be (economically) stored, water used to generate it by spilling it over a dam can be. This connects current decisions and future opportunities: spilling water over a dam to generate power today means that water is not available to generate tomorrow. Thus, as with storable commodities, the problem of the optimal (and competitive) operation of a hydropower system is inherently a dynamic programming problem.

This is a first-order issue in some markets, such as the Pacific Northwest of the United States and Canada, and Scandinavia.[19] Fortunately, the methods of this chapter can be combined with the methods of the rest of the book to address this problem. Specifically, a combination of the seasonal storage model in Chapters 6 and 7 with the load dynamics and fossil-fuel supply curve modeling of this chapter can be used to construct a structural

---

[19] It is not important in other markets, such as Texas in the United States, where virtually all power is generated by non-hydro sources.

model of a hydro market. The "stock" of water behind dams represents the analog to inventories in the storage model. Natural changes of this stock occur seasonally, because of snowfall, for example. Moreover, these changes are random, and information about future changes flows continuously. Thus, a model with a random load process and a process describing the flow of information about water availability represent a reasonable way of characterizing a market with an important hydro component.

But I have done enough for now. That is left as an exercise for the reader, giving you an opportunity to put all the tools of this book to work. Good luck!

References

Anderson, R., and Gilbert, C. 1988. Commodity Agreements and Commodity Markets: Lessons from Tin. *Economic Journal* **98** 1–15.

Baldwin, W. 1983. *The World Tin Market: Political Pricing and Economic Competition.* Durham, NC: Duke University Press.

Barone-Adesi, G., and Gigli, A. 2002. Electricity Derivatives. Working paper, Universita della Svizzera Italiana.

Bellman, R. 1957. *Dynamic Programming.* Princeton, NJ: Princeton University Press.

Bessembinder, H., and Lemmon, M. 2002. Equilibrium Pricing and Optimal Hedging in Electricity Forward Markets. *Journal of Finance* **57** 1347–1382.

Carter, C., and Revoredo, C. 2005. The Interaction of Working and Speculative Commodity Stocks. Working paper, University of Cambridge.

Chambers, M., and Bailey, R. 1996. A Theory of Commodity Price Fluctuations. *Journal of Political Economy* **104** 924–957.

Cont, R., and Tankov, P. 2003. *Financial Modeling with Jump Processes.* New York: Chapman & Hall.

Deaton, A., and Laroque, G. 1992. On the Behavior of Commodity Prices. *Review of Economic Studies* **59** 1–23.

Deaton, A., and Laroque, G. 1995. Estimating a Nonlinear Rational Expectations Commodity Model with Unobservable State Variables. *Journal of Applied Econometrics* **10S** S9–S40.

Deaton, A., and Laroque, G. 1996. Competitive Storage and Commodity Price Dynamics. *Journal of Political Economy* **104** 896–923.

Duffie, D. 1996. *Dynamic Asset Pricing Theory.* Princeton, NJ: Princeton University Press.

Duffy, D. 2006. *Finite Difference Methods in Financial Engineering: A Partial Differential Equations Approach.* New York: Wiley.

Elliott, R., and Kopp, P. 2004. *Mathematics of Financial Markets.* New York: Springer Finance.

Epstein, L., and Zin, S. 1989. Substitution, Risk Aversion, and the Temporal Behavior of Consumption and Asset Returns: A Theoretical Framework. *Econometrica* **57** 937–969.

Eydeland, A., and Geman, H. 1999. Fundamentals of Electricity Derivatives. Pages 35–44 in Jameson, R. (ed.), *Energy Modelling and the Management of Uncertainty.* London: Risk Publications.

Eydeland, A., and Wolyniec, K. 2002. *Energy and Power Risk Management: New Developments in Modeling, Pricing, and Hedging.* New York: Wiley.

Fackler, P., and Miranda, M. 2002. *Applied Computational Economics and Finance.* Cambridge, MA: MIT Press.

Fama, E., and French, K. 1988. Business Cycles and the Behavior of Metals Prices. *Journal of Finance* **43** 1075–1093.

Geman, H. 2005. *Commodities and Commodity Derivatives: Modeling and Pricing for Agriculturals, Metals, and Energy.* West Sussex: Wiley Finance.

Geman, H., and Roncoroni, A. 2006. Understanding the Fine Structure of Electricity Prices. *Journal of Business* **79** 1225–1262.

Gibson, R., and Schwartz, E. 1990. Stochastic Convenience Yield and the Pricing of Oil Contingent Claims. *Journal of Finance* **45** 959–976.

Gilbert, C. 1988. Optimal and Competitive Storage Rules: The Gustafson Problem Revisited. In Guvenon, O. (ed.), *International Commodity Market Models and Policy Analysis.* Dordrecht, The Netherlands: Kluwer Academic.

Gjerstad, S. 2007. The Competitive Market Paradox. *Journal of Economic Dynamics and Control* **31** 1753–1780.

Gustafson, R. 1958. Carryover Levels for Grains: A Method for Determining Amounts That Are Optimal Under Specified Conditions. USDA Technical Bulletin 1178.

Hamilton, J. 1994. *Time Series Analysis.* Princeton, NJ: Princeton University Press.

Harrison, M. J., and Taksar, M. 1983. Instantaneous Control of Brownian Motion. *Mathematics of Operations Research* **8** 439–453.

Hilliard, J., and Reis, J. 1998. Valuation of Commodity Futures and Options under Stochastic Convenience Yields, Interest Rates, and Jump Diffusions in the Spot. *Journal of Financial and Quantitative Analysis* **33** 61–86.

Hirshleifer, D. 1988. Residual Risk, Trading Costs, and Commodity Risk Premia. *Review of Financial Studies* **1** 173–193.

Ikonen, S., and Toivanen, J. 2009. Operator Splitting Methods for Pricing American Options with Stochastic Volatility. *Numerische Mathematik* **113** 299–324.

Johnson, B., and G. Barz. 1999. Selecting Stochastic Processes for Modelling Electricity Prices. Pages 3–22 in Jameson, R. (ed.), *Energy Modelling and the Management of Uncertainty.* London: Risk Publications.

Joshi, M. 2003. *The Concepts and Practice of Mathematical Finance.* Cambridge: Cambridge University Press.

Judd, K. 1998. *Numerical Methods in Economics.* Cambridge, MA: MIT Press.

Kaldor, N. 1939. Speculation and Economic Stability. *Review of Economic Studies* **7** 1–27.

Keynes, J. 1930. *A Treatise on Money.* New York: Harcourt, Brace and Co.

Killian, L. 2009. Not All Oil Price Shocks Are Alike: Disentangling Demand and Supply Shocks in the Crude Oil Market. *American Economic Review* **99** 1053–1069.

Kogan, L., Livdan, D., and Yaron, A. 2009. Oil Futures Prices in a Production Economy with Investment Constraints. *Journal of Finance* **64** 1345–1375.

Kreps, D., and Porteus, E. 1978. Temporal Resolution of Uncertainty and Dynamic Choice Theory. *Econometrica* **46** 185–200.

Lucas, R. 1978. Asset Prices in an Exchange Economy. *Econometrica* **46** 1429–1445.

Lucas, R., and Stokey, N. 1989. *Recursive Methods in Economic Dynamics.* Cambridge, MA: Harvard University Press.

Mandelbrot, B. 1963. The Variation of Certain Speculative Prices. *Journal of Business* **36** 394–419.

Merton, R. 1973. Theory of Rational Option Pricing. *Bell Journal of Economics and Management Science* **4** 141–183.

Miltersen, K., and Schwartz, E. 1998. Pricing of Options on Commodity Futures with Stochastic Term Structures of Convenience Yields and Interest Rates. *Journal of Financial and Quantitative Analysis* **33** 33–59.

Miranda, M., and Rui, X. 1996. An Empirical Reassessment of the Commodity Storage Model. Working paper, Ohio State University.

Newbery, D., and Stiglitz, J. 1982. Optimal Commodity Stockpiling Rules. *Oxford Economic Papers* **34** 403–427.

Ng, V., and Pirrong, C. 1994. Fundamentals and Volatility: Storage, Spreads, and the Dynamics of Metals Prices. *Journal of Business* **67** 203–230.

Ng, V., and Pirrong, C. 1996. Price Dynamics in Refined Petroleum Spot and Futures Markets. *Journal of Empirical Finance* **2** 359–388.

Nielsen, L. 1999. *Pricing and Hedging of Derivative Securities.* Oxford: Oxford University Press.

Osborne, T. 2004. Market News in Commodity Price Theory. *Review of Economic Studies* **71** 133–164.

Oskendal, B. 2003. *Stochastic Differential Equations: An Introduction with Applications.* New York: Springer.

Pindyck, R. 1994. Inventories and the Short-run Dynamics of Commodity Prices. *Rand Journal of Economics* **25** 141–159.

Pirrong, C. 1996. Metallgesellschaft: A Prudent Hedger Ruined or a Wildcatter on NYMEX? *Journal of Futures Markets* **17** 543–578.

Pirrong, C. 1999. Searching for the Missing Link. Working paper, Washington University.

Pirrong, C. 2006. Incorporating Outages into the Pirrong-Jermakyan Framework. Working paper, University of Houston.

Pirrong, C. 2007. Testing the Theory of Storage. Working paper, University of Houston.

Pirrong, C. 2008. Stochastic Volatility of Fundamentals, Commodity Prices, and Inventories. Working paper, University of Houston.

Pirrong, C., and Jermakyan, M. 2008. The Price of Power: The Valuation of Power and Weather Derivatives. *Journal of Banking and Finance* **32** 2520–2529.

Ramey, V. 1989. Inventories as Factors of Production and Economic Fluctuations. *American Economic Review* **79** 338–354.

Revoredo, C. 2000. On the Solution of the Dynamic Rational Expectations Commodity Storage Model in the Presence of Stockholding by Speculators and Processors. *Computing in Economics and Finance 2000.*

Ross, S. 1989. Information and Volatility: The No-Arbitrage Martingale Approach to Timing and Resolution Irrelevancy. *Journal of Finance* **44** 1–17.

Routledge, B., Seppi, D., and Spatt, C. 2000. Equilibrium Forward Curves for Commodities. *Journal of Finance* **55** 1297–1338.

Scheinkman, J., and Schectman, J. 1983. A Simple Competitive Model of Production with Storage. *Review of Economic Studies* **50** 427–441.

Schoutens, W. 2003. *Levy Processes in Finance: Pricing Financial Derivatives.* New York: Wiley.

Schwartz, E. 1997. The Stochastic Behavior of Commodity Prices. *Journal of Finance* **52** 923–973.

Schwartz, E., and Nielsen, M. 2004. Theory of Storage and the Pricing of Commodity Claims. *Review of Derivatives Research* **7** 5–24.

Shreve, S. 2004. *Stochastic Calculus for Finance II: Continuous Time Finance*. New York: Springer Finance.

Smith, V., Suchanek, G., and Williams, A. 1988. Bubbles, Crashes, and Endogenous Expectations in Experimental Spot Asset Markets. *Econometrica* **56** 1119–1151.

Stachurski, J. 2009. *Economic Dynamics: Theory and Computation*. Cambridge, MA: MIT Press.

Telser, L. 1958. Futures Trading and the Storage of Cotton and Wheat. *Journal of Political Economy* **66** 233–255.

Trolle, A., and Schwartz, E. 2009. Unspanned Stochastic Volatility and the Pricing of Commodity Derivatives. *Review of Financial Studies* **22** 4423–4461.

United States Senate Permanent Subcommittee on Investigations of the Committee on Homeland Security and Governmental Affairs. 2006. The Role of Market Speculation in Rising Oil and Gas Prices: A Need to Put the Cop Back on the Beat. Washington: Government Printing Office.

Verleger, P. 2010. The Big Freeze: The Dog That Did Not Bark. *Notes at the Margin* **14** 1–5.

Villaplana, P. 2004. A Two-State Variables Model for Electricity Prices. *Third World Congress of the Bachlier Finance Society, Chicago* (2004).

Welch, G., and Bishop, G. 2001. An Introduction to the Kalman Filler. Working paper, University of North Carolina at Chapel Hill.

Williams, A., Ledyard, J., Gjeerstad, S., and Smith, V. 2000. Concurrent Trading in Two Experimental Markets with Demand Interdependence. *Economic Theory* **16** 511–528.

Williams, J. 1996. *Manipulation on Trial*. Cambridge: Cambridge University Press.

Williams, J., and Wright, B. 1991. *Storage and Commodity Markets*. Cambridge: Cambridge University Press.

Wilmott, P., Dewynne, J., and Howison, S. 1993. *Option Pricing: Mathematical Models and Computation*. Oxford: Oxford Financial Press.

Working, H. 1933. Price Relations Between July and September Wheat Futures in Chicago since 1885. *Wheat Studies* **9** 186–238.

Working, H. 1949. The Theory of the Price of Storage. *American Economic Review* **39** 1254–1262.

Yanenko, N. 1971. *The Method of Fractional Steps*. Berlin: Springer.

Author Index

Subject Index

Printed by Printforce, United Kingdom